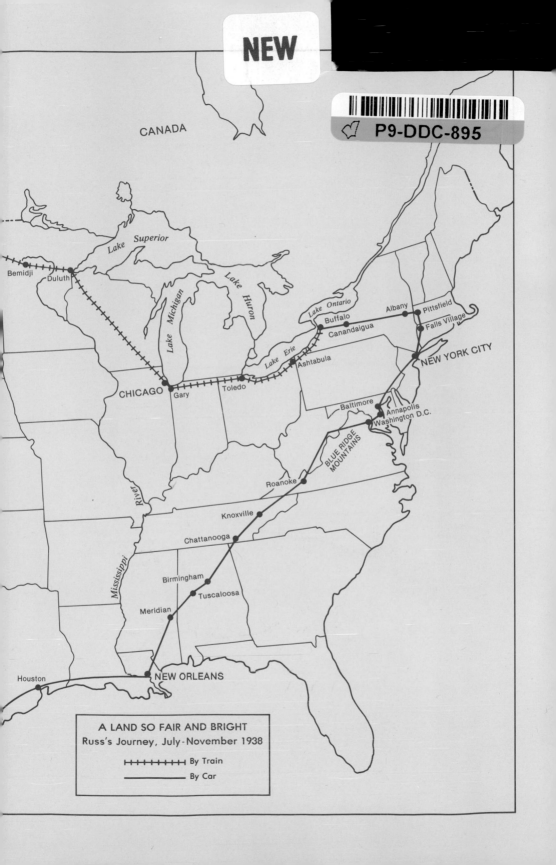

CANADA

Lake Superior

Bemidji  Duluth

Lake Michigan

Lake Huron

Lake Ontario

Buffalo  Albany  Pittsfield
Canandaigua  Falls Village

Lake Erie

Ashtabula  NEW YORK CITY

CHICAGO  Gary  Toledo

Baltimore
Annapolis
Washington D.C.

BLUE RIDGE
MOUNTAINS

Roanoke

Mississippi River

Knoxville

Chattanooga

Birmingham
Tuscaloosa

Meridian

Houston  NEW ORLEANS

**A LAND SO FAIR AND BRIGHT**
Russ's Journey, July - November 1938

┼┼┼┼┼┼┼┼┼┼ By Train
─────── By Car

# A Land
# So Fair
# and Bright

By the same author:

Hard on the Wind

# A Land
# So Fair
# and Bright

═══════════════════

*The True Story of a*
*Young Man's Adventures*
*Across Depression America*

RUSS HOFVENDAHL

SHERIDAN HOUSE

First published 1991 by
Sheridan House Inc.
145 Palisade Street
Dobbs Ferry, NY 10522

Library of Congress Cataloging-in-Publication Data

Hofvendahl, Russ, 1921–

    A land so fair and bright : the true story of a young man's
adventures across depression America / Russ Hofvendahl.
      p.    cm.
    ISBN 0-924486-10-4 : $22.95
    1. United States—Description and travel—1920–1940.  2. United
States—Social life and customs—1918–1945.  3. Depressions—1929—
United States.  4. Hofvendahl, Russ, 1921–    —Journeys—United
States.  5. Railroad travel—United States.  I. Title.
E169.H684  1991
917.304′917—dc20

                       91-11287
                         CIP

Cover and text design by Jeremiah B. Lighter

Cover painting, "Threshing Wheat" by Thomas Hart Benton,
courtesy of the Sheldon Swope Art Museum, Terre Haute, Indiana

Printed in the United States of America

ISBN 0-924486-10-4

*For my children Laurel Camille,
Kathleen, Steve and David*

*With love—and my thanks for
being who you are.*

# ACKNOWLEDGEMENTS

It is my privilege to acknowledge the contributions of those individuals who have done so much to make this book possible.

In chronological order they are:

Marie Olson, my cousin, who carefully gathered together all of the post cards, letters and the diary which her mother, my beloved Aunt Doris, had saved for so many years. Marie delivered this material to me, after Aunt Doris' death, and suggested that it could make an interesting book. I hope she was right.

Beverly, my wife, who was always and invariably the first to read the latest script after I wrote it in longhand on my yellow, legal-size tablets. She read the material carefully and criticized it unsparingly. In a very real sense, this book is the product of a collaboration with her. She had the good sense and moral fortitude to stand her ground in making those suggestions, however much I may have disagreed initially, which contributed so much to the end result.

Bev Cusimano, my secretary, who took the handwritten script, with my deletions, inserts, and directional scrawls, and turned it into a neatly typed, readable manuscript. She accomplished this, remarkably, without missing a beat in terms of keeping the flow of legal work moving through our office.

Ellen Wilson, my editor who, tactfully but firmly, clarified the syntax of my sometimes convoluted prose and whose faith in this book never faltered. The importance of her contribution cannot be overstated. Without exception, when I reviewed Ellen's editing, I could only wonder why it was not written that way in the first place.

D. Warner Johnson, dedicated traveler by sidedoor Pullman, fellow member of the National Hobo Association, and accomplished photographer. Warner generously made his comprehensive collection of railroad photographs available for my selection of those too few illustrations which appear in this book. I only wish we had the space to use them all.

The editors at Sheridan House whose professionalism, patience, and understanding have earned my enduring gratitude.

My heartfelt thanks to you all!

# 1

Clinging to the catwalk in a prone position on the top of the boxcar, I bounced and jolted through the Canadian night. There had been times in my life when I had been miserable, but nothing like this. It was July 1938, and the Canadian Pacific railroad simply did not have the money to maintain its track and roadbeds. For a hobo riding the top the result was sheer misery—or death if he lost his grip and rolled off.

It was bitterly cold as the train chugged into the foothills of the Canadian Rockies, jarring and swaying over the tracks, the occasional mournful *whohoohoo* of the engine's whistle drifting back to me from twenty-five cars ahead, the wind like an arctic blast. Finn Bering was stretched out on his belly just ahead of me, enveloped in his blanket. His bulk broke the whistling wind slightly, but not enough.

There was no moon that midnight, but the stars were bright in a dark-blue velvet sky. There wasn't much freight traffic heading east out of this small town, and we knew we had the right train for Kamloops Junction—made up now in the New Westminster railroad marshaling yard, the engine huffing steam far up the line, impatiently awaiting the conductor's highball.

"Russ, there's no empties on this freight. Ve've got to get out of New Vestminster for sure now. Only choice is to ride the top." But for a Scandinavian tendency to pronounce a *W* like a *V* and a *J* like a *Y*, Finn spoke excellent English.

"Okay, Finn, so let's ride the top!"

Finn, who had already hoboed from New York City to Los Angeles, knew better. At age sixteen, I lacked Finn's experience on the road.

"It's going to get cold up there. It von't help much, but get one of your blankets out so you can wrap it around you."

"It's not that cold. I don't want to break my roll."

1

Finn paused momentarily where he was kneeling, pulled a blanket off his roll, and retied it. He looked at me. "Suit yourself."

I was beginning to learn that Finn told me once what was right and then dropped it. Moments later we climbed the ladder to the top, stretched out, and were on our way.

God, how right he was, I thought, as I shivered and hung on to that catwalk like a human leech, my bedroll carrying line hooked on my left arm. There was too much train noise for conversation. All that was left was to think about the chain of events that had carried me to the top of this boxcar, bouncing and jolting through the night.

# 2

It was July 12, 1938. The telephone rang at my Aunt Doris's home in the City. I picked up the receiver.

"Hofvendahl?"

"Yes."

It was Bent Jorgenson, ship's chandler and factotum for many of the foreign vessels that docked in San Francisco.

"Got a berth for you on the *Dagmar Salen*. Swedish freighter out of Stockholm. Bound for the Far East. You want it?"

"You bet!" I didn't ask about the berth, pay, quarters, or anything else. All that mattered was that I was shipping out again!

My first seagoing voyage had been a hard one, on a codfishing schooner to the Bering Sea the year before, but sea fever had permanently infected me.

"Okay. Be at my office by three this afternoon. She's shovin' off at five. Don't forget your seaman's papers."

It was then one o'clock. The call was not totally unexpected. After fruitless hours of haunting the U.S. Maritime Union hiring halls, during my last semester of high school, I had heard of Jorgenson's sideline of filling sudden vacancies in the crew roster of foreign vessels. The shipping companies paid him for his services, and I never thought to ask, with shipping so tough on the West Coast, why Mr. Jorgenson fulfilled this particular function. The answer lay in the long hours and small pay, which even then made it difficult for the foreign lines to fill a vacant berth in an American port. With my merchant seaman's papers, and some real seagoing behind me on the schooner *William H. Smith,* I represented more experience than he could usually muster for a shorthanded foreign merchant vessel. He had guaranteed me a berth when I first met him in his office, but warned me that I would be shipping out on short notice. Since that meeting my seabag had basically been packed, and I was ready for the call.

At 3 P.M. sharp I was in Jorgenson's office on Battery Street. He spoke to the man in his office. "Captain Olafson, this is your new hand."

The captain was of medium height and powerful build. He had the unmistakable command presence of a merchant skipper. His English was broken, but he communicated. He glanced at my papers.

"Hofvendahl. I see ya shipped on a vindyammer. Ya know how to work?"

"Yes, sir!"

Without otherwise acknowledging my presence, he turned to Jorgenson, nodded once, and strode out of the office.

Jorgenson looked at me. "You're goin' to be workin' on the *Dagmar Salen*. Thirty dollars a month, good food, good quarters, but you'll put in the hours. You're shippin' as a messman."

"Messman!" The disappointment in my voice couldn't be concealed. I wanted to ship out as an ordinary seaman.

"That's right. Take it or leave it. I got plenty other people ashore, glad to get any berth."

"I'll take it, Mr. Jorgenson, it's just..." My voice trailed off.

Jorgenson looked at me and his expression softened slightly. "I understand, son, but you do want to ship out. There's not many berths today—even on the foreign vessels."

I nodded.

"Okay. These are the ship's articles. Sign here."

I signed.

"The *Dagmar Salen* is berthed at Pier 37. Better report aboard now."

My seabag slung on my shoulder, I hiked over to Pier 37.

The *Dagmar Salen* was a trim vessel. I had been aboard foreign ships of almost every flag that steamed into San Francisco, and the Scandinavian vessels were the cleanest and most shipshape. She was painted a gleaming white. The Swedish flag was snapping in the breeze at her stern. The yellow cross on the blue background was simple and bright. My spirits lifted as I started up the gangway.

The duty mate at the head of the gangway gave me a hard look as I reached the deck.

"Hofvendahl, Sir, new messman."

He didn't say a word. Simply stared at me and jerked a thumb aft to a midship companionway. The hell with it, I thought, someone will tell me where to bunk. Just as I reached the companionway, a tall, good-looking young man came out on deck. He looked at me quizzically.

"You the new messman?"

I nodded. Then, encouraged by his smile, I stuck out my hand. "Russ Hofvendahl. You know where I'm bunking?"

"Yah. You're in my cabin." He returned my handshake with a firm grip. "Finn Bering. Come on, I'll show you."

I could hardly believe my eyes when Finn led the way into our cabin. It was downright spacious, with two wide berths attached to the forward bulkhead, our own washbasin, a chair, and a porthole.

I brightened up again. "Say, these quarters are pretty good!"

"Yah, that they be, and the food is good too, but Yesus, how they vork you on this vessel."

I had heard of the long hours the crew put in on the foreign ships—all but the black gang who did strictly four on and eight off the clock around due to the heat of the engine room.

"What do you mean?"

Finn looked at me with a small smile. He was about six feet one inch in height and had a strongly chiseled face topped with a head of curly golden-blond hair. His eyes were startlingly blue. His body was trim and muscular, tapering from broad shoulders to slim hips. He looked to me to be the very picture of the legendary Viking.

"Vell, I tell you, Russ. I shipped out of San Pedro on this vessel. I been vorking a good sixteen hours a day since the day I come aboard. Didn't even get to go ashore in Frisco, and ve'll be shovin' off in about an hour."

"What's your job?"

Finn looked at me with the perverse pleasure an old con expresses when he greets a new inmate. "I'm a messman—like you."

My heart dropped a bit. I sure didn't like the sound of no shore time. I had been looking forward to the exotic ports of the Orient.

"Why such long hours?"

"Vell, they operate these ships cheap, basically undermanned and no unions like on the American vessels. Take my vord, they keep you going from five in the morning until after nine at night."

Just then the ship's steward stuck his head through the cabin entrance and said something in Swedish.

Finn answered and then turned to me again. "They don't speak much English aboard, even though they'll be carrying a small passenger list out of San Pedro—mostly Yanks. The captain knows I speak English. I got orders to lead you around until you know enough to get the vork done. Come on, it's time to set up for the night meal."

Thus began my routine of setting up a fifteen-dish smörgåsbord as a preliminary for the two main meals, and the same setup for mid-morning and mid-afternoon mug-ups. There were at least four different kinds of pickled herring, assorted cold cuts, and various cheeses. It was all delicious and the messmen were welcome to what was left, but every dish had to be washed and dried after every setting. In addition I had the responsibility for cleaning and squaring away the cabins of the three mates who were the deck officers. I served as waiter at breakfast and the two main meals and washed the dishes afterward.

That afternoon, despite the first faint stirrings of alarm that Finn's words had evoked, I rushed out of the galley to watch the dock hawsers cast off as the engine bell rang full astern, and the *Dagmar Salen* slowly backed away from Pier 37. The surge of excitement I felt as I watched the Embarcadero begin to slide past was cut short by the brusque voice of the steward. I couldn't understand the words, but the abrupt tone and the curt gesture toward the galley were unmistakable. Get to work!

And work I did. I got one glimpse of the Golden Gate Bridge through the dining-salon portholes as we steamed under it, but my vision of standing at the rail of this trim freighter as I watched San Francisco slip astern was rudely shattered. It was about nine that night when I dried the last cup, stowed it, and walked to my cabin.

Finn had arrived just a moment before and was stretched out on the lower bunk, his hands clasped behind his head.

"Vell, Russ, vhat you think of the *Dagmar Salen*?"

"It's a trim ship, but you were so right. They really work you. I wouldn't mind so much if someone at least said thank you or whatever the hell they say in Swedish. But they not only don't say it, the steward, the mates and the cook act like they're really pissed off at me."

"Don't sveat it, Russ, it's not you. It's yust the vay they're used to treating everyvun." He looked at me speculatively. "New Vestminster is in British Columbia—about ten miles east of Vancouver. I understand that the ship's officers are going to take some time off, half at a time. That means ve'll be cutting down on the galley duty. Ve may even get off this bloody ship ourselves for an hour or two. I may not be aboard vhen the *Dagmar Salen* shoves off."

I gulped. Deserting ship was pretty heavy, treated as a felony in the United States and Canada. The shipping companies did not waste much time or money trying to find a deserting seaman. But, if he chanced to fall into the hands of the law, the punishment was swift and severe—to make up for those deserters never apprehended.

I stared at Finn, started to open my mouth, and then decided to say nothing. I climbed into my upper berth and fell into an exhausted sleep.

Finn shook me awake at four the next morning. Whatever his feelings about a messman's life on the S.S. *Dagmar Salen,* it didn't lessen his infectious good humor. He grinned as I stared sleepily at him.

"Come on, Russ. Ve got vork to do. Let's get going."

The motion of the ship told me that we were plunging into a heavy sea. It was blowing strong out of the northwest. After a quick shower I went out on deck and stood by the rail for a moment, looking toward the east, where the first rays of the sun were preceded by a series of horizontal streaks of crimson, yellow, and purple. I breathed deeply of the fresh sea air and, for a moment, hoped that Finn could be wrong about this ship and this voyage. I did feel so alive there on the deck as the bow buried itself in the rolling swells, flinging showers of spray almost all the way aft to the midship superstructure where I stood leaning on the rail.

Then I heard the steward's sharp voice. All that I could recognize was my name, but the tone and intent were the same as before. Get to work, now!

I had just set the table for the elaborate forenoon mug-up for the ship's officers and thought that I would have at least a few moments for myself when the steward appeared out of nowhere. He was a medium-sized man, dark hair plastered to his head, and a mouth that seemed to be permanently fixed in a down-at-the-corners disapproving grimace.

"Coom!" He was carrying a bucket of sudsy water in one hand and a short-handled stiff scrub brush in the other.

I followed him out of the dining salon and down the companionway. He stopped at the hatch that opened onto the main midship deck. Setting the bucket and the brush on the deck, he vigorously pantomimed the scrubbing of the bulkhead, which was my next assignment. I looked at the already gleaming white bulkhead and thought bitterly—no wonder these Scandinavian ships always looked so sparkling—these people never stopped working.

It probably was a combination of many factors, but inevitably I began to think about Finn's plan to jump ship in Canada.

On the one hand, simply feeling the life of this sturdy vessel as she drove ever northward into the heavy seas was like a tonic for me. But the few moments I was able to steal for myself out on deck, watching the never-ending motion of the sea, breathing that invigorating air, only emphasized the contrast between that feeling and the relentless, never-ending grind of my inside work. It began to sink in that, if anything, seeing the ports of the Orient mainly from the deck of this ship would be worse than not seeing them at all.

Finn and I took our meals together in the dining salon before setting up for the ship's officers' meals. The food was ample, well-prepared, and ran heavily toward roasts, soups, and some really outstanding Swedish pastry. Our only chance to talk was while eating, as we were too exhausted at night to spend much time talking in our cabin.

He was just nineteen, three years older than I, and one of the most fascinating men I had ever met. He was a Dane, born and reared in Copenhagen. He had finished the Danish equivalent of high school at age seventeen, then had one year of compulsory army service, and shortly thereafter had shipped on a Danish freighter for the United States. He had left home with the unabashed intention of deserting ship as soon as he hit a U.S. port because he had always wanted to see the States. He did so two days after his ship docked in New York City. His English was excellent, but was marked by the British accent of one who had learned the language in a European school. He chuckled when he told me what it was like trying to get by in Manhattan the first few days.

"I'd talked to a good number of English travelers and a few Yanks back home in Copenhagen, and I thought I could speak the language pretty vell, but Yesus those New Yorkers! They talk so fast and they pronounce some vords as I never heard before like 'New Yoisey'—it took me avhile before I figured that vun out."

"How did you get along there, Finn?"

"Vell, I got a job on a dairy farm out on Long Island. I vanted to get out of the city until my ship vas gone. Those Sixth Avenue employment agencies—there vas plenty of yobs, they yust didn't pay too vell. Anyvay, I used to spend summers on a farm my uncle had near Glostrup. I knew how to milk cows. That's all that Long Island farmer cared about, and they didn't talk as fast out there as the city people, so I got used to understanding American."

Finn was justifiably proud of the fact that his family name descended from a remote ancestor, Vitus Bering, the Danish navigator, for whom the sea was named. The fact that I had made a voyage to the Bering Sea on a windjammer the year before was about the only thing in my background that compared with the adventures he had already experienced, but it created a bond between us. Finn was determined that some day he would sail to the Bering Sea also, just to see the body of water named for his ancestor.

Returning to Manhattan from the Long Island dairy farm, he hung around the waterfront until he signed on as a wiper in the black gang of a Norwegian freighter bound for South America. A wiper is the least-skilled member of the engine-room crew, and is treated accordingly, but Finn was happy to get any berth at the time. He had fond memories of the South American ports—particularly Rio de Janeiro.

"Ah, Russ, that Rio is something. Your ship come in this harbor and you smell the tropics, you see those hills growing up to the sky, the palm trees, it's beautiful!" He looked at me a moment, remembering that San Francisco was home to me. "Frisco looked beautiful too, but they never let me off this ship to really find out. Even if I did, don't think I'd have had as good a time as I had in Rio." He grinned reminiscently.

"You know those Rio girls hadn't seen any guys with a body vhite like mine." Finn's face and forearms were tanned to a deep-bronze but the rest of his body was milk-white, as I remembered the Scandinavians on the schooner.

He was not at all boastful, the memory still amused and aroused him, and he was trying to keep his account factual.

"I'm not saying that I vas the first vun in Rio, of course, but for these girls I vas. I don't think it vas me really, but they vere so dark and I suppose the men they knew vere pretty dark too. Anyvay, the engine-room gang had pretty good shore time in Rio vhile we vere tied up there—yust barely keeping steam on. So the first night ashore I met this lovely Carioca girl and ve got along fine. They're pretty relaxed about sex down there and she yust took me to her room in her home, vith her folks and a couple of sisters sleeping right near us. Portuguese is vun language I don't speak, so I'm not sure yust vhat she said, but I'll never forget the look on her face vhen I peeled my clothes off. She yust stared at me, then damned if she didn't get up, run out of the room, and come back with her sisters. I'm pretty vorked up by then. I'd stripped Maria's clothes off and was yust ready to climb aboard vhen she dashed off. I'm standing there ready for action vhen the three of them come back. I'd guess they probably ranged from fifteen to eighteen years old, but they vere vomen believe me! Anyvay, I sure vould have lost it vhen the three of them showed up, but they all started touching me at once. I kept hearing that "*blanco, blanco!*" vhich I knew meant vhite. Maria vanted to let her sisters vatch, but I said the hell vith that and chased them out of the room. But before the night vas over I'd had all three of them, and it vent that vay the whole veek ve vere in Rio. I yust barely managed to drag myself aboard vhen ve finally shoved off." He grinned again. "So now you know vhy I like Rio so much!"

Indeed I did.

# 3

The steward personally served Captain Olafson and his family in their private quarters on the bridge deck, and I never had occasion to ascend to the master's living area. From the main deck below I did catch occasional glimpses of Mrs. Olafson, their two young children, and their pet monkey from the Philippines. It seemed to me that this captain, following his career at sea but surrounded by the important elements of domesticity, really had it made.

As we steamed north, the conviction that this particular ship was not for me began to grow. If Finn had not planted the seed, I'm not sure just what I would have done, but the idea of jumping ship was deepening in me.

Finn had been paid off and discharged from the Norwegian ship in New York the preceding April, and was finally ready to embark on his dream of seeing the United States. The foreign-born eighteen-year old with twenty dollars in his pocket, no real idea of what he was confronting, no experience on the road, and little experience in American ways, blithely set out for the Pacific Coast of the United States. He exhausted his small store of capital getting out of the East, where hoboing was tough and dangerous, and then caught his first freight in Louisville, Kentucky. From there he made it all the way to Los Angeles by sidedoor Pullman; with his quick intelligence he was wise in the ways of the road by the time he got there. He had held a number of temporary jobs, lived in flophouses, and spent his spare time haunting the San Pedro piers looking for a berth on a Scandinavian ship. Armed with his Danish seaman's papers, a bona fide discharge from the Norwegian freighter, and speaking the language, he was a welcome addition to the ship's complement of the *Dagmar Salen* which had just lost another messman. Two weeks later I met him aboard ship at Pier 37.

We were eating dinner together the fourth night out, due to berth in New Westminster the next day at 1100 hours. The ship would be berthed there for two days. I spoke in a low voice. "Finn, you still thinking about jumping ship?"

He had not mentioned the subject again after that first time, rightly concluding that it had made me distinctly uncomfortable.

He didn't say anything, just looked at me and nodded.

Given some of the impetuous decisions I had already made, including shipping out as a messman on the S.S. *Dagmar Salen,* I hardly qualified as a long-range planner. Still, just getting off the ship was only the first step. I was worried about what we were going to do as illegal aliens in Canada, and just how we would get across the border back into the United States.

"What do you figure on doing once we're ashore?"

Finn was suddenly animated. "Russ, it's getting close to vheat harvest time on the prairie. Ve can make big money there. I've talked to hoboes who've ridden the rails in Canada. They tell me it's a lot easier than the States. Clean yungles, plenty of good vater, not too many railroad bulls. I figure ve can beat our vay east, go to vork in the harvest, make a stake, and then decide vhat to do."

Next to ships, railroads were a passion of mine, in part, no doubt, a product of my close association with my beloved railroading Uncle Jerry Sleight. I could feel a thrill of excitement.

"Sounds good to me, can I come along?"

Finn shoved out his right hand, gripped mine firmly, and nodded emphatically.

His next words sent a chill down my spine. "I haven't qvite figured out how yet, but by God I'm leaving vith my seabag."

"Jesus, Finn, it looks like we'll get to go ashore in New Westminster from what the steward told you. Then we can just take off, but I sure don't like the idea of trying to get a seabag ashore too."

Finn stared at me, a determined look on his face. "You know, Russ, they've had a hell of a turnover of messmen on this vessel. Not vun of them has left vith anything but the clothes on his back. These bastards are not going to have our gear. I don't know how yet, but ve're going to do it!"

The next day at eleven the *Dagmar Salen* gently eased up to the long pier at which two other merchant ships were berthed, one at least a ship's length forward of us and the other a ship's length astern. I loved to watch the deckhands sail the small heaving lines ashore, to be followed by the heavy hawsers attached to them, the operation occurring simultaneously at the bow and at the stern. There was a good deal of seamanship involved in coordinating this docking operation—controlling the tremendous inertia of a ship this size by the gently careful use of the engines, now forward a touch, now astern, getting the bow and stern lines ashore and secured on the heavy bollards on the dock at just the right instant. The deckhands of the *Dagmar Salen* were professionals, and Captain Olafson commanded the entire operation from the bridge with practiced skill. Then we were tied up and secure, with just the slightest creaking of the pier as we snugged onto the bollards. A few moments later the gangway was slung and lowered. Captain Olafson strode down the sloping surface, carrying a briefcase, to clear the ship for this Canadian port.

I had already become rather adept at locating the steward and finding out where he was likely to be so as to steal a few moments on deck whenever I could. Now the gangway fascinated me. I saw it as the road to freedom, and my spirits soared when I looked at it. I soon realized that I was staring at the duty mate at the head of the gangway, where one of the mates was always stationed around the clock when the ship was in port. I wasn't looking forward to going down that gangway for the last time with the duty mate's eyes drilling into me. I really wasn't all that sure I could bring it off without suddenly breaking down and babbling out a confession.

Finn's crazy fixation about getting our personal gear off made my mind whirl, and I *knew* that was going to ruin everything.

Finally, with a despairingly fatalistic shrug of my shoulders, I darted off the deck and back into the galley just before the steward appeared.

That afternoon, at about three o'clock, I was starting to set the table for the afternoon mug-up when Finn called to me from the other end of the dining salon.

"Hey, Russ, hold it, ve got shore time for two hours."

"Shore time! Do you mean it?" I couldn't believe it.

Finn smiled broadly. "I mean it! Don't know vhat's gotten into the steward, but he told me ve've got two hours off. Let's make the most of it."

Half an hour later we had climbed a short, steep, tree-lined walkway that overlooked the harbor and led to a Canadian Veterans of World War I clubhouse. The Canadian beer was strong, much stronger than our U.S. beer, and it came in large bottles. We paid ten cents for a bottle that contained almost a quart of liquid. About halfway through my second beer I was beginning to feel definitely mellow, and gave a start when I realized that Finn had been gone for quite some time, while I was staring down the green slope of the hill at the port. I could see my vessel in the distance, and it looked just as shipshape to me as the first time I had seen her in San Francisco tied up at Pier 37. I felt a sudden twinge, and then I thought of those sixteen plus hour days, slaving away under the steward's compulsive orders, and my resolve firmed up. One way or the other, I was jumping ship here.

Just then Finn came walking up to our table, followed by a balding, agreeable-looking man about forty years old. He was strongly muscled and weighed about two hundred pounds.

"Russ, my countryman Eric Yensen."

We shook hands and, as pleasant as Eric was, I could not quite account for Finn's air of self-satisfaction. He leaned forward conspiratorially. Involuntarily I did the same, as did our new companion. I gave a start when I realized that Eric Jensen was at least half again as mellowed out as I was, and he was nodding confidentially right along with Finn.

"I knew I'd find a way. Eric's an old sailor himself and he's a Copenhager too!" Somehow, when I heard the word "sailor," I realized that our new-found friend was about to become an integral part of our felonious leave-taking of the S.S. *Dagmar Salen*. While I was feeling a definite glow myself, I wasn't feeling all that comfortable about bringing a total stranger into our plans. Still, I thought, I didn't really know Finn all that well, either, just a few days earlier.

Finn spoke in a low voice.

"Eric's been ashore here in New Vestminster for ten years now. He's still a Danish citizen but he's legal here, got a Canadian vork permit, and a vife, and a house about a quarter mile from here. He's going to help us and ve're going to show those bastards!" Eric Jensen was nodding and beaming as Finn talked.

The pieces were falling into place now. I could see why Finn was feeling so pleased. Not many deserting seamen had a sanctuary just a quarter mile from the docks. But another cold chill raced down my back when I heard the word "wife". As far as actually jumping ship was concerned, we had decided that we would casually walk off the *Dagmar Salen* just before she cast off, hopefully when the duty mate's attention was turned elsewhere. The problem was that was almost two days away, and I had zero confidence in the ability of Eric Jensen to keep this undertaking a secret from his wife. It seemed as if half the town of New Westminster would soon know of our plans.

Eric sat up suddenly. "Ve need some more beer!" He weaved uncertainly toward the bar. While he was returning rather unsteadily with three more of those large bottles, Finn continued to unfold the plan.

"Ve haven't qvite figured out how ve're going to get the seabag off first, but vhen ve're ready to yump her, Eric's going to come aboard and get the mate tied up some vay vhile ve stroll off."

"Jesus, Finn, isn't he taking a hell of a chance? He may be here legally, but he's still an alien. If they find out he's mixed up in this he could be in real trouble."

Finn beamed proudly. "Yah, but he's a Danska! He vants to help. He's really homesick, and vhen he finds out I'm from Copenhagen there vas no stopping him." He raised his voice slightly as Eric Jensen slammed the bottles of beer down on our table. "Eric vas a ymnast back home in Copenhagen, that right?"

Eric fairly glowed. "Yah, I show you!"

Before either of us could think of something to stop him, he had drawn himself into a poised, if slightly unsteady, forward position, arms outstretched, and launched himself into a series of forward handsprings. Fortunately, there was a clear space about twenty feet from where he started. Every time he completed a forward handspring and landed on his feet I could feel the floor shake. The bartender had his back turned when Eric sprang into his first handspring, but the thunder of the initial landing brought him whirling around. We were almost the only patrons in the place, but there were a few Canadians sitting at a table against the far wall. I didn't know quite what to expect, but I was totally unprepared for the polite round of applause the performance had produced. It began to dawn on me that our friend was, to put it mildly, a rather well-known character in these parts. This depressed me even further when I thought about how essential secrecy was to our plan.

Eric returned to our table, breathing hard, but looking very pleased with himself. Feeling definitely self-conscious, but wanting Eric to know that we too appreciated him, Finn and I added our applause to that of the bartender and the other patrons. Our gymnast all but scuffed his shoes and tugged his forelock, but it was quite apparent that he was happy with our appreciation of his performance.

I decided that the environment was right to try to make some impression on him.

"Eric, we really appreciate your helping—"

He put up a protesting hand. "Nothin', nothin', for a fellow Danska."

"I know, but still I don't want you and your wife getting in trouble over us. For her sake don't tell her what we're planning. Okay?"

He looked at me owlishly for a moment. "Thas right, ya be right. I not tell her."

Finn glanced at the clock on the wall. "Ve've got to be getting back to the ship now, Eric. I'll meet you here tomorrow same time and ve'll vork out the details." Then we left.

I didn't know it at the time, but I had just had my first and last liberty in New Westminster. The next day the steward told Finn that one, but not both, of us could have liberty that afternoon. It went without saying that Finn should go to solidify our plans with Eric Jensen.

I was somewhat relieved when Finn returned to the ship that afternoon considerably more sober than he had been the day before. He wouldn't talk about our plans for the morrow at dinner, telling me that we would nail it all down in our cabin that night.

That's when I got the final word. We would each stow two blankets, clothing, personal effects, and other gear, in my seabag.

Finn had tested the size of it and, carefully packed, it would just fit through our porthole. Our cabin was on the outboard side of the ship from the pier and one of us would shove the seabag through while the other took it out on deck.

"When we going to do this, Finn?"

"Seven o'clock tomorrow morning."

"Seven in the morning! Why not tonight when it's dark?"

"Because they got guards and floodlights on that pier until six-thirty in the morning. 7 A.M. vhile the ship's at a berth and everyvun aboard's going to be eating breakfast. Eric vill be vaiting yust inside the varehouse on the pier near the stern. He'll have that seabag out of sight in no time."

I nodded gloomily. "I hope you're right, Finn." Then another thought struck me. "It's really going to take two of us to get that seabag through the porthole, Finn, and we're both supposed to be serving breakfast in the Officer's mess. How do we handle that?"

Finn nodded thoughtfully. "That's going to be close. Ve'll only need a minute or two, but both of us gone at the same time could be a problem. Of course there are enough times vhen ve're both out of the dining salon in the galley together." He thought some more. "Tomorrow really load up their plates that first serving. I'll slip into the galley, go out the starboard hatch, and get around to the deck outside our cabin. You duck out and slip the seabag through. If anyvun says anything or tries to stop you, yust tell him you have to piss. Okay?"

There wasn't any point in arguing now. I nodded glumly. We were committed.

At seven the next morning I placed a heavily laden plate on the table in front of the first engineer and glanced up as Finn disappeared into the galley. I looked around quickly and saw that the steward was nowhere in sight. Now was the time.

Moving rapidly, but trying to look unhurried, I left the dining salon, crossed to the port companionway, and ran to our cabin. Quickly I went to the porthole. "Finn?"

"Yah, I'm here. Get it out!" We had packed the seabag carefully the night before and had stowed it on the deck under Finn's berth. I rolled it out and hoisted it to the porthole as fast as I could. Just as it started through I heard the sound of quick footsteps in the companionway and the steward's angry voice, "Hofvendahl?"

Oh, Lord, I breathed, as I gave the seabag a final push. It stuck two-thirds of the way through. God knows on what, but it was firmly wedged. A seabag half-in, half-out of that porthole was as incriminating as a signed confession. I could hear the steward turning the knob of the cabin door. "Pull, Finn," I whispered in anguish as I gave one last desperate push. The seabag disappeared through the porthole as I whirled to face the angry steward. "Hofvendahl!" He sputtered in Swedish, gesturing toward the dining salon. I nodded my head as placatingly as I could under the circumstances, and rushed by him to resume my duties.

About five minutes later I carried a load of dirty dishes into the galley and saw Finn at the sink washing dishes. The cook's back was turned, and as soon as Finn saw me he grinned, gave a large wink, and nodded his head once. I heaved a sigh of relief. At least we had the goddamned seabag off the ship.

The steward disappeared into his cabin at about ten-thirty. I glanced at Finn working in the dining salon with me. He raised his right hand with fingers outstretched, clenched them once, and repeated the gesture twice more. Fifteen minutes! The departure hour of eleven had been chalked on the small blackboard hanging on the bulkhead near the head of the gangway. For this part of our plan, we had agreed that I would simply stay close to Finn and basically do what he did. At a quarter to eleven he beckoned to me and I followed him out to the deck, around the aft end of the superstructure, and waited there about twenty feet aft of the duty mate at the head of the gangway. Just as we arrived I heard footsteps ascending the gangway and the unmistakable voice of that intrepid Danska Eric Jensen. I couldn't understand what he was saying in Danish, but the tone was jovial and it sounded as if he were asking (and assuming) permission to come aboard. The mate responded angrily, and then we heard a small commotion just forward of the gangway.

"Come on!" Finn whispered. It was now or never!

As we cleared the aft starboard corner of the deckhouse, we could see the mate's back and Eric facing us. Both of their voices were raised angrily now. We didn't run down the gangway but we moved fast. Just as we reached the bottom, the mate looked over the side and shouted at us.

Finn replied reassuringly in Danish. He whispered to me. "I told him ve'd be back in a minute. Don't run, for Christ's sake!" A moment later we were inside the long warehouse on the pier. We looked back once to see Eric angrily descending the gangway, shaking his fist at the mate who was responding in kind.

"Now! Let's move!" Finn broke into a run and I followed. Ten minutes later, completely out of sight of the harbor, he was pounding on the door of a modest, well-maintained little house. A pleasant-looking woman, obviously Mrs. Jensen, opened the door and shut it behind us without a word.

An hour later Eric Jensen arrived, grinning broadly. "Dey didn't shove off for anudder half hour, but she be on da vay! I vatched from up on da hill until I see her cast off. I tink you boys okay now."

We had done it—seabag and all.

# 4

Eric Jensen had a modest-paying night-watchman's job. He had given up the hours when he would normally have been sleeping to first quickly spirit off the seabag from the dock where Finn had flung it from the stern of the ship, and later to divert the mate while we walked off the *Dagmar Salen*.

He was obviously exhilarated by the role he had played in our accomplishment. Now he was telling us what to do next.

"Dey goin' to let de Mounties know dere's two sailors ashore. Dis be a small town. I tink ya best catch a freight out tonight after dark. I vant to get some sleep now, den I take ya to de yard."

I could see my seabag standing upright in the corner of the small living room. Mrs. Jensen wasn't happy with us or what her husband had done to help us, but she was cooly courteous. Finn told her how much he appreciated what they both had done; his personality was thawing her reserve.

"Mrs. Yensen, ve be out of here soon. No vun vill ever know vhat Eric did for us. I vant you to know ve thank you."

Then Finn went to work on the contents of the seabag. He had brought some light but strong line from the ship, and he showed me how to construct a compact blanket roll, with two loops around it, and a carrying line between. It was a good stout seabag, but the blanket rolls were more practical for our purposes now, and we thought it was the least we could leave behind for our friend.

About seven that evening Eric awoke, insisted that we have dinner with them, and that we take some meat sandwiches with us.

When it got dark we left the house, again with heartfelt thanks to Mrs. Jensen, and headed for the railroad yards.

The Royal Canadian Mounted Police were doing heavy duty in those days and part of their job, as we were to learn the hard way, involved confining hoboes within the borders of the provinces. It didn't make much sense to me, but at some level of the national government it had been decided that the wandering hoboes would, to the extent possible, be kept in the particular provinces wherein they originated, and prevented from moving from one province to another.

Eric was explaining some of this to us as we hiked through the darkness to the railroad yards about a mile from his house.

"De Mounties be pretty good people. Dey not like some railroad bulls. Von't rough ya up or anyting. I don't tink dey be lookin' hard for a couple sailors vith everything else dey have to do, but best ya get out of New Vestminster now."

When we reached the railroad yard, Eric left us in a darkened area near a freight-loading platform while he checked out the situation. He returned in about thirty minutes.

"Dere's a freight makin' up on de far side of de yard. Hobo tell me she be pullin' out for Kamloops Junction in about an hour. I tink you boys can handle it now, yah?"

Finn shoved out his hand and Eric clasped it strongly. I heard Finn speak. "Eric, I don't know how or vhen but somehow—"

Eric interrupted him, "Nay, Finn, for a fellow Danska, you'd have done de same for me."

I shook hands with Eric Jensen and added my thanks to Finn's. Then he was gone. It was quite typical of the road—to meet someone who, in one way or another, strongly affected one's life briefly and then disappeared as if he had never existed.

We found the freight train and had time to learn that there wasn't an empty boxcar or gondola in the entire line of railroad cars. That's when we climbed to the top and the train started rolling east.

With my hands numb from the cold, the entire front of my body aching and bruised from the pounding I was taking stretched out on my belly on that catwalk, I was beginning to wonder just how long I could hang on, when I realized the train was starting to slow down. I raised my head and looked ahead. Very faintly I could see the dim glow from the engine's firebox veering slightly to the right. As we slowed more and more, Finn stirred, getting the blanket off, and sitting up. He stared forward for a moment.

"Ve going off on a siding. Must be a through train heading our way. Yesus vhat a ride!"

"How long do you think we'll be here, Finn?"

"Hard to tell, but I guess at least ten minutes." I could see the white gleam of his teeth as he grinned at me. "Enough time to get a blanket off your roll if you vant."

I didn't say a word. Just went to work on my blanket roll.

As it happened we were about halfway to Kamloops Junction then. I climbed stiffly down the ladder to stretch my legs and relieve a bladder that felt like it was about to explode. I began to feel almost human again.

"Russ, I should have varned you more. You never vant to take a long ride on the top, but ve had to get out of that town."

"I know, Finn. I should have listened to you when you told me to get that blanket out. Are there going to be many more rides like this?"

Finn's voice was emphatic. "Not if I can help it! Ve're in the middle of novhere so ve got to ride it into Kamloops, but Eric tell me that's a pretty good-size division. Ve should be able to catch an empty box to the last division before ve start into the Rockies. Ve just take it vun day at a time."

Then we heard the long whistle of the onrushing through freight as it rolled by us on the main line.

"Come on, Russ, ve got to get back aboard."

I was not looking forward to stretching out on that catwalk again, but somehow, perhaps because I was dreading it so much, the reality was not as bad as I had feared. My blanket did help to break the wind, and it slightly padded the rough wooden surface under my body.

It was still a long night, but just as dawn was breaking we felt the train begin to slow again. Sitting up and looking forward we could see, fanning out in front of our train, the diverging rails of a main division. We were finally at Kamloops Junction.

# 5

We had five dollars between us, which was a goodly sum for our particular lifestyle. Once out of New Westminster there was no need to hurry and we really had to rest. We found the local hobo jungle by the banks of a clear rushing stream not too far from the railroad yard. The term "jungle," common usage for hobo camps throughout the United States and Canada, was a real misnomer applied to this wooded glen.

Finn was pleased to learn that what he had heard about the Canadian jungles was accurate, at least thus far. When we reached this secluded spot by the stream I felt as if I could camp here forever. There was a circle of stones marking the place for a cooking fire, some empty gallon tins neatly lined up near it, and even a small store of firewood.

We ate the sandwiches Mrs. Jensen had given us. Then wearily we unrolled our blankets, found a space near the stream bank with no rocks, and were asleep just as soon as we hit the kip.

It was almost three in the afternoon when I woke up, and I felt like a new man.

I took a long drink of water from the clear stream, then moved down to where I could wash up without disturbing the drinking area.

Finn sat up sleepily and stretched luxuriously. "Ah, that's vhat I needed. Ve go into town now and buy us some meat and spuds for a mulligan."

We made up our rolls and secreted them downstream a slight distance from the campfire location. It really wasn't all that necessary. The hoboes, in this part of the world at least, were basically hard-working men, down on their luck, simply trying to survive. It was rare indeed for anything to be stolen from a man's bedroll, but we decided that there was no sense in tempting fate. When we returned from town, with fifty cents' worth of beef for a stew, potatoes, and onions, another hobo was just starting to build a fire. He looked up as we walked down the slope and nodded in a friendly way. He was on the small side, weather-beaten from a life outdoors.

Finn responded in kind. "Ve got plenty of grub for a good mulligan stew. You vant to join us?"

"That's mighty kind of you. I was aboot to start cooking up some spuds, but that's all I have." I recognized the Canadian inflection, the speech so much like that of the western United States, but with its occasional idiosyncrasies such as pronouncing "about" as if it is spelled "aboot."

Jack, the Canadian, was quite well informed as far as local rail traffic was concerned. First names were commonly exchanged on the road, but it was fairly unusual for a hobo to introduce himself by last name also. If it wasn't volunteered no one asked. He shook his head when we told him about the long ride from New Westminster on the top.

"Well, you don't have to worry aboot that out of Kamloops. There's a Canadian National freight heading for Blue River tomorrow morning aboot seven. I think you have a better chance to get through Jasper Pass on the Canadian National than over Rogers Pass on the Canadian Pacific. Should be a lot less rail traffic and a lot less hoboes up north. They may not be checking the freights as close up there. Should be aboot half-empty boxes on that train. Me, I'm on the way to Vancouver." Unless it was volunteered one did not ask. Jack didn't tell us why he was heading for Vancouver and we did not inquire.

Finn had appropriated two sets of eating utensils, enamel cups, and enamel bowls from the galley of the *Dagmar Salen,* which had been stowed in the seabag when it sailed off the stern. When we made our blanket rolls at Eric Jensen's house, one set went into each pack. As I smelled the heavy, savory aroma of Finn's mulligan I could feel myself salivating. It was beginning to get dark there by the stream, and the fire over which the stew was cooking cast a cheerful, flickering light on our camp.

Jack had broken out some coffee, and salt and pepper from his pack as his contribution to our repast. The strong smell of the coffee mingled with the smell of the stew, and suddenly I was ravenous.

Finn used his fork to prod the meat, then announced that it was ready.

Somehow, although it didn't really compare with our food on the ship, it seemed to me that I had never tasted anything as savory as that jungle mulligan and strong coffee.

Jack rolled into his blankets not too long after it got dark.

Finn and I stretched out on our blankets, a rounded rock as a pillow tucked under the end of the blankets beneath our heads, and looked up at the star-strewn sky. There was no moon to lessen the effect of the constellations, like diamonds fixed in the dark blue velvet of the nighttime heavens.

There was just a slight whisper of a breeze stirring the leaves of the trees, joined by the quiet murmur of the stream. Perhaps it was the reaction to the events of the last couple of days, but I felt utterly relaxed and at peace with the world. From time to time one or the other of us would get up to throw another piece of wood on the fire. We didn't really need the warmth, but it was so pleasant to watch the flames and the sparks that we were reluctant to let it die.

Finn had his hands clasped behind his head staring up at the heavens. "Russ, you see that Cassiopeia up there?"

I was awestruck. "What?"

"That constellation vhat looks like a *W*."

I stared hard, then finally, with Finn's help, located this group of stars across from the Big Dipper.

"That constellation vas named by the Greeks. Cassiopeia vas the mother of Andromeda. She vas chained to a rock—"

I interrupted him. "Where in the hell did you learn all that, Finn?"

He looked at me with some surprise. "In high school. I really enjoyed astronomy. Something about giving names to those beautiful groups of stars up there. That and the Greek legends—I don't know vhy exactly, but I liked studying that."

I was beginning to feel distinctly self-conscious about my own high school education—or lack thereof compared with that of my Danish companion.

"Did you learn English in high school too?"

"Yah, also German. Ve had to learn two foreign languages to graduate."

"Sounds like you worked pretty hard in high school."

"Ve did, but I'm glad now. Seems like I know qvite a bit about a lot of things."

I had to agree. I was beginning to appreciate the fact that the education Finn had acquired in his twelve years of schooling in Denmark compared very favorably, in a liberal arts sense, with that acquired by those few college graduates I had known. More than anything else, it seemed to me that Finn's education had equipped him with a resourcefulness and adaptability that I had rarely encountered.

He went on for another half hour or so, obviously enjoying himself immensely, pointing out the Ursa Major, or Great Bear constellation, of which the Big Dipper is a part, and others—recounting the ancient Greek myths identified with each. I wasn't always, or even very often, able to identify the shapes and figures in that starry sky, which he seemed to find so readily. Still it was a pleasure just listening to him because it was obviously such a source of satisfaction to him to exercise his mind and to inform me. Finally he gave a huge yawn.

"Russ, ve got to get up early. Make sure ve catch that freight for Blue River tomorrow morning."

"Guess you're right, Finn. Good night."

He was already drifting off. The last thing I heard was a sleepy, "Night."

I awoke about six the next morning. Back home in San Francisco my life was so tightly scheduled that, between getting to high school downtown in the morning from the outer Mission, where my Aunt Doris's home was located, getting back to the house for a quick nap and a change of clothes, and then back downtown to my night job in the Valet Shop at the St. Francis Hotel, I could hardly function without my serviceable Waltham wristwatch. I had Friday nights off and then worked a full day shift on the weekend. Since I went to work at 8 A.M. on Saturdays and Sundays, I was effectively in rather constant motion seven days a week. Once I had shipped out on the *Dagmar Salen* it seemed as if I had hardly looked at my wristwatch because someone else was constantly telling me what, where, and when, anyway.

Now, with a freight to catch this morning at a scheduled departure time, and probably others later on, my wristwatch began to assume a greater importance in my life. I didn't wear it on my wrist but kept it tucked in the left front pocket of my Levi's. I did this in part to protect it and in part out of self-consciousness. There were not many hoboes on the road in 1938 sporting wristwatches, and I didn't want to look conspicuous by being the exception to the rule.

I called to Finn. "It's five after six, think we'd better saddle up if we're going to catch that freight."

"Yah, I vant to have time to look it over, find vun of those empty boxes so ve don't ride the top this time."

We finished off the remains of the mulligan for breakfast, washed down by the cold, clear water from the stream. By the time I was awake Jack had already left—quietly so as not to disturb our sleep. We cleaned up the jungle, washed out the cooking cans, made sure the fire was doused, and left it as squared away as we had found it.

The Canadian National freight train was spotted in the yard where Jack had told us it would be. It was about twice as long as the freight out of New Westminster, and about a third of the cars were empty boxes.

Finn Bering was a natural-born teacher for starters. For another, he had learned some hard lessons hoboing across the United States, and he made it a point to impart his knowledge to me.

"Ve pick an empty box fairly near the caboose, but not too close. Both Eric and Jack say these crews not bother the hoboes, but if they do start casing the train they usually start from the front end vhen ve're on a siding. If ve're in a boxcar far enough back, there's a good chance they von't check the whole train."

He found what he was looking for about five cars forward of the caboose. The door was slightly ajar, and we could see the remains of the broken seal still dangling from the hasp.

"Russ, don't *ever* break a seal on a car. For some reason that really sets them off. If you ever get caught doing that—" He shook his head.

"What's so bad about that?"

"Don't really know exactly. I guess it's a lot of things. The trains are running across state lines in the States, and I think breaking a seal is a federal rap. There's usually not the type of freight in a boxcar that a hobo could steal, but I guess if a car shows up at the end of the line vith a broken seal, then they probably got to do a lot of papervork. Anyvay, like I said, don't ever break a seal, and if you see another hobo messing vith vun, you get out of there."

The floor of the boxcar was above waist level, but at a convenient height for Finn to put his shoulder to the door and roll it half open.

Being several inches taller than I, it was easier for Finn to put his roll inside the car, place his hands flat on the floor, and then spring in. It was harder for me but I managed. This was my initial sight of the inside of an empty boxcar, and my first impression was one of tremendous space. There were some large pieces of cardboard packing material strewn about, but otherwise it was empty.

"Sometime ve going to have to catch vun on the fly. Don't ever try to make it at the door, it's yust too high. You catch the ladder at the front end." We were standing at the half-open door of the boxcar as Finn was talking. His words became very emphatic.

"Remember, Russ, don't *ever* forget that—alvays the front end."

"Why is that?"

"Vell, sometimes a freight is going faster than you think. You yust can't hang on. If you trying to grab the iron on the front end and you don't make it you'll get bounced off the side of the car." He grinned ruefully. "It happened to me twice on the Santa Fe down in New Mexico—it don't feel good. But if you trying to catch that ladder at the back end, and she's going too fast to hang on, then you get tossed between the cars and under the vheels." He made a gesture of drawing his forefinger across his throat. My disregard of Finn's advice to break out a blanket that first night riding the top, and the consequences, made me an attentive listener. I never forgot his admonition—it was as important as anything he ever told me.

We heard the whistle sound, and then the successive clanks, as the slack was jerked out of the couplings the length of the train as the engine started to pull. We were ready when the jolt hit our car, but it still almost knocked us off our feet.

We stood at the open door watching as we wound through the maze of tracks in the yard and finally out onto the main line. The engine whistle gave a long *whohoohoo* and we were on our way.

Kamloops was not a large community, and we were soon out in the country. Lovely country it was there in British Columbia that July day. There were sparkling streams, lush meadows, and pine-scented forests. It felt as if we were on an uphill grade because the train didn't seem to be doing more than about fifteen miles an hour, although the gradient of a railroad track on a grade is not usually visually apparent. Being out of the wind inside our private sidedoor Pullman (the sardonic hobo term for a boxcar with its sliding sidedoors) and watching that lovely countryside roll by, I was really enjoying this ride. I decided to sit on the floor at the door and dangle my legs outside. This brought another warning from my knowledgeable companion.

"Russ, I like to do that too, but yust keep an eye out vhen you do. There should alvays be enough clearance for your legs, but you never know. Some breakmen forget and leave a svitch handle in, and it can take off your leg if your train's moving fast enough. Or if another freight is passing, and you're sitting there, sometimes there be a metal cargo strip flying loose that can cut hell out of you."

As Finn started talking I had pulled my legs back into the car. Finn smiled easily.

"It's yust that there be a lot of vays to get hurt on these freight trains. I don't vant to scare you, I yust vant to make sure you look out for yourself."

I nodded and resumed my position with my legs dangling. It was one of the most comfortable positions a hobo could find in a boxcar, and I eventually traveled a lot of miles sitting like that. But always after that I kept a sharp eye out forward for anything that could cause a sudden injury or amputation.

Jack had told us that it was about a ten-hour run to Blue River due to the grade. Three times we pulled off on a siding to make way for a through train heading west. The first time we kept a careful watch out to see if any of the crew were inspecting the train—ready to make a quick exit if it looked like trouble. But we saw nothing, and then we relaxed. We unrolled our packs, and our blankets, on top of some layers of cardboard. That made the jolting ride almost comfortable as we stretched out and dozed off from time to time.

After the stop at the first siding when no one approached our car, we decided to slide the door open on the other side. That was something I truly enjoyed. With both doors all the way open the effect, crossing a bridge over a rushing river as the scenery became ever more wild and beautiful, was spectacular. We were not just seeing this country, it was as if we were right in the middle of a vivid, exciting, and alive panorama.

Considering what lay ahead, it was fortunate in a way that the ride to Blue River was so enjoyable. The first leg of our journey had taught me to count my blessings when I had them—and have them I did in that boxcar rattling from Kamloops Junction to Blue River, British Columbia. I eventually traveled thousands of miles by sidedoor Pullman, but I never enjoyed any part of my odyssey more than this one.

# 6

About five that afternoon we felt the train slowing and heard the long sound of our engine whistle. From the boxcar door we could see the town of Blue River down the tracks. We had our blanket rolls tied, and we were ready to get off as soon as the train stopped.

We hadn't had any trouble with train crewmen or railroad bulls yet, and we didn't want any. So we were off the boxcar and moving across the web of tracks, out of the yard, just as the freight was slowing to a halt.

Blue River was a quiet community of about three thousand people in the heart of the western slope of the Canadian Rockies. The air was brisk and invigorating. The town was clean and comfortable-looking. We saw one logging mill and guessed that it and the Canadian National division yard were the main economic supports of this community. We didn't see any other hoboes or bindle stiffs on the main street, and this made us feel a bit self-conscious. But it tended to confirm Jack's advice to head north, with a better chance to get into Alberta through Jasper Pass on the Canadian National, rather than to try through Rogers Pass on the much more heavily traveled Canadian Pacific.

Our funds were now down to four dollars and fifty cents, but with the bounty of the wheat harvest waiting for us east of the Rockies we weren't too concerned.

As usual Finn kept a sharp eye out as we walked along the main street. Suddenly he stopped, pointing down a cross street.

"Russ, that look like a river yust beyond town. I bet the yungle's over there somevhere. Let's buy some grub at that store down the block, then ve head for the yungle."

We bought seventy-five cents' worth of provisions this time, which we figured would provide a good, ample dinner and breakfast—and some bread, cheese, and sausage to provision us for the next leg of our journey.

Finn was right—the jungle was just where he figured it would be on the banks of the rushing stream. It emptied into a lovely blue jewel of a lake about a quarter mile down from our camp. There were two cooking fires going when we reached the hobo camp, with four men around each. This jungle was just as clean and neat as the one in Kamloops. We exchanged greetings in a friendly way, and Finn asked if any of the 'bos were heading east.

A stocky young man at the nearest fire replied.

"Far as I know everybody here is heading east for the harvest. But we hear it's going to take some doing to get through the division at Red Pass."

Finn was quick to pick up essential information. "Vhy is that?"

"For some reason they've got a lot more Mounties on duty up there now. Goddamned if I know why, but the provincial governments are bound to keep us in B.C. and out of Alberta. Maybe they figure there's only so much work in the harvest in Alberta and they want it for their own men."

Only Finn and the young Canadian had been talking. Now an older man at the fire joined in.

"From what I hear there's only one chance of getting through Red Pass. There'll be a lot of empty boxes here out of Blue River, but those Mounties will have you rousted out of them sidedoor Pullmans so fast it'll make your head swim."

"What do they do to you if they catch you?"

"Nothing, really, but this time of year there's usually a forest fire going somewhere up there. I hear that they pull you off the freight, put you to work on a firefighting crew at seventy-five cents a day plus meals, and in about a week they buy you a ticket on a passenger train right back here to Blue River."

Finn was obviously shook up by this news. "Yesus, I don't vant to fight fire yust to buy a ticket on a bloody passenger train back here."

The other man nodded in agreement. "We all feel the same way, but I wanted to tip you guys off to what it's all aboot up the line aways."

"Vell, if you can't ride a box how do you expect to get through?"

"There's a lot of milled lumber shipped out of Blue River. Aboot the only chance you have is to ride a lumber car out until you're fairly close to Red Pass. Then you make a nest for yourself on top of the car, pull some planks over you, and hope you'll get through."

Finn's tone was skeptical. "The Mounties must have seen that a thousand times, vhy they going to miss it?"

"You're right, it's mainly a matter of luck. You see, there are so many lumber cars, and the freights are at the division in Red Pass such a short time that they just can't really check every car. Mainly what they do is walk the top of the loads. If you do a good job of getting yourself into that load, they won't be able to see you. The only way they'll find you is if they step on a plank on top of you and feel it give. If you're really lucky they may not have time to walk your car."

Finn nodded. "I see vhat you mean."

"One thing," the man continued, "for Christ's sake be careful where and how you burrow in. Stay away from the heavy lumber, the four by fours and six by sixes. Sometimes those freights start and stop with a hell of a jerk and they'll shift the load. That can make hash out of a hobo if he's in the wrong spot when that happens. We're all catching a freight out tomorrow morning aboot nine. We'll give you a hand if you want to come along."

"Thanks for the dope. Ve appreciate it, and ve'll be careful."

By then their mulligan was simmering and the cook was ladling it out into a varied assortment of good sized tin cans and other containers. When they had left the cooking fire, we moved in. Finn hadn't told me what he had bought at the butcher shop.

"What're we going to have for dinner, Finn?"

"Mountain oysters, ever have them?"

"Mountain oysters? What in the hell is that?"

Finn grinned. "Cattle nuts. They run qvite a few head of cattle up in these mountain meadows, and they save the nuts after they've castrated the yearlings. I had them the first time in a yungle down in Arizona. They're cheap and they're good."

I felt my stomach give a slight lurch. I wasn't used to anything quite this unusual in the meat line.

Finn saw the expression on my face and grinned again. "You'll like them, Russ, I guarantee it. Besides, it'll put lead in your pencil."

I put a good face on it. "Whatever you say, Finn, but right now I don't think I need any lead in my pencil—God knows when and if we'll have a chance to get laid hoboing on the road like this."

Finn was right, of course, the mountain oysters were rich, savory, and delicious.

When we had eaten our fill we again stretched out on our blankets and looked up at the starry heavens. I could tell that Finn was thinking hard.

"Seems like this is a good-sized group of hoboes, Russ. I think ve do better if ve stay over another day vhen there not be so many men all doing the same thing. Anyvay, this is a nice little town, and ve can take a svim in the lake."

He was my leader—in spades.

"Whatever you say, Finn. Show me some more of those constellations, will you?"

Finn was only too happy to oblige, and my astronomy lesson continued for another hour or so before we rolled into our blankets, breathing deeply of the crisp mountain air, and fell asleep almost immediately.

About five o'clock in the morning, I was awakened by a

sickening feeling in my stomach and a rising tide of nausea that threatened to spill over immediately. I just managed to get a decent space between me and the sleeping hoboes when I vomited violently. It seemed as if everything I'd eaten for the last week came spewing out. Finally, after another convulsive spasm I was done, and managed to find my way back to my blankets, collapsing in them without waking Finn, who was a sound sleeper anyway, or any of the other men. I had washed my mouth out at the stream and for a little while I felt almost normal. Then, just as dawn was breaking, I felt that terrible surge of nausea rising to my throat again. This time Finn was awake and looked at me in alarm as I struggled out of my blankets.

"Russ, vhat's the matter?"

I could only shake my head and lurch away. My stomach had been so thoroughly emptied by the first violent spasm that I had nothing left to heave. I simply retched helplessly, tasting the bitter bile in my mouth.

Then Finn was there beside me, holding a cup of cold water.

"Here, vash your mouth out, then drink the rest. Best you have something in your stomach to get out if you're going to heave like that."

I nodded gratefully, rinsed my mouth out, and gulped down the rest of the water in the cup.

Finn helped me back to my blankets and, as I slid weakly between them, placed his hand on my forehead. "Yesus, Russ, you be burning up!"

The other hoboes were up and about by then, and it was soon apparent to them that I was in no condition to travel.

The one who had talked to Finn the longest yesterday spoke to him again. "I wouldn't try it with your partner feeling this way. It's tough enough if you're feeling good."

Finn nodded without saying anything, and I felt a surge of relief when I remembered that he had already decided to stay over an extra day anyway. The way I was feeling just then, my stomach aching from the dry retching, and my body on fire, I didn't think that I could make it tomorrow, either, but at least we had planned for this day in Blue River.

Finn looked at the man. "Vhat do you think is vrong with him?"

He shook his head. "I don't know. You guys been traveling together. You been eating the same grub right along?"

"Absolutely the same."

"There must be something he ate you didn't, or something he did or didn't do that you missed. Can you think of anything?"

We both concentrated hard, and then I thought of something. I was barely able to whisper. "Finn, that last siding we were stopped on before Blue River, remember I got off and got a drink of water out of that stream and you didn't?"

The Canadian looked at me.

"What color was the water?"

"It was sort of greenish, but it was clean and cold."

"Glacial water, that's what you drank. Doesn't hit everybody but when it does it's murder. Fever and heaving. Good thing is that you'll be over it by tomorrow. You'll be miserable today, though, I guarantee you." His sympathetic look belied the unfeeling words.

Finn gave a sigh of relief. "Vell at least ve know vhat's ailing him." He looked inquiringly at the Canadian. "Is there anything I can do for him?"

"Not a damn thing. He's going to be heaving off and on all day. I think just keeping water in his stomach so that he'll have something to toss, and won't have the dry heaves—that's aboot all you can do. That, and try to cool down the fever."

The men rolled their packs, and they stopped to murmur a word of encouragement and luck to me as they left the jungle.

It was a long day for me, as I heaved at frequent intervals, regurgitating now only the cold river water which Finn constantly provided. That and a cool, damp handkerchief, which he dipped into the can of water he had carried up from the stream, and placed on my burning forehead. As briefly as I had known Finn Bering, the thought never crossed my mind that he would abandon me here in the hobo jungle in Blue River. I am sure that the thought never crossed his, either, as much of a potential handicap to his travels as I had become.

I don't think I became delirious that day, but I did doze off from time to time and my mind kept drifting back to my home in San Francisco with my Aunt Doris and her husband Mike Phillips.

It would be weeks before I finally wrote home—a brief post card from Fortuna, North Dakota—and sometime after that before I wrote a letter to my beloved Aunt Doris describing, among other experiences, how sick I had been in Blue River, British Columbia.

I didn't know that my Aunt Doris had saved everything that I had ever written to her. Shortly after her peaceful death at age eighty-three, her daughter, Marie, delivered a box of letters and post cards. They were the sum total of all of the communications I had ever written to my aunt from the schooner, and from various points throughout the United States when I hoboed from one end of the country to the other. There were others too, from college, from various foreign ports I had shipped to, and from overseas in the Pacific during World War II. But it was the cards and letters of this particular odyssey, including a description of how I felt at Blue River which, reading them, made it seem to me as if I had swung off the freight at Kamloops Junction only yesterday. Finally, I discovered that my ever-loving, devoted aunt had preserved a diary I had kept covering my journey, on the road, from New York City to New Orleans, across the gigantic state of Texas at its widest part, across the deserts of New Mexico and Arizona, and finally home to California. All of the cards, letters, and the diary are written in pencil, but more than half a century later, the handwriting is still legible. A glance at one of the letters, or a diary entry, and I can all but feel that boxcar rattling over the roadbed, with the warm wind sweeping over me in the open sidedoor, seeing the magnificent sweep of the North American landscape unfold before my youthful eyes.

By six that night I had stopped vomiting. Finn placed his hand on my forehead. "Vell, Russ, our friend vas about right. I know it's been a tough day for you, but you seem to be getting better." He looked at me inquiringly, and a bit anxiously I thought. "How about it. You think you be strong enough to catch a freight tomorrow?"

"I've felt better, Finn, but I'm going to be okay. As a matter of fact, the smell of that grub from the campfire makes me downright hungry."

Finn grinned. "Mountain oysters again, but you haven't eaten anything all day. Take it easy now."

He dished me up a bowl of the savory meat and potatoes, and went on talking.

"You dozed off for a couple of hours this afternoon and I vent down to the yard. Saw some lumber cars on a siding vhere they'll be making up a freight tonight. She pulls out about six in the morning. Found three cars loaded with vun-inch planks that should be vhat ve need. Think you'll be up to it?"

"Maybe it would be a good idea if we walk into town after we eat. I think I'm going to be okay but I'd like to try to get some strength back. I've been half asleep all day, and if I walk around a little it may make it easier to get a good night's sleep." I didn't realize then how prophetic my next words would prove to be. "I've got a feeling this next leg's not going to be too easy. I want to be ready for it."

After we ate we walked into town. It was light until quite late in the evening in this northern latitude, and Finn pointed out the lumber cars from the far side of the marshaling yard.

It was just beginning to get dark when we returned to camp about nine-thirty. There had been no sign of any other hoboes since the men had left that morning. As usual it looked as if Finn had figured this one right. Whatever our chances of getting through Red Pass might be, they should be better simply by virtue of the fact that two hoboes are easier to overlook than ten.

We awoke at five the next morning, and shortly thereafter found our freight. Finn located the three lumber cars he had spotted the day before. They were flat cars, with long stakes to secure the lumber on both sides, and short lengths of milled planks running across and inside the stakes at each end to contain the load of loose planks. There was no ladder, or course, and it wasn't easy clambering to the top, but we made it just as we heard the long whistle and the series of clanks down the line as the engine pulled out.

We were on our way to Red Pass, British Columbia.

# 7

As soon as we were under way Finn began to study the loosely stacked planks.

"Ve better get to vork, Russ. Ve have to move vun hell of a lot of lumber to get ourselves covered. Then ve got to be sure it's evened out on top so it looks okay."

We had been told that it was about a four-hour run from Blue River to Red Pass. There should be plenty of time to fashion our burrow but, characteristically, Finn set to work immediately. I was still feeling a bit weak from my stomach problem at Blue River, but I turned to with him. It wasn't easy on top of that swaying, jolting load of lumber, but eventually we had a space about thirteen feet long, two feet wide, and about two feet deep hollowed out. We made our wooden hole as far to the left side of the load as we could, hoping that if a Mountie did walk the top of this car, he might stay to the center.

We shifted the side planks slightly, so that when we did conceal ourselves the covering planks rested, at least as to one edge on either side, on a ledge of lumber. When Finn was satisfied that we had done everything we could, he spoke to me.

"Okay, Russ, climb in and move these pieces on top of you. Get your blanket roll long vays between your legs. I vant to see how it look. If I can't see anything, I'm going to step on the top, so be sure to brace it with your knees and hands."

I climbed into the space and moved two one-inch by twelve-inch pieces of milled lumber on top of me. They were both about six-and-a-half-feet long. It wasn't easy working in such a confined area, but I finally had myself covered.

My voice sounded muffled even to me. "How does it look, Finn?"

"Very good!" I could hear the satisfaction in his voice. "Brace yourself, I'm going to step on that top piece."

But for a crack of light it was like a coffin in there—the metaphor came unbidden to my mind. With my claustrophobic tendencies anyway, I sure as hell hoped we wouldn't be traveling this way too long.

Then I felt Finn's tread on the plank just above me where I had it braced with all my strength—palms upward, pressing hard. Despite all the pressure I could bring to bear, the one-inch plank gave slightly. As our friend in Blue River had said, it was going to take luck to make it through Red Pass this way.

When Finn stepped off the one by twelve, I flung both pieces off me—more vigorously then I realized.

Finn was smiling slightly. "Vhat's the matter, don't you like it in there?"

"Jesus, Finn, I hope we don't have to ride too long like that!"

"Don't vorry. I don't think I'm going to like that any more than you do. I figure ve'll climb in about ten minutes before Red Pass. Then it's yust a question of how long this freight is on the siding before they take her through."

I shook my head resignedly. "I guess it's the only chance we have of making it, Finn, but I sure wish there was another way."

"Vell, there isn't, so ve make the best of this vay. It looked good, but if a Mountie ever step on vun of those planks it's going to be all up vith us. I can't figure out anything to handle that."

Neither of us felt much like talking. Finn's plan for working the wheat harvest hung in the balance now. I tried not to think about the grim possibility of being tossed off this freight train, fighting fire for a week, and then being shipped back west. We were traveling through the heart of the Canadian Rockies and the scenery was spectacular. Soaring above us in the distance were the bare, jagged outlines of the magnificent range, snow-covered at the very top even at this time of year. Along the railroad right-of-way the forest crowded, the clean mountain scent of pine strong in the clear air; an occasional rushing stream of sparkling water tumbled down the side of the cut and under a culvert to dash out on the other side of the tracks.

Finn turned to me. "Vhat time do you have?"

I pulled out my wristwatch. "Ten-thirty."

"Let's finish our grub. Then ve climb in and keep our fingers crossed."

We had the planks over us when Finn spoke again as the freight was clanking to a stop.

"Remember, Russ, not a vord vhen ve're stopped. Sound really carries up here. Make sure you hold those planks level, but don't vear yourself out bracing them unless ve hear a Mountie valking the top."

"Okay, Finn." All we could do now was wait and hope.

We were stopped about ten minutes, which seemed like an eternity to me, silent in my wooden, coffin-like hole, when I heard voices on our side of the train.

"Looks pretty clean, Bill, you see any sign of men on this train?"

"No, but I'm going to check the tops of some of these lumber cars."

I heard one pair of footsteps moving away on the roadbed. For an instant my heart leaped. Maybe we were going to make it. A moment later I could hear the scuffing sound of someone climbing the load on our car, just as we had done back in Blue River. The sound of approaching feet on top of the load came nearer. It seemed to be centered on the lumber. Maybe we would make it yet. I quite literally held my breath, concentrating now on bracing the planks above me, not moving a muscle. The footsteps passed Finn, and had almost passed me, when I heard the first voice call out again. It was coming from our side of the train from the ground below about one car back.

"See anything up there?"

"No—" Then, with a step to the side of the load, I suppose by some malignant fate to better communicate with his partner, I could feel the plank above me give with the weight of a firmly planted foot. The voice was deliberate and businesslike.

"Hey, Joe, get up here and give me a hand. We may have a rider."

The next instant I felt my wooden cover lifted off, and looked up into the face of a uniformed Royal Canadian Mounted Police officer. His penetrating look pinned me like an insect in a laboratory display. It was all up with us. I stared despairingly back at him. It was my first sight of one of the famed Mounties. I could have done without the privilege. The officer was a tanned, clean-cut looking man in his early thirties. He wasn't wearing the scarlet coat of the dress uniform known worldwide. For this duty he was dressed in greenish khaki and was wearing a hard-billed police-uniform hat, not the broad-brimmed, peaked dress-campaign hat.

He looked at me almost regretfully. When he pulled the planks off me he also, of course, exposed Finn. "All right, my lads, on your feet now."

By then Joe, the other Mountie, was on top of the car. They both wore holstered pistols which looked to be of fairly heavy caliber. We had never given any thought to physically resisting the Mounties if they found us, but it probably had happened on more than one occasion when a hobo, desperate to make it through, simply abandoned his good sense. Bill, the Mountie who had stepped on my plank, spoke matter-of-factly. "Boys, we got a forest fire going aboot two miles from here. Grub's good, even if the pay isn't much. We can use your help."

Part of the process was obviously to size up our attitude. They moved and spoke rather casually, but I noticed that they kept their distance from us and both had their right hands near their holsters.

Finn had a magical ability to adapt himself to just about any situation, however adverse. He shook his head. "Ve vorked so hard on that hole."

Bill, the Mountie who had discovered us, smiled slightly. "I've seen a lot of them, lad. You boys were covered aboot as good as any. When I stepped on that plank, I sure didn't expect to feel it give."

Finn smiled ruefully back at him.

The Mountie spoke briskly now. "Toss your rolls over the side and wait until my partner is on the right-of-way. Then you climb down the same side."

We followed orders. There was never a time when one or the other didn't have us covered.

Finn feigned ignorance of what we already knew was the ultimate fate of the inducted firefighters.

"Ve haven't been eating too vell lately. You say the grub's good?"

Bill nodded. "That it is. The province pays only seventy-five cents a day; I'd guess we can use you for aboot a week."

His statement coincided with what we had been told at Blue River.

Finn shrugged resignedly. "Vell, if the food's good, seventy-five cents a day could be worse. Vhere do ve go?"

The Mountie looked at us appraisingly. Then they decided to let us find the firefighting camp without an escort.

Bill spoke again. "Follow the tracks aboot a mile down around that curve. You'll see a path to the left—it's well marked. Then follow it into the woods. It's aboot a two-mile hike from here to the base camp."

We didn't know it then, but these officers weren't risking too much turning us loose like that. More than one hobo who had decided to bypass the firefighting returned later, footsore and weary, defeated by the Canadian wilderness.

But Finn Bering, with unquenchable optimism, couldn't believe what seemed to him to be our good fortune.

We hiked down the tracks, away from the Mounties, by unspoken agreement not talking to each other. When he was sure that we had rounded the curve and were completely out of sight, Finn turned to me with a wide grin.

"Yesus, Russ, can you believe it? They turned us loose. All ve got to do now is find the next siding, vait for a freight through, and ve'll be on our vay again!"

I wasn't all that sure. "I don't know, Finn, those were pretty smart guys. I just don't think it's going to be that easy."

Finn was supremely confident. "Yust vait, you'll see. Let's valk!"

And walk we did. The problem was that there was no place to walk except between the rails over railroad ties. The route was basically cut through on the sides of mountains, with the terrain rising steeply on one side of the tracks, dropping sharply on the other. For us it was the Canadian National tracks eastward or nothing.

The ties were so spaced that it was too short a step from one tie to the next, but too long to be comfortable, even for a good-sized man like Finn, to step on every other tie with one normal pace. What added to the difficulty was that the ties were slightly elevated above the roadbed which consisted of crushed rock. As we proceeded along the right-of-way, we were constantly stepping on rough rock, then up to the hard, smooth surface of a tie, and back down to the rough rock. It was an uncomfortable walk at best, always threatening to trip you if you didn't keep an eye out for exactly where you were stepping. It was something like walking along a horizontal ladder.

This was wild, densely wooded country along the right-of-way, with the sere, naked peaks of the Canadian Rockies thrusting into the blue sky in the distance.

The sun shone brightly, but at this elevation it was not too warm. My bedroll weighed about ten pounds with the two blankets and the personal gear rolled inside. It really was not a burdensome weight, but the farther we plodded over those railroad ties the heavier it seemed.

The high-topped work shoes we each wore helped, but we hadn't been hiking an hour when I was sure that the Mounties knew exactly what they were doing back in Red Pass.

"Finn, you got any idea how far it is to the next division?"

"Not real close, but I took a look at a railroad map at Blue River the second time I vent into town. Yasper is the next division. I'd guess it's about thirty miles from Red Pass. Anyvay, don't vorry about it. Ve catch a freight some time today, the next siding."

As it turned out, Finn's estimate was off by just about fifty percent. It was forty-four miles from Red Pass, British Columbia, to Jasper, Alberta—for pedestrians like us, every foot of it over that bloody right-of-way.

I was trudging alone, keeping my eyes on where I was stepping so as not to stumble on one of the elevated railroad ties, when I heard an exultant shout from Finn.

"There—Yellowhead vun mile!"

Sure enough, the block-lettered railroad sign at the edge of the right-of-way said just that. Finn was a bit smug. "See, vhat I tell you, Russ. Ve rest vhen ve get to Yellowhead. Then the first freight through that stops on the siding ve climb aboard and ve're on our vay. If ve have to vait for a vhile ve'll buy some grub." Painfully, we trudged that mile and then we saw the sign announcing "Yellowhead." Despite the signs, Yellowhead consisted of absolutely nothing except a double set of railroad tracks, the main line through the Rockies, and a siding to accommodate a secondary train letting a mainliner through. There was not even a section shed in sight. The only evidence that any human being had ever set foot in this wilderness was the railway roadbed and the tracks themselves. Finn was a bit nonplussed, which was unusual for him.

"Vhy in the hell they give a name to a bloody siding?" He didn't expect an answer from me or bother to answer his own question. "Vell, it doesn't make any difference. Ve'll park ourselves about the middle of the siding and catch the first freight that pulls over and has to vait for a through train."

Wearily I dropped my blanket roll in the scrub brush, just off the siding about halfway down the tracks. We had been hiking then about three hours steady. It was a good deal warmer than it had been earlier in the day and there was very little breeze. The one factor that eased the pangs of hunger was the sparkling, leaping streams of cold mountain water that cascaded down and under the culverted road-bed about every mile or so. It was not greenish, I noted with relief, and I drank my fill. It not only assuaged my thirst but it gave me a full feeling so that I wasn't feeling too hungry—yet.

We hadn't been stretched out five minutes when we heard the distant sound of a train whistle coming from the west.

Finn was on his feet excitedly. "Come on, Russ, this may be our freight! Get ready!"

I got myself achingly to my feet, slung my blanket roll, and waited. I had hardly done so when a Canadian National passenger train came thundering through Yellowhead, two long sounds of the whistle crying derisively to us it seemed to me. We sank back to the ground, and about half an hour later we could hear the distant sounds of another train coming from the west. We listened carefully. The slower chugging, laboring noise made it almost a certainty that it was a freight this time. And so it was. It too rolled through Yellowhead without a pause. It was going much slower than the passenger train but far too fast for us to even think of catching it on the fly.

Finn's training as an infantryman in the Danish Army helped on that difficult march. He wasn't a soldier by choice but had put in a year of compulsory service after high school. He emphasized the necessity of taking care of our feet. Periodically we stopped and bathed them in the cold water, drying them on the single towel we each carried in our rolls. It did seem to help some, but each time it was more of a task to get my shoes back on.

Finn made up his mind after the freight rolled through Yellowhead.

"Come on, Russ, this is probably yust an emergency siding. Ve hike on to the next one. Bound to be something more there."

The weariness I felt in my legs, the ache in my feet, the beginning of the gnawing pangs of hunger in my stomach, almost caused me to rebel. Then a dawning realization of just how serious our predicament could be forced me to my feet to stumble on over those damnable railroad ties.

In addition to his greater strength and maturity, Finn had the further advantage of the responsibility as commander of this small foot force. He was always thinking, planning and, as we started down the tracks again, he asked me for the time.

I pulled out my watch. Then I stopped. "What in the hell difference does it make?"

Patiently he explained. "Those be mileposts to the center of the siding. I vant to get some idea how much time ve be making. I don't plan to hike all the vay to Yasper, but"—his voice trailed off—"you may be right, Russ, about those Mounties and vhy they didn't take us to the firefighting camp. If ve got to valk it all the vay to Yasper without food I vant to have some idea vhat ve up against."

I pulled out my watch. "It's two-thirty now."

Finn nodded, and we walked haltingly on over the ties. When we reached the milepost on the eastern end of the Yellowhead siding he asked me for the time again. I looked at my watch.

"Two fifty-five."

"Okay. Ve be making about two miles an hour over this damn track. Ve left Red Pass at about eleven-thirty." He did some mental arithmetic. "If ve keep at it steady to dark, then start early tomorrow morning, ve should make Yasper tomorrow afternoon sometime even if ve don't catch a freight."

"My God, Finn, the way my feet are feeling now I just don't think I can do it."

Finn's tone of voice was at once encouraging and admonitory. "Like I said, Russ, I'm sure ve'll catch a freight somevhere along the right-of-vay, but vithout food ve von't last forever. Ve better plan on hiking it all the vay if ve have to."

In a way Finn's mistaken estimate of the distance between Red Pass and Jasper was a blessing. By his reckoning we had covered about a third of the distance. If I had realized then that it was forty-four miles to Jasper instead of thirty, with about thirty-four miles yet to go, that knowledge might have defeated me.

On we trudged. We were stopping more frequently now, and each time that I bathed my feet it was harder to get my shoes back on.

After an eternity, another railroad sign slowly came into view— "Wildhorse one mile."

Finn probably wasn't feeling much better than I was, and he may have felt the pangs of hunger to an even greater degree with a larger body to sustain. The sausage and cheese sandwich I had eaten just before we pulled into Red Pass this morning was only a faint memory now. I was sure that Finn was feeling just as starved as I was. Still, he felt the responsibility for getting us into this, and he made his voice as briskly cheerful as he could.

"Vhat time is it now?"

I stopped and pulled out my watch. "About six forty-five."

Finn nodded. "I think these places about seven miles apart. Ve'll take a rest in Vildhorse, maybe buy some food there." For a moment he forgot, or deliberately chose to disregard, what he had said earlier about maybe having to hike it all the way to Jasper without food.

When we reached the signpost identifying Wildhorse, it was a replica of Yellowhead—nothing but a double set of tracks. Finn shook his head. He did seem a bit discouraged.

"Ve rest for about ten minutes here, then ve'll go till ve find a stream about dark." He tried to grin. "That'll give us something to put in our stomachs tonight and tomorrow morning before ve start."

I didn't even bother to reply. Somehow I got to my feet again. It was about eight-thirty when Finn decided we would camp for the night. There was a small shelf of ground a safe distance from the side of the right-of-way, a clear stream flowing nearby.

After I had spread my blankets I started to unlace my shoes. Finn looked at me for a moment, and kept his voice casual.

"Russ, I think ve best unlace our shoes much as ve can, but I don't think ve better take 'em off. I'm afraid ve not get them back on. My feet look pretty svollen. Those blisters you got on your feet—" He didn't finish the sentence, simply shook his head.

As totally miserable as I was, I was asleep the instant I rolled up in my blankets. Before I knew it, Finn was shaking me awake the next morning. I sleepily opened my eyes, squinting at the grandeur of a crimson dawn coloring the distant peaks to the east.

Finn's tone was gentle. "Come on, Russ, the sooner ve start the sooner ve get there."

I realized then that he had given up hope of catching a freight. We had to do this on our own. I almost cried out with pain as I stood up and felt the sudden burst of fire in both feet.

Then on we struggled. We were crossing more trestles now as the tracks traversed deep mountain ravines. Finn brought up the rear today, I think to make sure that I didn't simply give up.

We hadn't seen a train, either passenger or freight, since the two yesterday. About ten-thirty, laboriously making our way across the third trestle we had crossed this morning, I realized Finn had stopped behind me. Involuntarily, I stopped too. Crossing those trestles was really brutal. There wasn't even the roadbed between the ties. It meant mincing across from tie to tie or taking the long half-step half-jump from every other one to the next alternate tie. The rocky bottom of the ravine, about two hundred feet below, waited under us if we stumbled.

Suddenly there was a terrible urgency in Finn's voice. I was so numb I had heard nothing.

"Russ, there's a passenger train coming. Go as fast as you can!"

We were more than halfway across, past the point of no return, and while it didn't really matter to my conscious mind by then, somehow the instinct for self-preservation took over. To a degree, I did move a bit faster over those terrible, life-threatening railroad ties, urged on now by Finn's shouts to move it, and the ever-increasing roar of the onrushing train. We were about eight feet from the end of the trestle when I could feel it shake with the movement of the wheels starting across.

"Russ—go!

I kept on, as fast as I could, not even considering the choice between death beneath the wheels of the iron monster or death on the rocks below. Just three feet from the end, the roar of the train enveloping me, I felt a blow to my body that sent me flying through the air, off the right-of-way and tumbling down the slope. At the same instant we were surrounded by steam and the screaming sound of the train's sanded braking. The engineer had finally seen us, too late to stop, but his full emergency braking attempt slowed the juggernaut the bare instant it took for us to escape with our lives. That sound stopped and the train rushed past us. I looked up once from under Finn's body to see the end passenger car flashing by. It took me a moment to realize that at the last possible instant, when

Finn realized that I wasn't going to make it in time, he drove his body into mine and flung us both off the right-of-way a split second before the engine roared by.

We lay there for a moment.

"Thanks, Finn." The words were hardly adequate, but it was all I could get out. Finn simply nodded.

The rest of that day passed in a semiconscious blur for me. We drank water, we passed three other named sidings—none with a vestige of human habitation—and we stopped more and more frequently.

Finn had already calculated that the sidings were about seven miles apart, and that he had badly underestimated the distance from Red Pass to Jasper. If anything the knowledge seemed to strengthen his indomitable will.

The last time we stopped that day it was after dark. I told Finn that I had had it.

"It's no use, I can't get up again."

His tone was cold and hard. "Goddammit, Russ, you vill get up! Ve only a mile from Yasper now, I reckon."

I didn't have the strength to debate him about his prior reckoning of distance, I simply knew that I couldn't get to my feet one more time. But I was wrong.

I felt my wrists grasped by an iron hand, and as if my arms were being jerked out of the sockets, Finn got me on my feet the last time.

He was finally right. The lights of Jasper came into sight a lifetime later. We had made it.

# 8

A jungle fire flickered in the distance and, after so many tortuous miles, the right-of-way leveled out so that we could walk off that accursed roadbed. Mercifully the hobo jungle in Jasper was on the west end of the railroad yard. We half stumbled down a bank to the fire crackling cheerfully by the side of a stream. A lone hobo was there, cooking. It was then about nine at night, and even in the dim light he could tell something was wrong with us.

"Where you boys come from?"

Finn muttered, "Red Pass."

"Red Pass! There ain't been a freight east since yesterday afternoon."

We just looked at him. Then I replied, "Nobody knows that any better than us, believe me!"

"Then how in the hell—" He stopped in disbelief. "Don't tell me you walked it over those bloody tracks?"

Finn nodded. "Ve sure did."

"How long since you had any grub?"

"Yesterday morning," I answered.

"Well, I got plenty of mulligan here. Help yourselves."

There really wasn't all that much stew simmering in the cooking can over the fire, but we gratefully accepted his generous invitation.

As the food went into my stomach it seemed as if the same burning sensation returned to my feet—and a terrible feeling it was.

Sometimes it was as if Finn read my mind. "Russ, tonight ve better get our shoes off. I think ve soak our feet good in that cold vater ve be pretty much okay tomorrow."

As painful as the cold water felt, and as difficult as it was to totter back barefooted the short distance from the stream to our blankets, Finn was right. When I woke up the next morning, I was ravenously hungry, my legs ached, but I was feeling almost normal again. At one point the day before yesterday, when I had bathed my feet, I had two blisters on the small and third toes of my left foot as large as the last joints on those particular digits. There were two on my right foot at the same places and about the same size. During the subsequent hiking all of those blisters had broken. The cold-water soak had wrought a small miracle last night. This morning there were shriveled patches of skin half covering the red flesh underneath, but no sign of infection. If I could just give my feet a rest in the clean pair of socks I gingerly pulled on, I was sure the blisters would heal rapidly.

Our host of the evening before, a Canadian by the name of Johnny, was one of the very few who had successfully concealed himself in a load of milled timber, and had been lucky enough to avoid having his hiding place disclosed by the tread of a Mountie. Like us, he was bound for the wheat harvest farther east. He was a man in his late twenties, and had been hoboing for some years in the Canadian west. He was quite knowledgeable as well as talkative. When we awoke the next morning, he was squatting on his haunches, sipping a tin can of hot coffee, staring at us, and still figuratively shaking his head.

"You know, boys, I've made that run four times now by freight. I don't rightly know whether or not any other hoboes ever made that hike, but you're the first I've met who've done it." He did shake his head this time. "Jesus!"

Now that we had made it, Finn's good humor was fully restored, and I was in a better mood myself.

Finn spoke to Johnny. "Vhere do you figure on finding vork in the harvest?"

"Well, it's a little early yet. They haven't started cutting and bundling. I figure to head east to Edmonton, lay over there for a while, then go south and east to get some work stooking first."

I looked at him. This was a new word to me. "Stooking, what's that?"

"They call it shocking in the States. It's when you go down the rows and stack up the tied bundles of wheat, usually three at a time, so the wheat'll dry and be ready for threshing."

Finn spoke again, "How are ve going to find out vhether ve can get vork or not?"

Johnny's tone was authoritative. "Don't worry about that. Those farmers need help when they have to get the wheat stooked up and drying. The word'll be out in every jungle on the prairie when there's work."

Finn changed the subject. "You vere very kind to us last night, Johnny, sharing that mulligan. You know vhere ve can buy some eggs? I'd like to fix us a big scrambled eggs breakfast."

Johnny's eyes lit up. "There's a little farm aboot a mile from here where I borrowed a couple of eggs yesterday."

"Vell ve don't have a lot of money, but ve got some. Vhat do you think he'll charge us for a dozen?"

Johnny thought a moment. "Probably about fifteen cents. Why don't you let me go get them." He gave us a quick smile. "I'd guess neither one of you feels much like walking."

Johnny was back in about forty-five minutes. "That farmer was really a nice guy. I think he was so surprised at a hobo wanting to buy something, instead of stealing it, that he threw in this chunk of butter and half a loaf of his wife's homemade bread."

Finn was a good jungle cook, and while he didn't have a skillet, that rich melted butter on the bottom of a cooking can combined with the dozen fresh farm eggs to produce an omelet that would have done a French chef proud. The omelet and the homemade bread made a breakfast as delicious and satisfying as any I had ever had.

When we had finished our repast, we scrubbed the cooking can clean with sand from the stream and water heated over our cooking fire. We left the jungle campsite squared away as we had found it and with a small pile of wood for the next travelers to use these accommodations.

We didn't see a sign of any Mounties, railroad bulls, or anyone else in the Jasper yards. It was as if that barrier at Red Pass insulated British Columbia from Alberta, and the authorities did not concern themselves with those few Knights of the Road who might slip through. Johnny had decided to travel with us as far as Edmonton. We found an empty boxcar on a made-up freight train, and were on our way about ten in the morning.

In a rather short space of time, I had been thoroughly exposed to the rigors of the road. On the one hand, it had made me a realist. However pleasant it now was to roll down out of the Canadian Rockies, sitting in the open door of our sidedoor Pullman, feeling the warm air flowing over me, my stomach full, I had no illusions about what we might encounter ahead. On the other hand, it had engendered the capacity to live for the moment and enjoy my present circumstances. Hour after hour we rolled on. The vastness of the Canadian prairie was as impressive in its way as the majestic mountains had been in theirs.

About an hour before we pulled into Edmonton, we tried to plan out our route with Johnny, who was going to wait out the slowly approaching northward march of the wheat harvest. We were down to about two and a half dollars now. Finn was impatient to get working.

"Johnny, I don't mind bumming vhen ve have to, but I'd like to get as far south on our money as ve can and get a yob. Vhere do you think our best chance is?"

"I'd say south Saskatchewan. They ought to be stooking aboot now or not too long from now. For some reason they're not watching the freights too close between Alberta and Saskatchewan. If if were you, I'd ride the Canadian National down to Calgary and catch the Canadian Pacific east."

That night we rolled up in our blankets in the Edmonton jungle, and the next morning said good-bye to Johnny. There was a connecting spur line between Edmonton and Calgary, but we waited a bit too long to catch our southbound freight. We had cased the train from one end to the other without finding an empty boxcar, although there were gondolas on the train carrying gravel. As we stood by the tracks near a sealed boxcar the train started to pull out. Finn was decisive.

"Russ, ve catch this vun on the fly now! Get that gondola coming up. I'll get the next one."

When I had sold newspapers back home in San Francisco several years earlier, I frequently worked the city streetcars, which meant catching them while they were moving, and often getting off the same way. With a bundle of papers under one arm I had only my right hand free to grab the vertical rail at the running board. I knew from this experience how important it was to match the speed of the car as I jumped on. The principle of catching a freight on the fly was exactly the same. You had to be running as fast as the train was moving, or the jerk on your arms was too great. This was the first time we would try to catch a moving train, but with my personal experience, and two hands to grab with, I felt no qualms.

I started to run with the train, my bedroll bouncing, the carrying sling across my chest. Finn was running too, a bit more slowly, dropping behind me. As the front end of the gondola approached I speeded up, grabbed the iron with my hands, and leaped for the bottom rung. My right foot hit the metal step and slipped through. For a terrible moment my foot was inches from the grinding wheel of the front truck of the gondola, my left foot dragging behind me, bouncing off the roadbed. I thought for an instant of dropping off completely, but the train had speeded up then to the point where it would have meant certain death to go backward off the ladder, even assuming that my right foot would clear the ladder going off and I wasn't hung there with my body caught by one leg, being dashed to a pulp along the right-of-way. The thoughts did not come slowly and rationally. They were instantaneous flashes of knowledge. I knew that my only chance for salvation lay in the strength of my arms. With an effort that cracked my arm muscles I did a pull-up on the upper rung of the ladder to which I was clinging in desperation. I started to sweat with the effort and the terror, and my hands were slick with perspiration, slipping slightly on the iron rung that I clung to so grimly. As the freight gathered frightening speed, I slowly and agonizingly pulled my body up until I could plant my left foot on the bottom rung, my right foot still close to the spinning wheel. Once I had my left heel locked on the rung, I pulled my right foot through until it too was planted there. For a brief moment I pressed my body against the ladder, my legs trembling violently with exertion and the terrible realization of what had almost happened. Then, very carefully and slowly, I climbed the ladder to the top of the gondola and tumbled over the side onto the load of gravel.

Finn had caught the gondola behind me and had already crossed from that one to the car I had finally caught. I lay on the gravel breathing heavily. He looked at me.

"Russ, you look vhite! Vhat happened?"

I shook my head. Finally I told him. "I don't know why, Finn, the train wasn't going too fast when I grabbed the ladder, but my right foot slipped through and my left leg was dangling."

"Yesus!"

"I thought about dropping off for a second, but the train speeded up so fast I was sure I'd be killed if I did that. I just hung on and finally managed to pull myself up and get my feet on the ladder. I don't know what I did wrong."

Finn's voice was reassuring, but I could see the grave concern in his eyes. "You didn't do anything wrong, Russ. Like I tell you, this be a dangerous vay to travel. Sometimes these things happen. You made it—that's the main thing."

There was a space between the end of the gondola and the slope of the load of gravel that provided enough room to stretch out and be protected from the wind. I lay there with the prairie sun beating down on me, as the freight rolled on, and gradually the trembling in my legs subsided. Five hours later we were in Calgary, the next division.

We caught a Canadian Pacific east out of Calgary. There were more hoboes traveling now and little or no policing of the railroad yards and trains. By unspoken acknowledgement, the authorities accepted the fact that the golden bounty of those wheat-laden plains required the sweat and muscle of the wanderers who sought only a chance to work for their food.

Little by little our small cash reserve dwindled as we bought food from time to time, asked in the jungles about available work in the harvest, and then moved on.

We now traveled in empty boxcars almost all the time. From Calgary to Medicine Hat, Swift Current, Moose Jaw—the place names a colorful mirror of this western country. At Moose Jaw we had spent our last money and still there was no sign of work. Finn studied the railroad map at the Moose Jaw depot.

"Ve're yust guessing now anyvay, Russ, but I think if ve get off this main line and head farther south there not be so many men and ve have a better chance to get a yob."

For once he was right, but there turned out to be a hard road between Finn Bering's plan and its implementation. There was a short string of empty boxes on a freight heading southeast out of Moose Jaw on a secondary rail line. We climbed aboard one of them when the train was made up and ready to go. There was not another hobo on this particular train and that should have told us something. Nor was there the slightest evidence of railroad security. We strolled along the right-of-way, like a couple of passengers selecting a cushioned coach for its particular amenities, until we found a boxcar with some clean cardboard packing remnants strewn about the floor.

It was a slow, halting ride to Weyburn, Saskatchewan, which took about five hours. When the train stopped we climbed off and dropped our blanket rolls in the local jungle. It was not an inviting scene. There was no sparkling stream dancing by, and only a few sticks of firewood. What we could see of Weyburn in the distance was equally dispiriting. The railroad division towns, like Medicine Hat and Swift Current, had a certain vitality to them, even in this Depression year, which the constant traffic and activity of a main railroad line created. The small prairie towns like Weyburn had once been prosperous communities serving as supply centers for a thriving agricultural economy. Now they were windswept, decaying places, their populace trapped like the farmers by a vicious cycle of poor whcat-crop years with high prices and little grain to market, or abundant crops with prices so depressed that it was equally catastrophic for farmers and merchants alike.

Finn looked at me quizzically. "You ever done any begging, Russ?"

I was indignant. "Hell, no, I've always earned my keep!"

"Vell ve got no choice now." He smiled. "I'm a pretty good bummer. Ve got no money and no yob. So you hike down to the far end of town and start hitting the houses. Don't yust ask for food. You always ask if there's vork you can do, okay? I'll start at this end, then ve'll meet back here in a couple of hours."

This would not be the last time on the road for me to beg for food, but it was the first time in my life that I had confronted this humiliating necessity, and it seemed to me to be the worst experience yet. I couldn't understand Finn's ready acceptance of this fact of life on the road.

The houses were small on the outskirts of town. They were all weather-beaten, some looking as if they had never been painted. Most had scanty, parched-looking vegetable gardens in back. The main road through Weyburn was unpaved.

It didn't look to me as if the occupants had enough to eat themselves, much less something to spare for a handout. I steeled myself and knocked at the back door of a house standing by itself on the far corner of town.

A tired-looking, middle-aged woman in a faded dress opened the door behind the screen. She stared at me.

"Ma'am, do you have some work—"

She slammed the door in my face.

Somehow this type of rejection was as humiliating for me as the need to beg was. It was as if I weren't even worth an explanation. Doggedly, I continued on.

I selected the houses at random so that my attempts at begging would not cause a door to be slammed in my face in a house adjoining the one I had just tried, but it did no good. Time after time I hardly opened my mouth before the same thing happened. Occasionally there was a murmured "sorry," but the result was always the same.

I pulled out my watch. It was almost time to meet Finn back at the jungle. I was growing desperate, and hungrier and hungrier. I decided to try one more time.

The lady who opened the next door at least listened to me.

"I'm sorry, there really isn't anything that needs doing." She stared at me for a moment. "How long has it been since you've eaten anything?"

"Yesterday morning, ma'am."

"You wait here on the back steps. I'll fetch you something."

She returned with a large bowl of rhubarb and a spoon. It wasn't my favorite food by a long shot, and the flavor seemed particularly sour to me, but it filled my stomach. I thanked her for her kindness and headed back to the jungle.

When I got there, Finn was stretched out on his blankets, his hands clasped behind his head, looking remarkably satisfied.

"Vell, how did you do, Russ?"

"Not too good. But the last place I hit I did get a bowl of rhubarb. It's helped some. How did you do?"

Finn grinned at me. "Good. I offered to vork, of course, but I didn't have to. There's only a few good-sized houses in this town, and they're all up at this end vhere I started." His tone was apologetic. "I'm sorry, I didn't know that vhen I told you to start at the other end."

"That's okay, Finn, I probably would have screwed it up anyway. What did you get to eat?"

"A full roast beef dinner. And five roast beef sandwiches. Here."

He reached inside a paper bag and pulled out a large sandwich. The slices of bread were obviously homemade and somewhat rough-ly cut. As Finn handed me the sandwich, I could see the thick slabs of roast beef and the heavily buttered insides of the slices. Compared with that bowl of rhubarb, this was something else. As I bit ravenously into the sandwich, Finn watched me appraisingly.

"You know, Russ, that look on your face vhen you started out—I could tell it vas really bothering you. Did you ever change that look vhen you knocked on those doors?"

"I don't really know. Probably not."

"Look at it this vay. Vhen vun of those vomen answer the door, they don't have much anyvay, and they see you standing there looking mad. You're probably lucky you got that bowl of rhubarb." He grinned sympathetically.

"You're probably right, Finn, but Jesus I hate to beg!"

"I'd rather vork than beg myself, but let me ask you—vouldn't you enjoy giving somevun something to eat if he needed it and you had it?"

"Well, sure, but—"

"So try to think of it that way. You look pleasant but hungry— that's not hard these days—and you're giving them a chance to do something that'll make them feel good."

Finn changed the subject. "They tell me at the grain elevator that they're really looking for men to stook vheat in Estevan now."

"Where's that?"

"It's about fifty miles southeast from here. There's another spur line running down there I'm told. The town's close to the border vith the States."

"Is there a freight heading that way?"

"About four in the afternoon tomorrow. Ve each have another sandvich tomorrow morning, and save the last two yust in case. Then ve catch that freight, and I hope ve find a yob in Estevan."

I noticed with some interest that my friend's unquenchable

optimism seemed to be tempered now with a bit of caution. He was conserving our rations and only hoping for a job. It was obvious that Finn Bering was also becoming more of a realist.

The freight out of Weyburn was short—not more than ten boxcars—all empties and no caboose on the end. It was the first time we had seen one made up quite like this.

"Finn, why all these empties, and nothing else on the train?"

"I don't know." He shrugged. "I guess if the harvest is getting close down around Estevan they may be setting up these empties to haul grain."

"Why don't they have a caboose coupled up? We've never seen a freight yet without one. There's something wrong with this train."

"Yah," Finn's tone was thoughtful. "You may be right. Anyvay, this is the only freight out and it's heading in the right direction, so let's climb aboard."

We got into an empty about the middle of the train and were soon on our way. Away from the towns the golden stands of wheat undulated in the slight breeze that blew over the prairie. At widely spaced intervals we could see the farming homesteads, always bordered by a stand of trees. They were lonely-looking places to me but, with the maturing crop surrounding them, they did not convey the air of desolation that Weyburn had.

The freight rattled along slowly, doing about ten miles an hour. Once in a while the right-of-way veered near an unpaved, dusty, two-lane road. We never saw a motor vehicle of any description on that road. The freight we were traveling on was the only sign of life in that tremendous expanse of sky and prairie. We rolled through the small town of Midale. Then an hour or so later, about seven that evening, we felt the train slowing. Finn looked at me with a puzzled expression.

"I figure ve got another two hours to Estevan. Vonder vhy ve stopping here."

We both stood up and peered out of the open door. All we could see was a network of railroad tracks with not a sign of human habitation. As the train began to stop, with the usual jarring clanks of the couplings, we saw lines of boxcars standing immobile on each of the sidings. In the distance there was a line of old passenger coaches. Then our freight stopped and we climbed off. Looking down the line of cars, we watched as the engine uncoupled and steamed off away from us. A few minutes later it was on the line back to Weyburn.

I was dismayed. "Finn, didn't you say this freight was bound for Estevan?"

"That's vhat they tell me in Veyburn. But this sure as hell is no town. Let's check out those passenger cars. May be some other hoboes here."

We hiked down the tracks and then over to where five very old Canadian Pacific coaches stood forlornly on a far siding, the paint peeling from their sides. Despite a growing sense of foreboding, there was something fascinating about the silence, the number of empty boxcars quietly waiting, and finally that line of passenger cars. It was like a railroad ghost town.

We climbed the high step of the last coach in the line and mounted to the vestibule. The door into the car was tightly shut, but we finally forced it open and started down the coach. We could see gas lamps spaced along the upper sides of the car and straight-backed velour-covered coach seats. The windows were so dust-covered that only an eerie light penetrated the interior. The only sound was our own footsteps. "Kind of spooky, isn't it Finn?"

"Yah, these cars must be fifty years old at least."

We forced our way though two more cars and were just starting down the fourth when we heard a weak voice coming out of the gloom.

"Who's that?"

Finn was walking ahead of me and stopped so abruptly that I bumped into him. I could feel my heart pounding—the sound of a human voice in that old railroad graveyard of coaches really startled me.

Finn replied, "Yust a couple of hoboes." He peered down the gloomy interior. "Vhere are you?"

"Right here."

I saw a slightly built figure rise from a seat about half way down the car and emerge into the aisle.

He was a young man, about twenty-one, rather small, with blond hair. He looked vulnerable and fragile. Finn's voice was loud in the silence of the ancient coach.

"Vhat in the hell are you doing here?"

The man smiled weakly. "I don't mean to be nosey but I could ask you the same question."

"Because somevun tell me that bloody freight vas going all the way to Estevan. Ve're looking for vork in the harvest. By the way, my name is Finn, this is my partner Russ."

We shook hands.

"Glad to know you, I'm Roger. Been here since yesterday. They told me the same thing in Weyburn."

He swayed slightly. Finn moved toward him. "You okay?"

"Just weak. I haven't eaten anything since the day before yesterday—and not too much then."

Finn's voice was concerned. "You better sit down, Roger."

We faced each other on an old set of coach seats, a visual parody of genteel travelers riding the cushions two or three generations ago.

We both stared at Roger, who was obviously about done in. Then Finn got up, moved across the aisle, and started to unroll his pack on the seat opposite us. His back was to me, but I knew what he was going to do. He moved back to where we were sitting and thrust the bag containing our two remaining sandwiches at our companion.

"Here. You need this vorse than ve do."

Roger gulped as he snatched the bag and looked at Finn, his eyes glistening. He started to say something but couldn't get the words out. He wolfed down those two large sandwiches as if they were delicacies plucked off a tray at a cocktail party.

All I could think of, watching him devour our remaining food, was the void in my own stomach. I had the feeling that the only way we were going to make it to Estevan was by foot. It had to be at least twenty miles from this godforsaken cemetery of railroad cars, and now we would be doing it without food. Then, with something of an inner bravado, I thought—we did it without food for forty-four miles over railroad ties, we can sure do it for twenty over a road.

I remembered Finn's brief lecture yesterday about giving when you had it, but somehow it did not erase the memory of our food disappearing into Roger's mouth.

When he had swallowed the last morsel, he leaned back and looked at us. "You know, I don't think I could have lasted much longer. You guys have really saved my life."

I felt a twinge of guilt as he thanked both of us. I was not that sure I was capable of the sacrifice Finn Bering had just made. One thing—my Danish friend practiced what he preached.

"Vhat vere you planning to do, Roger, before ve showed up?"

"God, I just don't know. It's so damn lonely here—I haven't talked to a soul. The engine uncoupled from a line of boxes and then just took off back up the line toward Weyburn."

"That yust vhat happened to us. Vhat kind of place is this?"

"Well I've heard that the Canadian Pacific has some old sidings with a lot of empty track scattered across the prairie. I'm told that they use some of them for storage yards just to get them out of the main divisions. My guess is that's what this is. I walked the tracks aways south yesterday, probably aboot half a mile, but it sure doesn't look like there's been any trains over them for a long time. There's grass growing in the right-of-way now. What do you figure to do?"

I could tell that Finn Bering was about to garner another recruit.

"Vell, ve got no reason to stay here, and I think you be right about this being some type of storage yard. Vonder how long these old passenger coaches been here?"

Roger shook his head. "Beats me."

Finn continued briskly.

"So, ve know that road's got to take us to Estevan. I reckon it's about twenty miles..." he broke off with an embarrassed grin, looking at me and remembering his estimate of the distance from Red Pass to Jasper. "Anyvay, ve going to turn in early tonight and start hiking first thing tomorrow morning, maybe before daybreak, vhile it's still cool."

Roger looked at him. "Mind if I go with you?"

Finn grinned. "You're velcome, Roger, don't think you got any more choice than ve have. By the vay, is there any vater around here somevhere?"

Roger shook his head. "None that I've been able to find. I thought I was more thirsty than hungry until I saw that grub of yours." He smiled ruefully. "Now I'm really thirsty again, but it's best not to think about it."

"If Estevan be tventy miles avay," Finn shot me a sideways glance, "I think ve make it in maybe six or seven hours. Vhat time is it now, Russ?"

I kept a straight face and pulled out my faithful Waltham. "Eight o'clock."

"Okay, ve hit the blankets now and ve start down that road four tomorrow morning vhile it's still dark."

It was black the next morning. No moon, only the stars in the velvet sky above us when we got under way—as Finn had planned. I had some difficulty swallowing when I woke up but, by working my jaw muscles, I managed to generate enough saliva to moisten my mouth and throat.

The first couple of hours went fairly well, and I blessed Finn's good sense in starting this early in the dark.

As we started walking down that dusty road, in order to bolster the morale of his troops or perhaps his own, Finn began to reminisce about his wheat-harvest experience back home in Denmark.

"You know it's hard vork in the harvest, but there be good things about it too. My uncle in Glostrup had forty acres of vheat, and it vent through the same cycle they talk about here. First it vas cut and tied into bundles. Then ve stooked it, as they call it here in Canada. Ve vorked hard, but my uncle vas a good guy. He put a beer keg on a vagon about mid-morning, and the horses pull it out to vhere ve're working."

"Beer keg!" Suddenly I wished that Finn had left this part out. Dawn was just breaking then, it was still cool as we trudged along the road, but the mental image of a cold mug of beer drawn out of a keg was almost too much for me. I couldn't even work up any saliva by then.

Finn Bering, however, was lost in his own memories.

"Yah. A beer keg. Cold it vas too, and it tasted good. Our Danish beer is strong, like Canadian beer, but ve sveat so much that you sveat it out qvick. Then mid-afternoon the vagon come out again." Finn smiled reminiscently. "Uncle Gustav have a very pretty neighbor girl. Vunce in a vhile she ride the vagon out. She played the accordion very good. Afternoons ve have good Danish smörgåsbord vith the beer. Then that girl playing music—it vas something."

"Jesus, Finn, you should have paid *him*." I was trying to be sarcastic, but the way it came out *I* would have paid anyone to stack bundles of wheat just to enjoy that cold beer and food.

"No, Russ. Like I said, believe me, ve work hard but all that helped. I don't know how they do it here in Canada, but those things help so much, and keep you vorking so hard, that I vouldn't be surprised if they did something like that here."

I really couldn't tell whether Finn actually believed it, was trying to convince himself, or was just trying to keep my spirits up. Whatever the reason, I decided to keep my mouth shut and we trudged grimly on.

We didn't rest for the first two hours, but when the sun rose in that hard, light-blue metallic sky we simply had to take a break every forty-five minutes or so. I started to sweat and was surprised that my body could generate that much moisture. Roger had not said a word since we started, but I noticed that he was dropping farther and farther behind.

It was like walking across a landscape retrieved in memory from a nightmare. There was not a sign of life. There were no intersecting farmroads. Every once in a while I wondered whether we truly were on the road to Estevan. From the slight elevation of the boxcar on the right-of-way yesterday we had seen an occasional farmstead in the far distance. Today we saw nothing.

About ten in the morning we collapsed on the bank by the side of the road. Roger was some distance behind us, trudging slowly.

"How far you think we've come, Finn?"

"God only knows. I think ve're doing better than ve did on those tracks out of Red Pass, but probably not much. I think ve have maybe another three miles or so yet."

Roger reached us and stumbled over to the bank. I spoke to him.

"How you doing?"

"I'm not sure I can go much longer. If we see a farmhouse somewhere I'm going to head for it. They got to give me a drink of water."

Finn and I looked at each other.

"Vell ve so close to Estevan now, I think, Roger, that it's best you hang on, make it into town."

"I know, Finn, but I haven't had any water for longer than you two, I really ain't sure I can make it without something to drink."

Finn merely nodded, and five minutes later he clambered to his feet, slinging his bed roll as he did. When we hiked, we carried the rolls by the sling over one shoulder. Climbing aboard a moving train, we slung them diagonally across our backs, the slings crossing our chests. Roger tried once to get to his feet but sank back to the roadbed. Without a word Finn grabbed one hand, I grabbed the other, and we hauled him up. He swayed slightly, then muttered, "Thanks. I'll keep trying."

About half a mile down the road was a right angle turn. It was almost the first bend we had seen. It had to mean something.

Onward we labored; the sun was merciless now. As we cleared the turn we saw in the distance a cluster of buildings. To our right a farmroad intersected the highway. Down that road, about halfway to our destination, we could see the characteristic stand of trees that marked a farmstead.

Roger looked at us.

"You know, if it hadn't been for you two, I'm not sure I would have made it. Right now I've got to have water so bad that I'm heading for that farm."

Finn nodded understandingly. "I know, Roger, but I yust don't feel like hiking all the vay to that farm, and then back, vhen ve can be in town about the same time. But you do vhat you vant."

We shook hands weakly, and Roger limped down the private road toward the farm. We continued on.

For once Finn had figured it right. It was about two and a half miles down the dusty thoroughfare to Estevan—a community that made Weyburn seem like a bustling metropolis. It didn't matter. We both saw it at the same instant. A horse trough filled with water. We broke into some kind of shambling half run and, as we reached the trough, simultaneously immersed our heads in that blessed liquid. There was a greenish sort of straw-filled scum on the surface, the temperature was tepid, but it didn't matter to either of us. Halfway down, the water was clean and cool. I swallowed and swallowed, finally emerging, gasping for air. Finn did exactly the same. Then we sat on the ground with our backs to the trough. I looked at him.

"Finding this goddamned wheat harvest of yours is tougher than I thought it would be, Finn."

He just looked at me.

At that moment a stocky farmer, clad in bib overalls and a straw hat, strolled over to where we sat on the dusty main road of Estevan. He had an amused look in his eyes.

"You boys lookin' for work?"

We were finally there.

# 9

We struggled to our feet, the water dripping from our hair.

Finn answered the farmer's question. "Ve sure are!"

He replied, "I can pay you a dollar a day, and you'll get plenty of good food."

I was incredulous. "A dollar a day!" After all that we had been through, we might as well still be on the S.S. *Dagmar Salen*.

His tone was understanding. "I'm sorry, boys, it's all I can afford. There are some other people in town looking for men. They can't pay any more than I can. You're welcome to find out if you don't believe me."

Finn, as usual, was pleasant and tactful. "Ve believe you. It's yust that ve hear for so long that they pay good money in the harvest..." His voice trailed off.

"I know. More than one of the men on the road have told me that. I think in the States, on a threshing crew, you can make more, but times have been tough up here."

"Vhere's your place located?"

"It's aboot twenty miles west, a couple of miles north of the border." Our prospective employer had shrewdly calculated that his references to higher wages in the States, and the locale of his homestead being just north of the border, might be enough to tip the balance for a couple of workers he badly needed at that point.

Finn shoved out his hand. "My name's Finn Bering. This is Russ Hofvendahl. Ve'd like to vork for you."

We were introducing ourselves to a stable member of society here, not a drifter. Last names were appropriate under these circumstances. When we shook hands I could feel the hard calluses, and felt self-conscious about my own relatively soft hands.

"Glad to know you. I'm Fritz Hoffman. Throw your rolls in the back of my truck over there, and we'll head for my place."

He led the way to a battered-looking 1930 Model A Ford truck with sideboards and a tailgate built onto the flatbed. We tossed our packs in the bed of the truck, and the three of us climbed in. With Finn's large bulk occupying the right of the seat, and Fritz behind the steering wheel, I was squeezed in the middle, straddling the gear shift where it stuck up from the floorboards.

Expertly Fritz retarded the spark, choked the carburetor, and turned the ignition. The Model A coughed reluctantly a couple of times and then sputtered into life. Fritz pushed in the clutch, shifted into low, and we were off. He made a U-turn in the deserted main street of Estevan, then turned off, and on to another unpaved, dusty road heading west.

It didn't take long to leave Estevan behind. It was a smaller, more woebegone version of Weyburn. There was a one-pump gas station at the edge of town. The chief structures were a one-story bank, with a wooden framework, on one side of the main street, and a one-story general store on the opposite side, with a small wooden

Lutheran church next to it. There were still hitching rails fronting the wooden sidewalks. A small cluster of single-story dwellings drifted aimlessly off to the prairie on both sides of the main street. They may have been freshly painted once, but now they were all a nondescript brown.

It was as quiet as our walk into Estevan. We saw no other traffic, but from our greater elevation from the seat of the Model A we could see occasional, widely scattered farmsteads in the distance across the prairie.

We rode in silence for a while. "It's kind of lonely country out here, isn't it," I said.

Fritz smiled briefly. "Suppose it is if you're not used to it. Me, I was born on our place, grew up there. It's really all I've ever known."

"How big is your farm?"

"Two sections, 1,280 acres."

He was a man about thirty-five years of age, blue-eyed, with short-cropped blond hair. He pushed his straw hat back on his head, and I saw how startlingly white his forehead was above the deep-bronze of the lower part of his face.

Fritz Hoffman lived a life that was new to me, unlike anyone I'd ever known in my city-oriented experience.

"Don't you ever get lonesome out here?" I knew my question was on the personal side, and I could feel Finn stir uneasily. Maybe this man did enjoy our company, or perhaps just a chance to talk to someone, not part of his day-in, day-out environment, was more important to him than even he realized.

"Not really. I have a good wife and two great boys. They're seven and six now. We all work so hard, even the kids at their chores, guess we just don't have time to get lonely." He glanced over at Finn. "You from the old country?"

I could feel Finn stiffen slightly. Then he relaxed. "Yah, Denmark."

"I thought so. My dad was from Germany. He homesteaded out here in 1898. When he died in 1927, I took over the place. First two years I made enough on wheat to pay off my two brothers for their interest in the farm and buy a new tractor." He shook his head. "It's been damn tough goin' ever since. If I have a good crop, can't get a price for it. If we get hurt by hail, or something else, it seems as if the price is out of sight, but I got no crop to sell."

We rode in silence for a while, then Finn spoke.

"How much vork do you have for us, Fritz?"

His tone was apologetic. "Not too much. I got one field of

wheat that's cut and bundled. I've really got to get it stooked up and drying. Probably about four days."

Ever since my involuntary response to the news that we would be working for a dollar a day, and Fritz Hoffman's advice that his farm was located just a couple of miles north of the border, the three of us knew without a word being exchanged that we would be heading south back to the States at the earliest opportunity. I felt sure that we would be well-fed by the time we took off, and with four dollars each in our pockets we would certainly be in far better shape than we had been. We obviously were not going to make the big money in the wheat harvest that Finn had talked about aboard ship on this job, but it was a start in the right direction.

We rolled into the Hoffman place about two in the afternoon. There was a neat-looking farmhouse painted white, a large red barn, and a stand of cottonwood trees that shaded the house. I could see a small orchard of fruit trees and a well-tended vegetable garden behind it.

Fritz parked the truck and we climbed out. We had told him about our dry hike twenty miles into Estevan, and even though there was plenty of daylight left to get some stooking done, he had decided that it would be better for us to rest up today. Also, it was Sunday and, as I was to learn, Fritz Hoffman was a devout man who preferred not to work on Sunday unless there was no other choice.

A rather pretty woman, dressed in a plain housedress, came out of the back door of the farmhouse as we drove up.

"Margaret, this is Finn and Russ. They're going to give me a hand on the stooking. I've been bragging on your food so it better be good!"

There was an easy way between these two—fortunately I thought, living out here so isolated from everything.

"How does roast pork and apple pie sound?"

I looked at Mrs. Hoffman. "Nothing ever sounded any better to me in my life, ma'am." I could feel myself salivating, and I simply couldn't stop myself from blurting out, "What time were you going to have dinner?"

Fritz grinned at me, then looked at his wife. "These boys haven't been eating too regular, honey, do you think we could eat a bit earlier today?"

"Sure. How about five o'clock?"

Again I couldn't stop myself. "That's great!"

Fritz said, "Grab your bedrolls, and I'll show you where to bunk."

He led us to the barn. I could smell the warm scent of the two milk cows stabled there. A hog pen was located at the corner of the barn, and its somewhat sour smell mingled with the aroma of fresh hay in the loft. There was a good-sized chicken coop about fifty feet from the barn.

"There's some clean hay in the loft. Spread your blankets there. Got my own well here. Plenty of good water. You can use one of the buckets there if you want to wash up."

I could tell that Finn was pleased with the Hoffman homestead.

"Ve'll be fine, Fritz. This be a nice place you have."

"Thanks." He stared at the distant fields. "Like I said, it's really all I've ever known. It does mean a lot to me."

Then he left us, and we climbed the ladder to the loft. We spread our blankets on the clean-smelling hay. I stretched out on mine, and sighed.

"You know, Finn, the money doesn't seem nearly as important as the way these blankets feel."

"Yah. It does feel good. I bet Mrs. Hoffman is a good cook too."

"Kind of wished you hadn't said that. I don't know if I can last another couple of hours."

"You vill. Anyvay, this be a good time to scrub out some clothes."

We each had one complete change of clothes and a bar of Ivory soap. Now we turned to our jeans, shirt, socks, and shorts that hadn't been changed or washed for too long. We spread them on the roof of the chicken coop to dry, and just as we finished, Mrs. Hoffman called from the back door. "Come on, boys, supper's ready."

It looked like every farmhouse I had ever seen. The front door led into a parlor that was furnished with uncomfortable-looking chairs and decorated with framed family photographs. I stood for a moment at the entrance to the parlor just off the kitchen, taking it all in. I recognized Fritz and Margaret in wedding attire. A robust, mustachioed man surveyed the parlor grimly from an oval frame centered on one wall. I surmised that this was Mr. Hoffman senior. Neither the front door nor the parlor, visible from the large kitchen, looked as if they were ever used.

The back door led directly into the kitchen. It was a large, comfortable room, dominated by a black cast-iron stove against one wall and a large oak table in the center of the room. There were aromas wafting from that old woodburning stove that had my salivary juices flowing like a mountain brook.

The table was covered with red-checkered oilcloth, set for six, with serviceable white crockery and heavy metal eating utensils. There was a napkin at each plate circled by a distinctively colored napkin holder. The napkins were reused by the same person for a number of meals. With all of her washing done by hand, Margaret Hoffman simply could not afford the luxury of freshly laundered napkins for each meal.

We were introduced to Martin and August, the seven- and six-year-old boys. They were sturdy, small replicas of their father, shaking hands with us self-consciously, round blue eyes taking us in.

As we took our places at the table, all of the Hoffmans bowed their heads. We did the same. Fritz gave the blessing.

"Lord Jesus, we give thanks for your bounty and ask that we may be worthy of it." He paused briefly. "And, Lord, thank thee for bringing Finn Bering and Russ Hofvendahl to this house to help in our labors. Please watch over them and protect them from misfortune. Amen."

He was a simple man, absolutely incapable of trickery, particularly when talking to his Lord. Still, I thought wryly as I sat there with my head bowed, I've never heard anything in my life that made me want to work as hard as I could for this man—whatever the wages.

Then Fritz began to carve the juicy roast pork while Margaret ladled up creamy mashed potatoes, a side dish of cold, absolutely delicious applesauce, and crisp green peas. There were ample plates of butter on the table, and I had my mashed potatoes and green peas liberally covered with it when Fritz addressed me.

"Pass your plate, Russ, let me put a couple of slices of pork on it."

Then Margaret spoke up. "Before you get started, let me get some gravy on those potatoes." These were only momentary delays, but the way my stomach was rumbling by then I didn't know whether I could last until, finally, the loaded plate was resting on the table in front of me.

I made a particular effort not to wolf down my food, but I wasn't too successful. I could see Finn out of the corner of my eye. It seemed to me that he was trying to restrain himself also—without any more success than I was having. After I had finished that first wonderful plate of food, I finally looked up to meet Mrs. Hoffman's gaze. She was looking at me with a combination of sympathy and pleasure. She spoke softly.

"You were really hungry, weren't you, Russ?"

"Guess I was, Mrs. Hoffman—"

"Please, call me Margaret."

"Okay, Margaret. I *was* hungry, but I tell you that was about the best cooking I ever tasted."

Finn joined in. "Yah, Fritz promised us good food, but I never expect anything this great."

There was pride in Fritz Hoffman's voice. "Everything on this table, except the salt and pepper, comes right from this place, and Margaret does most of it. I butchered the hog, but she tends the vegetable garden, churns the butter, does it all."

Margaret Hoffman heaped our plates a second time. As I was getting toward the end of that portion, I finally began to slow down.

Fritz looked at me and grinned. "You getting tired of this food, Russ?"

I smiled back and shook my head.

Margaret's tone was brisk. "You boys be sure to leave room for apple pie."

I could hardly believe it. That wedge of hot, flaky apple pie, the rich sweet juices mingling with the heavy cream, which was so thick that it had to be spooned out of the pitcher, completed our banquet.

Finally we were replete. There really wasn't much dinner-table conversation to interfere with the serious business of eating in this family, but the warm, comfortable kitchen was obviously the heart of the household. When we were all finished eating, the boys cleared the table, and Fritz leaned back in his chair contentedly—lighting up a briar pipe.

"It's none of my business, boys, but I *am* curious. How did you end up in Estevan?"

Finn was a natural-born storyteller, and he had long since decided that we could trust these people. So he told them the story of our ship, how we had left it, and all that we had been through traveling to Estevan, Saskatchewan.

Fritz and Margaret had solid grade-school educations, and they were both intelligent. But Calgary, Alberta, was the most distant city they had ever visited. I am sure, over the years, that more than one itinerant worker had entertained them with stories of travels on the road. It did seem, however, that they had never met anyone like Finn

Bering before. They were fascinated by his descriptions of his home in Copenhagen, his adventures in New York City, and the South American ports he had visited. San Francisco was of particular interest to them, and I told them about the magic of my hometown, the City by the Golden Gate, with an enthusiasm and eloquence that surprised even me as I was talking.

I was equally fascinated by the life they led on this lonely spread on the prairie.

"How hot does it get here in the summer, Fritz?"

"It runs aboot a hundred through August. Then it starts to cool off."

"What's it like in the winter?"

The Hoffmans looked at each other.

"Then it gets cold, Russ. Hit fifty below last January—for five days straight."

"Fifty below! Isn't it tough to keep things going when it gets that cold?"

"It is that. We got to watch the stock real close then. We stay pretty comfortable here in the house, but I got to chop ice off the trough every day, and I got to be outdoors seeing that the animals get fed and watered. You get used to it. Not too bad until the wind comes. Then, a strong norther blowing, you really feel it."

I could only marvel at these people who lived an isolated life without complaint, their nearest neighbor five miles away.

There were a hundred questions I wanted to ask—what did they do if someone got sick, or hurt in an accident in the winter, could they use that outdoor privy without leaving part of their backsides frozen to the seat? Then I noticed Finn almost imperceptibly shaking his head. He knew that my questions, at the least, would sound critical of their way of life; at the worst, they might give offense to these decent people. I kept my mouth shut.

We had all enjoyed the conversation, but I suddenly realized that my head was nodding. Our early start this morning, the twenty-mile hike to Estevan, and all of the food I had devoured—it was all too much.

Fritz pulled his watch out of the pocket in the bib of his overalls.

"My God, it's eight o'clock already. I've really enjoyed talking with you two, but I think it's time to call it quits for now. I'd like to get started about six tomorrow morning."

I stretched out on my blankets and the next thing I was aware of was a rooster delivering a strident greeting to the morning.

Margaret Hoffman's breakfast of bacon, eggs, hot cakes, and fried potatoes was just as ample and splendid in its way as our banquet the preceding evening had been. By 6 A.M. we had finished breakfast and had hiked out to the field, which seemed to me to stretch to the horizon. On the way to the field we saw the two boys returning from the chicken coop, each carrying a basket of fresh eggs.

Fritz efficiently showed us how he wanted the bundles of wheat stood up, leaning against the others in a three-bundle pyramid, and stacked in an orderly row marching across the limitless field.

We each took a row, starting at one side of the field, and went to work. The bundles were not particularly heavy but, after an hour, the constant bending over to grab the tied cylinders of cut wheat, straightening up to stack them, and then bending over again, began to take its toll. I could see Fritz, some distance from me now, going down his row like a machine. Finn was also working well ahead of me by then. I felt a certain regret that I had ever listened to Finn and his stories of the damned wheat harvest. Then I remembered Fritz Hoffman's benediction the night before. I would not let him down even if I couldn't match his pace. Grimly I continued on down the row. By ten in the morning the sun was beating down and I could feel the sweat pouring off my body.

Just then I heard a faint shout and looked up to see Fritz beckoning us to him. Finn had stooked up about a quarter more than I had, but was still far short of what Fritz had accomplished. We trudged across the field to where he was waiting. He had completed one row and about a quarter of another starting back in our direction.

He was sitting on the ground, an earthenware jug of water and an enamel cup between his legs.

"You boys are doing fine. You don't break once in a while, and get some water down, this sun can finish you."

Gratefully Finn and I sank to the ground beside him.

"I didn't notice you carrying this water out this morning, Fritz."

"I didn't. Spotted some jugs around the field yesterday aboot where I figured we'd need them. Left a cup with each jug."

It simply never occurred to me that for a dollar a day Fritz Hoffman might be getting his money's worth out of us. All I could think of was how well we had been treated, and how much slower I was.

"I'm sure not getting them stooked up very fast, Fritz."

"That's okay. I can tell you're working steady. First time you ever do this, it's not as simple as it looks."

He glanced at Finn. "I can tell your partner here has stooked wheat before."

Finn Bering was uncharacteristically quiet. "Yah. That's right. But Yesus you could fit vun of them whole farms in Denmark in yust this vun field."

Fritz nodded and looked around the horizon. "I guess these spreads out here are pretty big compared with the old country."

Then we returned to work.

At noon I heard the faint halloo again and looked up to see Fritz waving us toward the farmhouse, shimmering in the noonday heat, a long way from where we were. Finn had apparently not heard him and was toiling doggedly down his row.

"Hey, Finn, time for chow!"

He straightened up slowly, shaded his eyes with one hand, and then started walking toward me. We trudged across the field in the direction of the farmhouse. I couldn't resist it.

My expression was serious. "Finn, when we going to see that wagon with the cold beer and sandwiches? I would really like to hear some accordion music too."

He whirled on me and, for a second, I thought I had pushed him too far. Then he started to grin.

"Vell, I got to admit it's not like Denmark. You know, vun day and ve have all the vheat stooked up at home. I don't know how ve going to get yust this field stooked up in four days."

"The way Fritz works I think we'll get it done."

Finn nodded his head glumly. I knew he wasn't looking forward to three and a half days more of that labor any more than I was. We washed off at the pump, and then sat down to another of Mrs. Hoffman's delicious meals.

We returned to the field about one o'clock, the sun a searing ball of heat in the blue sky. We broke twice that afternoon for a drink of water and a brief rest. By six in the evening I wasn't sure I could bend over one more time when, once again, I heard Fritz Hoffman shout at us across the field and motion in the direction of the farmhouse.

I never really knew whether we did as well as Fritz told us we were doing, or whether he simply had an instinctive knowledge of how to get the most out of his workers. As nearly as I could judge it looked as if, between us, Finn and I were stooking up about two-thirds of what the boss was doing by himself. Still, it was critically important for him to get this wheat up and drying at just this time. He couldn't get it all done himself, and we did make the difference for him.

I thought Margaret looked at us a bit anxiously that night at supper. "How're you feeling, boys?"

Finn looked at her and smiled. "Ve're okay, Margaret, really."

She continued to look rather searchingly at me.

"Well, I do feel it in my back some, but I'll be okay."

Her husband interjected.

"Don't worry about these two, Margaret. They're good boys and they're working steady. Not like some of those bums we get once in a while."

My resolve was strengthened once more by his encouraging words, but when I heard the rooster sound wake-up time the next morning I wasn't sure that my back was going to make it. As I started to rise from my comfortable bed on the hay I could feel a stab of pain in my lower vertebrae.

"How's your back feel, Finn?"

"Not too good."

However, and surprisingly enough, by mid-morning I was working steadily, and the ache in my back was gone. On and on we toiled, now more used to the terrible monotony of this labor, the burning heat of the sun, and the neverending bending and straightening.

By the end of the third day, as we stopped our labors, I could see that there was just about one day of stooking left.

That evening at supper Fritz confirmed my inexpert appraisal.

"Like I said, you boys have really worked steady out there. One more day will do it."

Finn spoke up. "How soon vill you be threshing?"

"I'd guess aboot ten days now. There's a threshing outfit working this way that I've talked to. I'm sure I can get you boys on if you want to stick around."

We didn't even want to ask what the wages were on a Canadian threshing crew. We were anxious now to get back to the States.

Finn shook his head. "Ve appreciate it, Fritz, but ve vant to head south. They should be threshing in North Dakota now, shouldn't they?"

"I'm sure you won't have any problem getting on a threshing outfit down there. But mind you, be careful when you cross that border. There's not likely to be any patrols out on the prairie, but they watch the border towns real close."

"Vell, it's no problem for Russ. The States is home for him. I don't think they hear about a couple of sailors yump the *Dagmar Salen* out in New Vestminster. But for me—all I got is my Danish seaman's papers—if they do pick me up I'm pretty sure they'll figure I'm no Yank real qvick."

"I've got some American dollar bills. When I pay you off I'll give you those instead of Canadian." Fritz smiled briefly. "Just do me a favor. If they do pick you up, don't tell them you been working at the Hoffman place. I'd just as soon not have the Canadian border patrol nosing around here accusing me of helping men cross the border. They work pretty close with the Americans you know."

Finn grinned. "Don't vorry, ve forget ve ever know you Fritz."

Four days of stooking exactly, just as we had been told. One more day of backbreaking labor under that burning sun, and we were finished.

I stood at the edge of the field that evening and looked at the neat rows of stacked wheat stretching in parallel lines into the distance.

Fritz stood quietly next to me. "What're you thinking about?"

"I don't know exactly." I smiled at him. "If I had known what stooking was, no matter how great Margaret's cooking has been, I'm not sure you'd have gotten me out here. Still, looking at that field, I'm kind of proud of what we got done."

"It's a funny thing, Russ. I've been doing it all my life, and I feel the same way. It never lasts you know. Those rows will be there until the threshing machine starts chewing them up. Then I'll be planting in the spring and watching it come up again. I suppose knowing that it'll be this way again, maybe that's why I feel good looking at that field myself." He smiled self-consciously. "You don't *have* to be crazy to be a farmer but it helps."

That night Margaret Hoffman outdid herself. Fritz had a side of beef hanging in the underground sod cold house, and we each had a T-bone steak so large that I had to deal with mine in two sections in order to have enough room on my plate for baked potatoes and vegetables. The steak was pan-fried but cooked to a perfect medium-rare. The crisp green string beans were heavily mixed with fried bacon chunks and slathered with rich butter. Dessert was a cherry pie made from black tatarians that Margaret had picked and canned earlier in the summer. I told myself that somewhere in the world there must be another cherry pie this delicious—but I wasn't convinced. Then I remembered to tell Margaret the same thing. I was never sure which I enjoyed the most, the taste of her food or the expression on her face when I complimented her on it.

As was the case with every meal we took with the Hoffmans, their two boys, Martin and August, cleared the table and started doing the dishes as soon as we were through eating. Most impressive to me was the fact that they did it without being told. They simply went to work.

The next morning we turned out about five, used to rising early now, and rolled our packs. There was plenty of work waiting for Fritz on the place after four days of stooking wheat, but he took his time eating breakfast. This morning there were scrambled eggs and sausage patties, plentiful as always, accompanied by biscuits and Margaret's delicious coffee laced with heavy cream. In the brief time we had dined at this table we had become friends. Our backgrounds were as different and unusual to them as theirs was to to us. We were all reluctant to say good-bye—knowing full well we would never meet again.

Finally, Fritz stood up, pushed his chair back from the table, and walked over to a cupboard. He pulled out a porcelain cookie jar and extracted some loose bills. Carefully he went through them until he had separated eight American dollars. He handed four of them to each of us.

"You know, Fritz," I said, "I really feel like we should be paying you. You sure were right, back there in Estevan, when you said we'd get plenty of good food."

I could see Margaret beaming behind him, a delighted look on her attractive face.

"Well, I got to admit that wife of mine is a pretty fair cook. But four days stooking under this sun." He shook his head. "Four dollars isn't much. I just wish I could pay you more."

Finn was anxious to get moving. "Vhich vay is the border, Fritz?"

"Come on, I'll show you."

We shook hands with Margaret and the two boys, shouldered our packs, and followed Fritz. He led us to the corner of the field where we had labored so hard.

"Those rows run basically east and west. The border's about

two miles due south. Just try to keep the rows at aboot a right angle to your direction of travel as long as you can."

"Vill there be anything marking the border vhen ve get there?"

"Not a thing. But aboot a half mile farther south you'll see a dirt road that runs east right into Fortuna, North Dakota. The country's kind of rolling down there. If I were you I'd stay well off that road because the patrol may be driving on it once in a while, then get on into Fortuna. It's not a very big town. The border patrol cars are marked, so it shouldn't be too hard to spot 'em if there's any around. If it's all clear in town there's a Great Northern spur that runs more or less southeast to the main line. Don't know if there's any freights running but you can find out."

We shook hands hard. Then he turned and strode away. We started walking south across the prairie.

# 10

We hiked across the fields, and it wasn't nearly as tough as I thought it would be. The days we stooked on Fritz Hoffman's place, going down the long rows of bundled wheat, had gotten us used to walking on the uneven ground. It certainly wasn't like walking on a dirt road, but it sure beat trudging those endless miles over railroad ties.

It was a bright, sunny day and not too hot this early in the morning. About nine o'clock we topped a small rise and saw a dirt road running generally east and west. Easterly in the distance there was a small cluster of buildings. That had to be Fortuna, North Dakota. There wasn't a vehicle in sight on the road but, heeding Fritz's warning, we stayed off it and hiked over the fields toward town.

As we were trudging along I kept thinking about the dollar a day we had been paid for twelve hours of backbreaking labor on Fritz Hoffman's place. I didn't resent it because of my respect for Fritz and my recognition of the financial problems he faced. Still it got me thinking.

"Finn, remember back on the *Dagmar Salen* when you said that we'd make a stake in the harvest and then decide what to do?"

"Yah." His tone was defensive.

I was conciliatory. "I'm not blaming you for anything, I made up my own mind to jump ship. But you know, I'll bet things aren't going to be too much better just a few miles away across the border."

Finn turned and looked at me as we hiked along, then he simply shrugged. I continued.

"Let's suppose we can make three times what Fritz paid us. That's only three dollars a day. We're not going to make much of a stake at that rate."

"Yah," he said resignedly, "I guess you're right."

I had told Finn about my job at the Valet Shop in the St. Francis Hotel and how relatively easy it was for a presser to find work.

"Back home in San Francisco I can make forty cents an hour pressing clothes in a dry-cleaning plant. That's hard work too, but at least I know what I'm doing. I can make a lot more in eight hours working in a plant than I can breaking my back for twelve hours out here on the prairie."

Finn looked at me and smiled. "Don't think these folks out here spend much money getting clothes dry-cleaned, if that's vhat you have in mind."

I shook my head. "No, that's not what I have in mind. What I'm thinking is if there are all those jobs in New York City like you told me about there should be plenty of pressing jobs. Did you ever notice any listed at those employment agencies?"

"No, I didn't, but then I vasn't looking for a yob like that. I can't do that kind of vork." His tone was thoughtful. "Vhat are you thinking about?"

"Well, I've always wanted to see New York City anyway. It may be that shipping there will be as tough this fall as it was on the West Coast, but at least we'll have a shot at that. If we can't ship out I'm sure I can get work pressing, and I'll bet you wouldn't have any problem getting a job either." A thought struck me. "Finn, you never have told me when you plan to go home to Denmark. You ever give that any thought?"

"Yah, you know I been gone almost a year now, and I do miss the folks. Vouldn't be tough for me to sign on a ship bound for Denmark or Sveden, I'm sure."

I turned and looked at Finn as we walked along. He looked at me and then started to smile. "Hold it up for a minute, Russ, let's sit down for a vhile and talk."

We dropped our blanket rolls in the field and sat down on the soft earth, our lower backs cushioned against the packs. Finn clasped his hands behind his head and stared up at the sky.

"You be pretty good people, Russ. You never give me hell for that little valk ve take through the Rockies or anything else that happen. You know, I think you're right. I like to be vhere I can smell the sea anyvay, and it's a hell of a long way from here!"

I felt a sudden feeling of elation, more from having persuaded my leader about a possible course of action than anything else. As usual, Finn made up his mind decisively.

"Tell you vhat. Ve hook on vith a threshing outfit somevhere in North Dakota. Then yust as soon as ve have traveling money ve head for New York. Vhat do you think?"

"I think that's great, Finn. Like I said, I always have wanted to see that town. You're on!"

There was something about a definite set goal that really elated me, not to mention the fact that this city boy's days working the wheat harvest wouldn't last too long now.

We got to our feet, shouldered our blanket rolls, and walked on toward our immediate destination.

Fortuna was a veritable metropolis compared with Weyburn and Estevan. I felt a surge of emotion when I saw the United States post office with the Stars and Stripes fluttering above it in the morning breeze. I really had not been out of my own country all that long but, looking back over what had happened, it did seem like a long time. The sight of the post office gave me a guilty start.

"Finn, I haven't written to my aunt. If the shipping company tells her that I jumped ship in Canada she's really going to be worried."

"Vell, I don't think they bother vith that, but it's a good idea you write to her."

We studied the main street carefully. There wasn't anything we could identify as a border patrol car. We saw some men carrying blanket rolls like ourselves, a not unusual sight in the prairie towns this time of year. We went into the post office. I broke one of my dollar bills to buy a penny post card. Then, using a pencil attached by a chain to a table I wrote to my Aunt Doris. It would be the first word she would receive from me in more than four weeks. The card was dated August 5, 1938. The message was simple and direct.

*Dear Aunt Doris,*

*Another fellow and I jumped ship in New Westminster, British Columbia. We rode the freights about 1,500 miles through Canada to Estevan, Saskatchewan. We got a job there and worked four days. We left this morning because there was no more work. I am going to New York to ship out again, or maybe get a job ashore. I'll write more later.*

*Love, Russ*

When I was through Finn gave me an appraising look.

"Russ, you need a haircut. So do I. Saw a barber shop down the street. Let's get our hair cut, then ve decide vhat to do. Ve can afford it."

It was a one-chair shop with the striped red-and-white revolving pole just outside the entrance. The barber was a man in his forties and as garrulous as most of his fellow practitioners. Finn climbed into the chair first. He kept his answers to the barber's questions to a minimum, trying to avoid betraying his accent.

While he was getting his hair cut I read an old issue of *Time* magazine. The search for an actress to play Scarlett O'Hara was duly reported. An English actress, Vivien Leigh, was selected to depict the spirited, quintessentially Southern heroine of Margaret Mitchell's epic novel *Gone With the Wind*. I didn't usually follow that sort of Hollywood activity, but this particular search had been so well-publicized and had ended so surprisingly, with Vivien Leigh's anointment, that I read the article with considerable interest. No one could know then how inspired the choice would be—that Vivien Leigh's Scarlett O'Hara playing to Clark Gable's Rhett Butler would create one of the most memorable screen romances of all time.

When the barber had finished, Finn paid him the twenty-cent price of the haircut, and I climbed into the chair.

"Okay, young feller, how do you want it cut?"

"Pretty short, I guess. Give me a look in the mirror once in a while, I'll tell you when you've cut enough."

I thought about working under the hot sun on Fritz Hoffman's place, and it occurred to me that I might be more comfortable with a short brush cut.

Finn left the shop and seated himself on a bench in front, just on the other side of the plate glass window. I could see him occasionally staring warily down the street in one direction, then the other.

The barber went to work methodically with his hand clippers. I realized I *did* need a haircut rather badly when I felt the coolness on the back of my neck as the barber ran the clippers up.

"That friend of your ain't very talkative, is he?"

"I don't know." I thought of the hours Finn and I had yarned together, and the way he had talked to the Hoffman family. I really wasn't concerned about this small town haircutter informing on us but, until we got farther south away from the border area, we had to be careful. I tried to be friendly. "Guess he's a little hard to get to know. This your hometown?"

"Yep. Born and raised here. Times been pretty tough for the farmers, but I think some of the things Roosevelt's doing for them is going to help."

After working busily for about ten minutes, he stepped back from the chair, spun it in a half circle, and held a mirror behind me so that I could see the back of my head in the mirror on the wall. "How's that?"

I gulped. I wanted it short, but Jesus, the skin on my scalp glistened through the remaining bristle. Looking at the top of my head I could see that I had a brush about an inch high, if that.

Hastily I answered. "That's fine, don't take any more off."

"All right, then we're done."

He spun the chair again to where I could see Finn through the plate glass window. The white-striped barber's sheet was still securely snapped around my neck. Finn was looking to his right, and just as the chair stopped I saw a uniformed border patrol officer walk up and tap Finn on his left shoulder.

I felt a terrible sinking in my stomach. For an instant I thought of flight. I was still trapped in the chair. The next moment I had an incongruous flash of the Chicago gangsters I had read about, meeting a machine-gunned end, helpless in a barber's chair. Coupled with that mental image was the more relevant one of those public enemies nabbed by the G-men under just such circumstances.

As Finn shot a startled look at the officer standing at his left, I saw another one coming from his right.

The barber had stopped what he was doing. I was still in the chair under the sheet. He was staring at the tableau in front of his shop.

"You guys Canadian?"

"No."

"Well if you're legal you got nothing to worry about. But..." His voice trailed off.

At that moment the first officer looked through the window at me still in the chair. The connection was unmistakable. The similarity in our ages, the deep tans, one young man waiting outside the barber shop with a fresh haircut, the other inside just getting his—the first officer came into the shop. Finn extended his wrists as the second officer snapped the manacles on.

His tone was hard and businesslike. "He a friend of yours?"

There was no point in lying, with the talkative barber there to tie us together.

"Sure, but we haven't done anything."

"Didn't say you have. But he doesn't sound like an American to me. I hope for your sake you didn't help him make an illegal entry."

I swallowed hard. The possible jeopardy I was in hadn't hit me until that moment.

"Okay," he said to the barber, "get that sheet off him."

"Hold out your hands." He snapped the handcuffs on my extended wrists. The feel of those cold steel bands locking onto my flesh was a traumatic shock I could hardly believe. The feeling of helplessness was bad enough. The visual stigma of criminality was worse.

Their four-door Chevrolet was parked on a side street around the corner from the barber shop. Although they were both in khaki uniforms, they were adept at making themselves unobtrusive, keenly attuned to suspicious-looking strangers. Undoubtedly Finn's continuous, searching scrutiny of the main street of Fortuna had engaged their interest. He must have been looking in the opposite direction as they turned the corner, saw him, and quickly ducked back to set up their arrest.

They tossed our blanket rolls into the trunk and drove us to the local jail. Finn and I sat in back. I saw that there were no inside door handles. Even if I had wanted to jump out and run for it, it would have been impossible.

They said very little on the way to the jail. It seemed to me that, like the Canadian Mounties we had encountered, they were professionals who did not particularly enjoy what their duties required of them.

The jail had only one cell. They took off the handcuffs and put us in a windowless cell together, disappearing into another part of the building, each carrying one of our blanket rolls. The cell was about eight feet in length by about five feet in width. It contained a set of metal bunk beds, each covered with a thin mattress. There was a toilet stool with no seat in one corner, and absolutely nothing else.

When the barred steel door clanged shut, the sound was like a physical blow. The handcuffs were off, but this was worse. I was totally confined and helpless, subject to the control of absolute authority. When they left us alone we just stared at each other for a moment.

"Yesus, Russ, I'm sorry I get you into this. Me and my big ideas vith the vheat harvest. I know I'm on my vay back to Denmark vhen they open that roll and find my seaman's vallet. I yust hope they turn you loose."

It was not really until that moment that the prospect of being on the road by myself, without Finn's guidance, began to hit me. That was assuming that I wouldn't be spending the foreseeable future in a federal penitentiary for aiding and abetting an illegal alien to enter the United States.

"The guy that put the cuffs on me said something about helping an illegal entry. What do you think they'll do to me?"

"I'm not sure, but I hope nothing." His tone became bitter. "Vith all the men on the road these days yust looking for a chance to vork, I don't know vhy it's so wrong to cross that border. Like I said, I know vhat's going to happen to me. I think if you convince them you're an American and don't start any fights vith them, you'll be okay."

"Don't worry about that!"

About five minutes later they returned to the cell. One of them, Officer Whiteside, was carrying Finn's seaman's wallet with his papers inside. The other, Officer Smithson, was carrying mine.

Smithson beckoned to me. "Come on, Hofvendahl. I want to talk to you." He led me into the local sheriff's office, sat down behind the desk, and fixed me with a stern look.

"I know there's a seaman by the name of Hofvendahl somewhere. No one would make up that name. I just want to make damn sure he's you, that you didn't roll some drunk and steal his papers."

I was indignant. "I wouldn't do that!"

Smithson smiled slightly and his tone softened. "It probably doesn't seem like it to you, but rolling a drunk isn't even in it compared with aiding and abetting an illegal alien to enter the United States. I'll tell you one thing for sure. Your friend Finn Bering, if that's *his* name, is sure as hell an illegal."

The bitter irony of this situation just about had me undone.

Finn had led me all the way from our jumping the *Dagmar Salen* to this disastrous end in a small prairie town in North Dakota. Now *I* was staring a federal penitentiary in the face, accused of aiding *him*.

Despite the standard police practice of separating two accused for interrogation, it was not as if I could say anything to add to, or detract from, Finn's dilemma. Exactly the same situation applied to me. Finn was indubitably an illegal alien, and he would be deported. I was indubitably an American citizen, and should be released, except for that ominous-sounding "aiding an illegal entry." Desperately I now wished that we had had another moment or so in that cell so Finn could have given me some idea of what to say. I looked at Officer Smithson. I had heard his name used by one of the local deputies when we had first arrived at the jail. I made up my mind. Telling him the absolute truth wouldn't hurt Finn anymore, and it might help me. Officer Smithson was a trim, blue-eyed man, about thirty, six feet tall, with clean-cut features.

"Mr. Smithson." Something like a pleased flicker of interest lit his face briefly at the use of his name. He continued to stare at me.

"Finn and I did come down from Canada this morning, but this country is my home, and Finn, he's really a great guy. I sure didn't think I was doing anything wrong just hiking across the border with him."

"I can see that, but these days we got strict orders to keep out anyone illegal and nail anyone who's helped an illegal come in. You know, I do believe you're an American, but we're going to take you and your partner to our own facilities in Portal. It's about fifty miles east of here. We got some real experts there. They're the ones you have to convince."

"What do you think they'll do to me?"

"I just don't know. It may be that since we've got one illegal for deportation, and you don't really look to me like you're running an alien smuggling ring, they could turn you loose. One thing for sure, you better convince them you're an American!"

About four that afternoon we were handcuffed again, put in the back seat of the Chevrolet, and drove east. There was little or no conversation on the drive. The officers in the front seat were not talkative types, and Finn and I were both lost in a gloomy specula-tion about what the immediate future would bring.

Mile after mile we rolled over a two-lane paved highway, the prairie stretching to the horizon in all directions.

At ten minutes after five we pulled up in front of a squat

brown-bricked structure. The American flag flew above it, and "United States Immigration Service" was lettered in brass over the front entrance.

The feel of the place was different from the jail in Fortuna. It was at once more efficient-looking and more ominous. There were four cells at the rear of the building. Officer Smithson was genial.

"Like to give you boys private rooms, but we're filled up right now. You're going to have to share this one."

He unlocked our handcuffs and ushered us into the cell.

It was very much like the one in Fortuna, except that there was a barred window through which we could see a patch of blue sky. The bars lacing the front of it seemed somehow larger and more menacing to me. When that cell door clanged shut, I again felt an impact that was almost physical. It seemed to me that the very environment spelled deep trouble.

They permitted us to take our bedrolls into the cell. Finn turned to me. There was a pained expression on his face.

"You know, I don't mind for myself, I go home to Denmark sooner or later anyvay, but goddammit it, Russ, I feel so bad about getting you into this."

"It's okay, Finn." There really wasn't anything else to say.

Finn opened his mouth to speak again when we heard a peremptory summons from a different officer standing just outside the cell.

"Hofvendahl. Get out here. We're going to ask you some questions."

I was led from the cell to a sparsely furnished office. Two officers I hadn't seen before were sitting, one directly behind a desk, the other also behind it, but somewhat to the side. Officer Smithson was sitting in a straight-backed oak chair, tilted against the wall. There was a similar chair placed squarely in front of the desk where I was motioned to sit.

"So you claim you're an American." The officer behind the desk addressed me. "Who won the World Series last year?"

My heart sank. I just didn't follow baseball that closely.

"I—I just don't know. I'm sorry."

My interrogator's face had a grim look on it. I could hear Officer Smithson's chair hit the floor with a small sound.

"Okay. So maybe you don't know baseball, but there's not many American guys your age who don't! Who's the heavyweight champ?"

I breathed a small sigh of relief. I was on familiar ground now.

"Joe Louis."

"Who'd he beat for the championship?"

"Jim Braddock."

I stole a quick glance at Officer Smithson. It probably was my imagination, but it seemed to me that he nodded almost imperceptibly. It occurred to me that he may have told the federal people at the Portal headquarters that he was satisfied that I was an American. I suddenly felt as if I were doing battle for him as well as for my own freedom.

"Which came first, the Constitution or the Declaration of Independence?"

The question was shot at me from the officer at the side of the desk.

I gulped. I knew the answer, but I had to be right just about every time now.

"The Declaration of Independence."

"Who was the first president of the U.S.?"

"George Washington."

On and on it went. Questions about American movies suddenly coming at me in the middle of an interrogation about the Civil War. As time wore on I was gaining confidence, and it seemed to me that Officer Smithson had visibly relaxed.

Finally, about six-fifteen, they stood up. "You're doing okay, Hofvendahl, but we got an officer at this station who worked in Frisco. That's where you're supposed to be from, isn't it?"

"Yes, sir."

"Well, you can get some chow now. Then we'll have a few more questions to ask you about what you claim is your hometown." They stood up, and I rose with them.

As Officer Smithson returned me to the cell, he whispered to me. "They're good people. Just doing their jobs. I hope to Christ you *are* from Frisco because John Lawson spent ten years out there working for the service."

I wasn't back in the cell long enough to tell Finn what had happened before the door was opened again and two trays of steaming food were shoved at us. It could best be described, charitably, as typical institutional food. There had been a time in my recent past when I would have given a great deal for food of any kind. Now the memory of Margaret Hoffman's generous, delicious meals was too fresh in my mind for me to appreciate the stringy stew and lukewarm boiled potatoes. Nonetheless, we had not eaten since morning, and it had been a long day. I turned to with a will. I had hardly finished when Officer Smithson was opening the cell door.

"Come on, Hofvendahl. They're ready for you."

This time there was only one officer, John Lawson I assumed, sitting behind the desk. My original inquisitors were sitting in chairs at the side of the room with Officer Smithson.

Officer Lawson was a kindly looking man who looked to be about forty. He was graying and had rather piercing brown eyes, I realized with a start, when I seated myself in front of the desk and looked at him. Like the others he didn't use any notes and he began without preamble.

"What's at the bay end of Market Street?"

"The Ferry Building."

"What's at the other end?"

"Twin Peaks."

"What year was the earthquake?"

"1906."

These men were experts in interrogation. The questions came rapidly almost before I had answered the last one. But now I was on totally familiar ground. From my early years, when I had first gone to live with Aunt Doris, she had permitted me to roam the City on my skates, and I thanked God for that experience now.

"What's the name of the biggest park in Frisco?"

"Golden Gate."

"What's the district called to the north of it?"

"Richmond."

On he went. Questions about Chinatown, North Beach, the Sunset District, came shooting at me. They weren't hard to answer for me, but it would have been impossible for anyone but a native San Franciscan to answer them all. It seemed to me that Officer Lawson, toward the end, was on my side. It also seemed to me that he loved the City the way I did. Finally, about seven-thirty, he leaned back in his chair and looked at the others.

"I think this young guy's on the level. Why don't you get him back in the cell, and we'll talk about it."

Finn looked at me as the metal door clanged shut.

"How did it go?"

"Fine, I think. The way the last guy sounded at the end, at least he thinks I'm an American."

"Did he say that?"

"Pretty much."

"Vell, if he thinks you are I'm sure the rest of them do." His voice was really anxious now. "Did they say anything about aiding an illegal entry?"

"Not a word, but somehow they all seemed friendlier when they wound up."

Finn heaved a deep sigh.

"Yesus, I hope you're in the clear, Russ. Course if you are, this be the end of the line for us."

I had been so apprehensive about what the Immigration Service might do with me that the thought of parting from Finn Bering had left my mind. But he was right. If they turned me loose tomorrow, Finn would remain behind. There was no point in dodging the issue.

"I know. I really feel like hell about it, Finn, but I'm going to get to New York. From what I heard them saying, you'll be going to Ellis Island. I'll see you there—for sure!" I smiled wryly. "Somehow I don't think I'm going to get rich working the wheat harvest, even here in the States."

Finn smiled back. "Yah, you may be right, Russ, but you vork enough to get a stake for New York, okay?"

We both knew how slim the chances were that I would be able to see him in New York, but Finn, with his innate ability to say the right thing at the right time, did that now. He continued talking.

"Ve may not have much of a visit, but I'll see you there for sure. You know, you keep shipping, some day you get to Copenhagen." He grinned. "Then I show you a time! I'm going to write my address for you, but don't vorry if you lose it, there's not too many Berings in the phone book. You'll find me!"

So we talked, cheering up each other, into the night. We reminisced about the jungles in British Columbia, about how startled we both were when we stumbled into Roger in that old, deserted passenger car south of Weyburn, about Margaret Hoffman's food— all that we had done and experienced.

Finally, Finn yawned.

"Let's get some sleep, Russ. Vhich bunk you vant?"

"I'll take the top one."

I tossed and turned on the thin pad for quite awhile, but eventually sleep came.

In the morning we were fed a breakfast of oatmeal mush and fried potatoes.

About eight o'clock Officer Smithson was at the cell door. His expression was grim. My heart sank. Then he started to smile. "Come on, Hofvendahl, we want to talk to you."

Once again I was seated in the office.

Once more the first interrogator faced me. He was alone behind the desk now. He was a powerfully built man and seemed to be the senior officer present.

"Hofvendahl, you've convinced us you're a citizen." He paused and leaned forward, his hands flat on the desk. He spoke slowly, emphasizing each word.

"Aiding and abetting an illegal entry is damned serious. You may have thought you were just hiking into the States with a friend, but you were committing a felony. Do you understand?"

"Yes, sir."

"The department pretty much leaves it up to us. Let me tell you, you've got a friend in Officer Smithson."

I shot an involuntary look at him seated on the chair against the wall. He winked at me.

"Anyway, we've decided to turn you loose. So you grab that roll of yours and get out of Portal. If I were you I'd stay a long way south of the border."

"I intend to, believe me!"

Then I was back in the cell tying my blanket roll. Officer Smithson was standing just outside the cell door. I finished, straightened up, and slung my pack over my left shoulder. I looked into Finn's face. We had really said our good-byes last night.

It seemed to me that I could see tears in his eyes. I know that my vision was blurred.

We shook hands—hard, for a brief moment.

"Be seeing you, Finn."

"Yah, Russ." He nodded. "In New York—don't forget."

"I won't!"

Then I was gone. On the road, now alone.

# 11

The Great Northern train depot in Portal was painted a conventional yellow, with brown trim on the window sashes and doors. It wasn't very large, but there was a bed of well-tended bright-red geraniums on the street side, which gave it a homey look.

Finn had beat his way west by a more southerly route and had never traveled on the Great Northern railroad. The line that was reputed to be the most hospitable and least hostile to hoboes enjoyed that reputation among the Knights of the Road throughout the United States, and Finn had told me about it. I decided this was the time to find out.

There was a kindly looking ticket agent behind the counter. He was an older, balding man, probably about fifty, dressed in railroad black trousers, a black vest with a gold watch chain strung across the front, and black sleeve guards that contrasted with his white shirt.

"Excuse me, sir, do you happen to know if there's any freights due out south for the main line?"

He looked at me quizzically for a moment. "If I don't, reckon there's no one around here that does. Sure you don't want to buy a ticket?"

I shook my head. "I don't have the money."

"Where you headin', son?"

I had already consulted my map. I knew that the main line ran generally east and west through Minot, which was about eighty miles southeast of Portal. I figured that once I got on the main line I should be able to get some information on where the threshing outfits were working.

"Right now I'm heading for Minot."

He pulled a large gold watch out of his vest pocket, snapped the cover open, and looked at it. "We got a way freight due out of this yard at nine forty-five this morning. Empty boxes mainly. Should be making up right now. If you hike down the tracks that way," he gestured to his left, "you'll find it. We don't have a lot of traffic out of Portal. You can't miss it."

The Great Northern was certainly living up to its reputation! "Thanks very much, I sure appreciate it."

"We aim to please," he said dryly.

I hiked down the tracks to where I could see a caboose spotted with four boxcars coupled up ahead of it. There was an engine picking up an empty gondola, chugging by the stationary cars to a switch down the line from them. This had to be my train. I walked over to it.

For the first time that I could remember, I saw the logo of the

Great Northern railroad painted on the side of a boxcar—the proud white mountain goat with its forefeet planted defiantly. "See America First." The words were blazoned across the reddish-brown of the boxcar above the curved horns. For some reason the slogan amused me. It seemed to be addressed to those wanderers who were *really* seeing America first—at no profit to the Great Northern.

I picked an empty boxcar three forward of the caboose, tossed in my bedroll, and clambered in. From the slight elevation of the floor of the boxcar I could look out over the limitless prairie, wheat shimmering and rustling in the morning breeze like a golden sea in every direction.

I concentrated on the immediate problem of leaving Portal, North Dakota, behind me and made a conscious effort not to think of Finn Bering. But the ache was there, and now, as I stretched out on the floor of the boxcar, my head pillowed on my pack, I could control my feelings no longer. I was by myself; I hadn't even seen a member of the train crew yet. The tears came unbidden, in a rush that I could not control. Thank God I hadn't broken down back there at Immigration Headquarters and shamed myself and Finn. Finally, the emotion subsided, and I felt strangely relieved and quieted.

I knew from stories I had heard, and simply based on my own common sense, that there were scum traveling on the road these days. Men who were aggressive sodomists, some who were literally murderers; they represented a danger that hadn't really been a problem in western Canada. Whatever the hazard now, it was likely to get worse the farther east I traveled.

There was definitely safety in numbers. Finn and I had both been more secure traveling together. In addition to that was the fact that he had made all of the decisions. It wasn't that I was too concerned about making up my mind when I had to, but I recognized the fact that the road, and the hobo jungles, could be truly dangerous. It was easier when Finn was calling the shots and assuming the responsibility for the decisions made. I sat up and shook my head. The hell with it. As much as I missed him, he had already taught me a lot. I knew how to take care of myself. I had to smile when I remembered some of Finn's decisions. The basic one of making a stake in the wheat harvest wouldn't take any prize for long-range planning. Then, deciding to catch the next way freight through at Red Pass—that had been something else! Still, I wasn't smiling anymore, Finn had never hesitated. Now I had to do the deciding for myself.

I heard the clanking jolts from the front of the train moving back. My car jerked forward, and we were rolling south across North Dakota. I stood up, went over to the open door, and sat down with my legs dangling.

It was a warm day, and the breeze created by the movement of the train felt good on my face. It was a slow freight, but it stopped only twice on the way to Minot. I saw no sign of railroad bulls and I saw no other hoboes at all. The vastness of the North Dakota plain rolling endless miles to the horizon had a somnolent effect on me. I hadn't slept all that well last night anyway, and I dozed some of the time away as we rolled southward.

We pulled into the Minot yards about four in the afternoon. I found the jungle, another dry one, just south of the right of way.

A group of about ten men were sprawled out, some talking, others sleeping. No one was cooking up yet.

I approached them warily, but they all appeared to be working stiffs, set apart from the bums by a difficult-to-define air of self-respect and independence. As I entered the general area of the camp one of the men sat up to look at me.

"Howdy, Mac, where you bound?" He was a husky young man of about twenty-five. His tone was friendly enough and I replied in kind.

"I don't quite know yet, but I'm looking for work in the harvest. You got any ideas?"

"Well, there's two threshing outfits due to hit Minot tomorrow or the next day, we hear. We're hoping that they'll need all of us, but I kinda doubt it."

There was no threat in his voice or manner, but the message was clear. Jobs were hard to come by, these men were here first, and it would not be advisable for me to stay around and compete for work when there might not be enough for the men already on hand.

"Where would you head if you were me?"

"Well, Rugby is on the main line about sixty miles east. I know there'll be a freight through tomorrow morning, a hotshot bound for Grand Forks, but she's bound to coal and water up in Rugby."

"Why Rugby?"

"One place is just about like another here in Dakota this time of year, but it is a little bit north. Time may be about right to catch on with a threshing outfit. I've been through it a few times. Kinda nice little town. For some reason I never seen many 'bos there. Don't really know, but you asked."

I nodded again. "Makes sense. What time is that freight due out of Minot?"

He grinned. "Ten in the morning. Real bankers' hours for you. You're welcome to chow with us if you ain't got anything better to do."

"Thanks a lot. I will if you're sure it's okay. By the way, my name is Russ."

"Glad to know you, Russ, I'm John." He tapped the man stretched out near him. "This here is my partner Steve." Steve grunted.

"How long you been hoboing in this part of the country, John?"

"This is my third year in the wheat. Why?"

"Well, I heard that the Great Northern is pretty easy on hoboes, but this is something else. This morning in Portal I went into the depot to get a line on a freight out. That agent couldn't have been any nicer if I was buying a ticket."

John nodded. "Be grateful. It's the way this particular railroad is. I think someone at the top finally figured how many of us were riding the rods through this part of the country. What the hell, it doesn't cost them any money. Probably saves them a lot."

"How's that?"

"For one thing, they're not paying a lot of railroad bulls. There'll be a few scattered around in some of the main divisions like here in Minot and east in Grand Forks—just to keep an eye on things, but they're not spotted in every division on the line." He paused for a moment, collecting his thoughts. "It's a funny thing, but as long as I've been on the road it's always been that way with this line. Maybe they really mean that slogan of theirs—'See America First'!"

"Okay, but not paying a few railroad bulls can't save them all that much dough."

John stared at me. "You're right, Russ, what they save is the damage that's not done in hotboxes, fires, and general orneriness."

"What do you mean?"

"On the whole, I'd say the men on the road are pretty good people, but there's always a few assholes scattered around. Some of those characters would rather take the stuffing out of a wheelbox to start a fire than use kindling, even if it's right there in a jungle. Anyway, when that car gets rolling without that greased stuffing in the wheelbox, it don't take long to get a hotbox that'll freeze the wheel, stop the train, and God knows what."

I was still puzzled and it showed.

"You see, Russ, those of us who ride this line so much really appreciate it. If we see some bastard starting for a wheelbox to get the stuffing, or talking about using railroad ties for firewood on the Great Northern, we put a stop to it right away!" He nodded grimly. "I remember one guy in a division out in Washington. It was two years ago, and I was on my way to the apple harvest. He was a wiseass, and pretty tough too. Kept saying we were damn fools for thinking any railroad was okay, and by God he was going to start a fire as he damn pleased. Took four of us to get him to see the light."

"I get the picture, John. How far does the Great Northern run?"

"All the way from Seattle on the west coast to Duluth on Lake Superior." He looked at me shrewdly and violated one of the unwritten rules of the road. "You thinking about heading east after the harvest?"

I nodded. "Yeah. All the way to New York City. What's it like as you get east?"

"Well, I'll tell you. Guess I've ridden almost every line in the country at one time or another. Duluth is a little out of your way, but if I was you I'd ride the Great Northern all the way there. It's an easier ride than you're likely to find anywhere else."

"Then what should I do?"

"There's a lot of freight traffic south to Chicago." He shook his head. "It's a son of a bitch getting through that town. Those yards go on forever. You in a hurry to get to New York?"

"A little bit."

"Well, I'd plan on hiking it through Chicago. It'll take you awhile, but you'll save time in the long run. East of Chicago there's only one main line really and that's the New York Central. It's a real tough line for hoboes, but it doesn't get too bad until you get near New York State."

"What makes it so tough?"

"They've got about as many railroad bulls as they have crewmen, and they're real goons. I've seen them shoot hoboes off trains with rifles from the signal towers."

"You serious, John?"

"You're damn right I'm serious. It's tough country for hoboes back there. You're just going to have to take it a day at a time. When it gets bad enough you're going to have to hit the highway. That's not all that easy in the east, either, but it beats getting killed by a railroad bull."

"Sounds like there won't be many hoboes on the freights back there."

"That's right. But there are some. You listen to me now. They're as bad in their way as the railroad bulls are in theirs. Jockers, sterno bums—they're no good. For God's sake, stay away from the jungles when you get east of Chicago. Most of that scum would cut off your feet for your shoes."

There was no question about John's sincerity—or his eloquence. I felt a surge of apprehension wash over me thinking of the road ahead.

As if reading my mind, John said, "Look, Russ, you must have a good reason for wanting to get to New York. You look like a pretty smart guy who can take care of himself. I'm just trying to tell you what to look out for, okay?"

"I appreciate it, believe me!"

John looked around the jungle where someone had started a fire.

He smiled at me. "I did invite you to dinner, but that don't mean you ain't going to work for it." He pointed to the roundhouse about a quarter mile away. "Why don't you take two of those cans with the carrying ropes down to the roundhouse. They got an outside faucet there. We'll need water to cook up. Don't try to fill 'em too full. They get pretty heavy, and you'll just be spilling water if you fill them too much."

I was happy to be able to contribute this much and set out for the roundhouse, carrying an empty five-gallon can in each hand by the rope that was tied through the holes on opposite sides of the cans. Following John's directions, I returned with the two cans about three-quarters full. I placed them by the fire that was now blazing, sat down some distance away on the ground, my back resting against my pack, and waited for dinner.

I guessed that some of these men had been traveling together for a while. There were no spoken directions, or anything that even suggested organization, but things seemed to work efficiently in this particular jungle. One hobo was obviously chief cook, others gathered and maintained the wood supply, and I assumed that one or two of the others had been responsible for acquiring the meat, potatoes, and onions, which accounted for the savory aroma wafting out of the cooking can.

After dinner we relaxed around the fire, not really needing its warmth but grateful for the cheerful ambience it gave to the camp. I listened with considerable interest to the hobo yarns of tough railroads, sadistic railroad bulls, lucky scores when forced to bum, and the other stories that together created a verbal fabric of life on the road.

The stars were bright in the velvet darkness of the prairie night, and about nine the talk drifted to a halt as each of the men became lost in his own thoughts. They were indeed making a workable adjustment to a hard life, but it had not always been like this. Once every man there had slept between sheets and eaten regularly at a table. It was now getting toward the end of the Depression, but none of the men around the campfire knew that then.

I was sunk in my own reverie, hypnotized by the dancing flames, when out of the darkness I heard the easy, plaintive sound of a harmonica. I didn't recognize the melody but it was catchy. I tracked the sound with my eyes and saw that it was my friend John who was playing so musically. The hobo sitting to my right began to hum along with John's music. Then others joined him. Directly across the fire one of the hoboes started the chorus in a clear, strong baritone:

> Oh the buzzing of the bees
> in the cigarette trees round
> the soda water fountains
> Where the lemonade springs
> and the bluebird sings
> In the Big Rock Candy Mountains

He had a natural sense of pitch and carried the rest of the men with him, on key, as one by one they all joined in. John's harmonica came through sweet and clear. Then the final, half-defiant, half-wistful verse:

> In the Big Rock Candy Mountains there's
> a land so fair and bright
> Where the handouts grow on bushes
> and you sleep out every night
> Where the boxcars all are empty
> and the sun shines every day
> Oh, I'm bound to go where there ain't
> no snow, where the rain don't fall

And the wind don't blow, in the
Big Rock Candy Mountains

They finished together with a rollicking flourish as the last notes from John's harmonica died away. There was silence for a moment; then the baritone said, "Always did like that damn song." There were murmured assents from around the campfire. Soon it was quiet again as the men looked into the flames. John was truly accomplished with his small mouth organ, and now seemed to be expressing a poignant mood of his own. Soft and clear came the strains of "There's a Long, Long Trail Awinding." Some of the men hummed along, but there was no singing this time.

Quietly I moved away from the circle of the firelight and spread my blankets. I drifted off to sleep to the sound of John's harmonica still making easy music there in the hobo jungle.

# 12

The main-line freight rolled into Minot about nine forty-five. It stopped long enough for me to find an empty boxcar, and then we were rolling east through the small North Dakota towns—Surrey, Granville, Towner.

After about four hours I felt the freight slowing and I saw the milepost for Rugby, North Dakota. From where I stood in the open door of the boxcar, it looked like a pleasant town. The homes were small but well-maintained, and there were shade trees lining the residential streets. The business section was not all that large. I swung off and walked out of the railroad yard to the nearest road. Two blocks away, there was a neon sign with "Hotel" at the top and "Good Eats Cafe" at the bottom. It was about two-thirty in the afternoon. I was hungry, and I guessed that what appeared to be the only restaurant in town would probably be about as good a place as any to get some local information on work in the harvest.

Other than a pretty waitress clearing tables, there wasn't another person in the Good Eats Cafe. She didn't notice me at first, as I came in quietly and seated myself in a booth that was already set up.

She was so intent on her work that it was quite awhile before she realized I was there. As for me, I was enjoying watching her very much. She was about five three, with light brown hair pulled back from her face by a ribbon tied at her neck. She bent over to pick up a paper napkin from the floor, and I appreciatively noticed how snugly her hips filled her white dress. Her dress wasn't particularly short but, when she bent over, a good portion of the back of her thighs was exposed, and I felt a sudden straining against the crotch of my Levi's. At just that instant she turned around and looked me directly in the eyes. I could feel the color in my face as I started guiltily, certain that she could read the lustful thoughts that were tumbling through my mind. I didn't know quite what to expect from her at this point, but what I got was an amused smile. I'm sure she *did* read my mind, but it didn't seem to bother her. As she looked at me, I could see that her breasts filled the front of her dress just as compactly as her rear filled the other part. She had clear blue eyes, a pert nose with a scattering of freckles across it, and a wide, generous mouth.

"How long you been sitting there?"

"Not long."

She continued to stare at me. "You're new in town, aren't you?"

"Yes, ma'am. I'm looking for work with a threshing outfit."

"Don't call me ma'am! I'm not that old. My name's Sally."

She looked to be about twenty-one. "I'm sorry, Sally. I was just trying to be polite. My name's Russ."

"Okay, Russ, do you want to order something?"

"Yes ma'—I mean Sally." I looked hurriedly at the menu. Cheeseburgers were ten cents, so were milkshakes. "I'll have a cheeseburger with everything on it, and a strawberry shake, not too thick."

"Coming right up." She disappeared through a swinging door into the kitchen. I could hear the sizzling sound of a hamburger cooking on a grill, then the loud whirr of a milkshake mixer.

In a surprisingly short time she reappeared with a tray, carrying a cheeseburger, a metal container with the strawberry milkshake, and a tall glass. She set the tray on the table and poured the shake into the glass with one hand, placing the plate with the cheeseburger in front of me with the other.

"Mind if I sit down while you eat?"

"Not at all, Sally. Matter of fact, one reason I came in here was to find out if there's any jobs around Rugby in the harvest."

"You came to the right place. Oscar Peterson is coming back in about a half hour. He told me he was looking for three more men and asked me to keep an eye out for him. Oscar runs his own threshing outfit."

"What is he paying?"

"Two fifty a day plus meals. His sister's cooking for him, and I hear she's really a great cook."

I thought to myself, so much for the big money in the wheat harvest. Still, it was better than a dollar a day.

"I've been stooking wheat up in Canada, but I don't know all that much about working on a threshing outfit."

Sally smiled at me, showing even white teeth. "Don't worry about it. A strong back is the main thing they look for on a threshing crew."

I bit into my cheeseburger. It was delicious. I cleared my mouth with a swallow of cold strawberry milkshake.

"This is really good. Do you do everything around here?"

"Not quite. We have a cook who's here for a couple of hours during lunchtime and again for a couple of hours during dinner. In between times I can handle the short orders. In my spare time I run the hotel."

"The hotel?"

"Sure, didn't you see the sign?"

I nodded. "That's right. I did, but I don't ever remember seeing a hotel run out of a restaurant before."

"It's like this in most of the small towns in this part of the country. There's six rooms upstairs over the restaurant and a good-sized bathroom. I don't clean the rooms or anything like that, but the keys are over there by the cash register. I check them in and out." She paused and looked at me in a way that stirred my blood for some reason. "You looking for a room, Russ? Forty cents a night."

"I really can't afford one now. Maybe after I get a job I'll come back. A hot bath would feel good one of these days."

She got up from the booth, looking me in the eyes. Her voice was soft. "It would be nice to see you if you get back here."

This time, the way she said it made me glad that the lower part of my body was concealed under the table, as again I felt the sudden tension against my Levi's.

In terms of dealing with women sexually, I was physically very experienced, but socially I was about as virginal and uninformed as a young man could be.

The total commitment of time required by high school and my

job back home eliminated all but the most casual of contacts with girls of my own age. On the other hand, I had quite willingly relinquished my virginity in a Turk Street bordello in San Francisco just before shipping out on the schooner, and I had since become a regular patron of those establishments. It simply was easier, more convenient, and considerably less time-consuming to satisfy my physical needs in this manner. I found the ladies of the evening I met in the houses to be, without exception, pleasant, courteous, and very interesting conversationalists. I suppose my youth and obvious interest in them as individuals caused them to take some degree of pride in completing my sexual education, in a physical sense at least, to a remarkable degree.

I knew what to do when I got there, but getting there in a more conventional social sense had me stymied.

Somehow, for whatever incomprehensible reason, I felt certain that Sally was feeling about the same way I was, but I just didn't know how to handle it.

I was five feet ten inches tall, with a rather stocky build. My hair, or what was left of it after that scalping in Fortuna, was bleached light by the sun, and I was deeply tanned after the weeks of outdoor living. My blue eyes and generally regular features made my appearance much like that of many of the North European men whose people had settled in this part of the world. I had never given much thought to my looks one way or the other. One thing I was sure of, I wasn't bowling over this lovely young lady with my appearance. That damn haircut! Suddenly I felt very self-conscious.

I finished the cheeseburger and shake and cleared my throat. "Uh, where you from Sally?" She was leaning on the counter near the cash register, idly turning the pages of a magazine. She looked up.

"Grand Forks." She smiled at me again, and again I could feel the color rising to my face—then she took pity on me.

"Where you from?"

"San Francisco."

"Frisco!" The enthusiasm in her voice was unfeigned. She walked over and sat in the booth. "I've always wanted to see that place."

"You'd love it, Sally. The hills out there just climb up from the bay—"

As I was about to launch into an enthusiastic description of my hometown, the door to the restaurant opened. A lean, muscular man, about forty-five, walked in. He wasn't wearing bib overalls and that set him apart from the farmers. He wore a battered fedora that shaded blue eyes set in a lined, weather-beaten face.

Sally said, "Hi, Oscar. I got a hand for you."

Oscar Peterson walked over to the booth, eyed me appraisingly and, without preamble, asked, "Can you handle a team?"

For just a second I hesitated, stealing a look at Sally. Almost imperceptibly, she nodded.

Then I replied emphatically, "Sure!"

"Okay, you're hired. Meet me outside in ten minutes; I've got a couple more men I'm picking up."

He turned on his heel and was gone. I looked at Sally.

"Did he mean a team of horses?"

She looked at me, amusement in her eyes. "He sure did."

"Jesus, Sally. I don't know anything about horses. What'll I do?"

"Don't worry about it. They're going to start working the Johnson place tomorrow morning. Oscar will take you out there in a little bit, and you'll have the rest of the afternoon to learn how to handle a team."

I was dubious. "Like I said, I don't know anything about horses, but it sure seems to me it's going to take more than a few hours to learn how to handle a team."

She was insistent. "Russ, the men who work on these crews are good guys. You'll find someone out there who can help you. Besides, these farm horses are pretty gentle. Believe me, you won't have any problem."

I wasn't all that sure but, with the slight psychological nudge from Sally, the die was now cast. I was so concerned about what I had gotten myself into that, momentarily, my clumsy romantic foray left my mind.

"Well, if you say so. What the hell, the worst that can happen is he'll fire me. If he does," I was suddenly emboldened by the fact that at least for now there was no more time for romance, "I'll come back here and hold you to account!"

I thought her smile was particularly sweet and inviting, but she didn't say anything—just looked into my eyes.

I smiled back, then got up from the booth, and went outside to wait for Oscar Peterson.

# 13

He drove up in a battered pickup truck. One man was sitting next to him and one more in the bed of the pickup. Oscar called out to me.

"Toss your pack in the truck and climb in."

I did as he said and was barely aboard when the truck went chugging off down the main street of Rugby and onto the prairie.

As I seated myself on my pack, one hand grasping the top of the side panel, the other passenger, a freckled, red-haired young man, leaned forward and stuck out his hand.

"How be ya. Me name is Terence Finnegan. Just call me Terry."

"Glad to know you, Terry. My name's Russ Hofvendahl."

His eyes were bright blue, with a dancing sense of life and mischief beaming out.

He was dressed in bib overalls and wore a straw farmer's hat. Despite the dress, which was the same as that worn by most of the farmers and farmhands in this part of the country, there was something very different about him.

I must have been staring more than I realized. Terry chuckled and leaned forward.

"You wonderin' what's an Irishman doing out here with all these squareheads?" He spoke with a heavy brogue.

He startled me. I really hadn't quite defined the question in my mind, but Terry was certainly close.

I smiled. "Something like that."

"Well, I came across from the old sod two years ago. Got tired workin' in the big city on the East Coast and decided to try my luck out here. Most of us Irishmen are pretty good with horses, so I got on with Oscar Peterson as a bundle-team driver."

We had only known each other a few moments, but there was something about Terence Finnegan that I liked. I felt sure I could trust him. The main thing was that I *had* to trust someone after so recklessly telling Oscar that I could drive horses.

"Terry, I've got myself into a real jam. I told Oscar that I could handle a team. I don't know the first thing about horses."

His tone was incredulous. "Not anything?"

"Not a damn thing; believe me, I'm a city boy."

He leaned back against the cab of the truck staring reflectively into the distance as we bounced along. Then he looked at me again.

"Sure and it's not likely you're going to be anything much as a teamster, but we should be at the Johnson place in another ten minutes or so. That'll give me the rest of the afternoon to make a horseman out of you. One thing about it, these farm animals are well-broken and pretty gentle. I worked on a threshing outfit down in Iowa earlier this summer. What they do is the farmers who are going to have their wheat threshed lend a team or two to the traveling threshing outfit, and the farmers work it out among themselves, trading off teams, wagons, and the like."

"Terry, that's just the beginning. I stooked some wheat up in Canada, but I've never even seen a threshing machine. How does it all work?"

"Well, the threshing outfit comes on to a place like the Johnson farm where we're headin' for now. They got the threshing machine and a small tractor to power it. They usually travel with a cook tent and a sleeping tent. When we go to work in the morning the thresher sets up his rig more or less centered in the field where we'll be working. Oscar's machine can handle four bundle teams. They'll give you two rows to load. You take your team down the line between them and fork the bundles onto the bed of yer wagon. When you got a load you drive the team back to the threshing machine, toss the bundles onto the belt until you're empty, and then do the same thing over again farther away."

As Terry was talking I was trying to visualize it all, and it still seemed as if I had gotten myself into something that wasn't quite as simple as that damn Sally had made it.

Terry was looking at me intently. "Don't worry, Russ. Sure and you've got an Irishman lookin' after ya. I'll talk to Oscar when we get there. I'll just tell him you're probably not as good as me." He grinned. "Not many guys are at that! I'll tell him we want a good gentle team for you, and then we'll get you some practice on harnessin' up, maybe a bit of driving. It'll work out, believe me."

Oscar Peterson pulled into the Johnson farmyard, and we piled out of the back of the truck. He walked over to where I was standing with my pack at my feet and smiled pleasantly.

"You know, I was in such a hurry to get a crew together I didn't even get your name," He stuck out his hand. "I'm Oscar Peterson."

"I'm Russ Hofvendahl, Mr. Peterson."

"Just call me Oscar, all the hands do—" He looked as if he were going to talk some more, probably question me about my experience, I thought apprehensively, but Terence Finnegan was standing next to us and interrupted him.

"Oscar, where do they have our teams stabled? I want first choice!" His engaging grin belied the demanding words. Oscar smiled back at him and allowed himself to be led away by Terry. I heaved a sigh of relief and got out of sight behind the large red barn.

About fifteen minutes later, I walked into the dim interior where I could hear the occasional stamping of hooves, the soft whoosh of a horse exhaling, and the rustle of halters and halter lines. Halfway down the line of stalls I could see Terry's red head above the side of a stall. I could hear him murmuring to a large bay, his right hand gently stroking the powerful shoulder muscle on the left side. He looked around as I approached. He kept his voice low.

"Now then, Russ, say something easy to me so this great lad will know yer there. Don't ever surprise 'em when you come into their stalls."

"What'll I say, Terry?"

"Doesn't matter. Just the sound of your voice, easylike, so you don't spook him. This is Ned, one of your team. Come on in."

I gingerly eased into the stall, looking with awe at this mass of animal I was supposed to handle—and this was only one of them!

Terry grinned at the expression on my face.

"Don't worry so much, Russ. I already told Oscar that you may not be as good a hand with horses as he'd like, but I'd see that you got by."

"Did you tell him I never drove a team in my life?"

"Hell, no, I didn't tell him that! Now pay attention. You're going to start learning."

Ned had turned his large head as I eased into the stall. The luminous brown eyes stared at me out of a white patched face. He really is beautiful, I thought.

"We'll teach you first how to get Ned harnessed up. Then you can lead him outside, and we'll work with the reins a bit. After that you can harness up Josh, and then we'll put them on the wagon."

Thus began the most intensive course of instruction that I had ever experienced. Little by little I learned the nomenclature of the bridle, the collar, the traces; how the reins led back through the collar to where I was supposed to control these animals from the bundle wagon.

Terry was a born instructor, he loved horses, and the challenge of actually getting someone like me out in the fields to handle a bundle team appealed to his free spirit.

Ned and Josh were a magnificent team of matched bay geldings from a farm ten miles away. They were about fifteen years old, according to Terry, and had worked together for a long time. They were gentle and patient and that helped.

The barn was at the far side of the homestead, a good distance removed from the farmhouse and even farther from where Oscar was engaged in getting the threshing machine set up for tomorrow's work.

After I had harnessed and unharnessed my team enough times to satisfy my Irish mentor, the time arrived when I had to back my team to the bundle wagon, and hitch them up.

The wagons were flatbeds with a vertical four-foot-high rail-like structure rising at the front end and extending across it.

When I had the team hitched to the wagon, Terry said, "Okay, Russ, up you go. Let's see you drive that team."

The hours I had already spent with my horses, harnessing and unharnessing them, had given me a little confidence, but this was the moment of truth.

"Remember now, Russ, take it easy. Ned and Josh know what to do. Kinda go along with them."

I clambered up on the wagon, stood behind the forward section, and gingerly lifted the reins with a soft "giddyap". Obediently those lovely horses started out, Terry walking alongside, keeping a sharp eye on what I was doing.

"Turn them left now. Mind you keep those reins straight."

I tugged slightly on the left reins and we started to turn. When I had completed the turn, Terry commanded, "Now right."

I was concentrating hard on keeping the reins straight in my hands, and once again the steady tug on the right reins turned the team in that direction. Round and round the barnyard area we went.

I was worried when I climbed up on the wagon. Now that I was concentrating so hard on what I was doing I wasn't worrying any longer. As a matter of fact, I began to realize that I had rarely enjoyed anything so much as riding that bundle wagon behind this team of beautiful horses. Part of it was the total uniqueness of the whole experience for me. Another part of it was the satisfaction that I found in doing something that had seemed to be almost an impossibility just a few hours before, but mostly it was the sense of power I felt in controlling those tremendous animals.

Finally, Terry seemed satisfied. "Think you'll do, Russ. Let's get them into the barn now. It's about time for dinner."

When I unharnessed Ned and Josh the last time it seemed that they both looked at me with a somewhat different look in their eyes—maybe not respect, but at least acceptance.

The food in the cook tent was just as generous and almost as good as Margaret Hoffman's, and I ate my fill.

I turned in early that night, determined to get a good night's sleep and be rested for the next day's challenge. Instead, I tossed and turned on my cot in the sleeping tent for what seemed to be hours. When I finally did fall asleep, it was only to dream nightmarish scenes of horses with reins running under their bellies instead of over their backs, with me frantically trying to untangle a hopeless jumble of harness.

At four-thirty the next morning Terry shook me awake to face the new day and my life as a bundle-team driver.

We were out in the field about six, ready to go to work after a hearty breakfast. Oscar made the initial field assignments, but after that he was too busy keeping the threshing machine going, and the unloading coordinated, to pay too much attention to the location of the bundle teams. Terry and the other two drivers were experienced hands, and they worked methodically down the rows until they had a load. Basically, I followed their lead.

I tried to stay as close to Terry's wagon as I could in case I needed help, but I found to my pleasure that it was all going better than I had any reason to expect. I thought that I had worked hard on the Hoffman place, but I now realized that it was nothing compared with this. Hour after hour I pitchforked bundles of wheat onto that wagon, driving up to the conveyor belt, and then forking the wheat off the wagon and onto the belt.

By nine the sun was high and it was hot. The sweat rolled down my back as I worked grimly on. The fact that Oscar had believed me, and Terry had worked so diligently to educate me, made me determined that I would pull my weight on this crew. There were times when I wondered once again what I was doing working the wheat harvest under that North Dakota sun, but I hung on. It happened that the only space available when I drove the first load up to the threshing machine was on the leeward side of the belt. I remembered seeing Terry, who was busily forking his bundles onto the belt from the other side, pause briefly, look at me with a small grin, and then go back to work. At that moment I didn't know what was so amusing, but I soon found out. The chaff from the wheat blew out in a constant stream from a pipe onto a nearby growing stack, but the air from the leeward side of the belt was thick with the chaff where the wind had carried some of it from the end of the pipe. As I grimly worked my way down from the top of the load to my wagon bed, the sweat continued to roll off my body. The chaff settled on me like another coating of skin, clogged my nostrils, and made it difficult to breathe. It was about as uncomfortable an experience as I could ever remember. It wouldn't be too many years before the huge combines would eliminate the threshing crews by combining the harvesting and separating of the grain in one operation. In 1938, in that part of North Dakota, the wheat was still transported to the threshing machine by bundle teams, and the leeward side of the belt was indeed a miserable place to unload. Occasionally I would pause for breath and look at Ned and Josh. Their sweating backs gradually accumulated the coating of chaff too, as they stood patiently, heads down, until I had my load off and we started back to the field.

Once in a great while I reached the threshing machine with no other wagons there, and I drove up to the windward side. However, most of my unloading was done amid the swirling misery of wind-borne chaff on the leeward side of the belt, and the roar of the tractor and the threshing machine made it seem as if I were consigned to some farmhand's purgatory to labor there forever.

Despite the backbreaking labor and the too-frequent discomfort of forking off my load on the leeward side, the work was considerably more interesting than the stooking I had done up in Canada. That, and my growing confidence in my ability to handle my team, gave me a certain feeling of satisfaction. The munificent sum of two dollars and fifty cents per day for my labor also helped—although there was more than one occasion as I topped a load, forking the last bundles high above my head, my muscles aching, when I thought about my friend Finn Bering and the big money we were going to make in the wheat harvest!

By the end of the fourth day it looked as if two more days of threshing would finish our work on the Johnson place.

That evening, as always, I took care of my team first. I picked up a bucket and walked wearily to the hand pump to draw a bucket of water and try to get the day's sweat and grime off my aching body.

Terry was already there, off to one side, stripped to the waist and busily sopping his torso. He looked at me.

"Russ, as you've perhaps noticed, they don't waste any time in these parts telling you what a good job you've done."

I nodded resignedly. Terry continued to talk. "I just want to tell you that I think you've pulled your weight on this crew. I'm damn sure Oscar thinks so too."

"Why do you say that?"

"Well, he's a pretty smart guy, and he's got just about everything he owns tied up in that threshing machine and tractor—not to mention the rest of the gear. Anyway, he just couldn't afford to keep you on if you weren't doing the job."

"Do you think he ever figured out how green I was with horses?"

Terry grinned. "I noticed him studyin' you and your team pretty careful the first few loads you brought in, but you got by fine. Main thing is you did what I told you—just sort of went along with Ned and Josh 'cause they know what to do."

"You know, Terry, that's one part of this job I really like. In the morning, rolling out to the field, driving those horses while I'm still clean, it just makes me feel good looking at them."

"I know what you mean. I been around 'em all me life, but I still enjoy working with a good team. Just stick with this mick, Russ, and we'll make a horseman out of you yet."

Neither of us realized it then, but my equine Waterloo was fast approaching.

It happened about ten the next morning when I was topping off my third load. I laid the last bundle on top of the wagonload of wheat, sliding it off my pitchfork. I was working at the left front of the wagon, nearest to Ned, when Josh suddenly gave a terrified whinny and reared high on his hind legs, front ones pawing the air. For a split second I stood there. Then I dropped my pitchfork and jumped for the left lower corner of the rack and scrambled onto the wagon. I had just clawed my way to the top of the load, when Ned gave a start as Josh's hooves thundered down to the ground and suddenly they were off! I lunged for the reins that had been loosely wrapped around the center post of the rack, which was where I always left them as I walked the team down the rows of shocked wheat. The reins were just disappearing over the rack when I managed to grab all four at the very end. By then we were flying. I couldn't believe that these sturdy workhorses could run like that. Over the field we bounced, my bundles so arduously loaded on scattering off as we went. Ned and Josh pounded through the neat rows of shocked wheat, leaving them strewn behind. I didn't have time to think what my runaway team was costing in terms of man-hours. All I could do was to keep myself aboard the wildly careening wagon. Suddenly, we were flying toward Terry's team, which was drawing a half-loaded wagon. I was hollering "whoa" and God knows what by then. Terry took in the scene at a glance, and instantly leaped for the halters of his team. I could see them rearing and plunging out of the corner of my eye, Terry just barely controlling them as we flew by. I heard Terry yelling.

"Saw them reins! Saw them!"

I knew what he wanted me to do but it was beyond my power to accomplish it. I had my left arm hooked around the corner of the post, desperately hanging on for dear life, my feet bouncing off the bed of the wagon as we charged across the field. Little by little I got the slack out of the reins and then heaved back on them with all my strength. It did no good. If anything, it seemed as if those damn horses were running ever faster. To my horror, I saw us bearing down on the threshing machine. By then, Oscar and the other drivers realized there was a runaway team loose, but they were helpless to do anything about it. I had a flash of what Terry meant by sawing the reins, but I suddenly realized there was no way I was going to get them stopped before we charged into the machine. In desperation, I pulled on the right reins with everything I had and, at the last instant, they veered off to the right. It was the only thing I'd tried that worked even a little bit, and I kept pulling on those right reins. Ned and Josh were probably beginning to run themselves out by then anyway. I didn't have the strength to pull them down, but I was forcing them into a galloping circle to the right in a bare stretch of field when I felt the right side of the wagon surge up under me, and I went flying off. The last thing I saw before I hit the ground was Ned's sweat-soaked hind quarters and the wagon being dragged along on its left side. I did a full flip in the air and landed on my back with a sickening thud, the breath driven from my body. The next thing I was aware of was Oscar Peterson standing over me, and Terry, a moment later, looking anxiously down at me.

"You okay, Russ?" I could hear Oscar's voice.

I could barely talk. "Where's my team?"

Oscar jerked his head to his left. About fifty yards away was my capsized wagon, Ned and Josh still in their harness, standing there blowing and snorting.

"I'm sorry, Oscar, I don't know what happened."

"Were you on the wagon when they ran away?"

"No, I saw Josh rear up at something that scared him. I managed to climb on just before they took off."

"You mean you climbed on that runaway wagon?"

"I just didn't know what else to do. It seemed like I ought to be up there trying to do something."

I knew without his saying it that my team had cost Oscar some real expense in terms of damaged gear and bundles of wheat that had to be laboriously retrieved from where they scattered across the field. Still, there was no anger in his voice.

"Try to stand up. Let's make sure there's nothing broken."

With Oscar on one side and Terry on the other, helping me up, I got shakily to my feet. I shook my head to clear away the cobwebs. Gingerly I extended both arms, and then, holding on to Oscar and Terry, raised each leg in turn, bending my knees.

"Guess everything's working okay, Oscar, but I'm sure sorry they ran away on me like that. Whatever made them do it?"

Terry answered. "God only knows, Russ. May have been a gopher snake. Could have been anything. One thing, even though you dumped the wagon that's what finally stopped them. A runaway team can drag a wagon on its side for only so long." He stared at me again. "Did you say you jumped on as they started off?"

I nodded.

"Well, me boy, I'm proud of you. Ridin' one of them wagons behind a runaway team ain't my choice of a place to be."

Somehow or other, despite a feeling that my career as a bundle-team driver had just ended, I could tell that both Oscar and Terry were pleased with me for at least trying to get the team stopped.

It took all three of us to get the wagon back on its wheels again. I was relieved to see that none of the harness had been damaged in our wild charge across the prairie. Terry helped me to get the spilled bundles back on my wagon. We worked on each side of the wagon, pitching the shocks of wheat back on. When we had an area cleared, I led my team to the next piece of ground where the strewn bundles lay. Ned and Josh were their usual docile selves by then, but I couldn't help noticing that Terry watched me closely whenever I grasped Ned's halter and walked them forward. It was about eleven-thirty when Oscar told us we would break for the midday meal.

He watched me carefully as I climbed stiffly onto my empty wagon and drove Ned and Josh back to the barn.

After our usual substantial meal, Oscar found me sitting on the ground by myself, my back against the side of the barn. I wasn't dizzy any longer, but my body ached. The collision with the ground had severely shaken me.

He squatted on his haunches, pushed his hat back on his head, and spoke to me.

"Russ, you really worked hard, I'm sorry—"

"That's okay, Oscar, I know you can't keep a guy who doesn't handle his team."

He shook his head. "No, that's not it. I could tell right off the first morning you drove that you were new at it. But Terry told me he'd keep an eye on you and you managed." He paused, "Until this morning."

I shook my head. "Like I said, Oscar, I'm really sorry."

"Don't worry about that. Could've happened to any one of us. Never know what's goin' to spook a horse. And I really am proud of you catching onto that wagon and at least trying. Trouble was that you didn't know quite what to do then.

"You see, Russ, that team's borrowed, and sometimes damn fool horses can really hurt themselves when they run away like that. They just go crazy, they'll run over anything. I saw the way you got them turned away from the thresher—that was good work. Trouble is that if the farmer who owns that team knew I was letting a green hand drive them—and they did get hurt—well, he'd be on me. I just can't afford to take any more chances. Y'understand?"

"I understand, Oscar. You know, I was getting so I felt like I could really handle old Ned and Josh—kind of enjoying it too."

Oscar straightened up. "I'm going to pay you a full day's wages. You been working four days before this, so I'm going to give you twelve and a half dollars."

Oscar Peterson was one of nature's gentlemen. Despite his own financial pressures, despite the havoc my runaway team had wrought in the threshing operation this morning, he not only wasn't giving me hell, but he was paying me a full day's wages for less than half a day's work that had ended a total disaster.

I stood up and shoved out my hand. "That's really good of you, Oscar. I appreciate it."

Oscar shook my hand warmly. "You're welcome to feed with us for a while if you want."

"No thanks, I'll get back into Rugby. Then I'll be moving on."

"If you like, I'll let Johnson's boy use my truck and he can drive you into town this afternoon."

It was about three in the afternoon when I saw the "Good Eats Cafe" sign again. I hadn't thought too much about it until we reached the main street. In a rush I remembered Sally and the hotel she ran. By then my body was really aching, and nothing in the world appealed to me quite so much as soaking in a hot bath. I could sure afford the forty cents for a room, thanks to Oscar Peterson's generosity.

She was working by herself again when I limped in, but this time she saw me immediately.

"Russ! I thought you were working on Oscar's crew." She looked at me closely. "What happened to you?"

I had an abrasion on the side of my face, and I was moving slowly.

"It's kind of a long story, Sally. Remember you told me not to worry about not knowing how to handle a team of horses?"

She nodded.

"Well, I did worry, but I was doing pretty good until this morning when my team ran away on me, tossed me off the wagon."

"Oh, Russ—" There was genuine concern in her voice.

I felt her sympathy, but all I could think about was soaking in a tub of hot water.

"You got any of those rooms?"

"Every one of them. You can take your pick."

"How about the bathroom—plenty of hot water?"

"Plenty."

"Well, I could use a bath anyway, but I do feel kind of banged up. I think a long hot soak would be real good for me."

I registered, paid the forty cents for a night's lodging, and followed Sally up the rather narrow, steep flight of stairs to the second floor where the hotel rooms were located.

There was indeed something about this girl. Her feminine scent was strong in my nostrils as we climbed the stairs, and I could see her hips moving just ahead of me. It was all I could do to keep my hands from reaching out and touching that lovely posterior.

"Why don't you take this room right next to the bath. They're all about the same anyway. Come on, I'll open up for you."

She inserted a long steel key into the lock and let me in the room.

It suddenly occurred to me that this was the first hotel room I had ever rented in my life, despite all the first-class hotel rooms I had been in on my job back home. It wasn't much—one straight-backed chair, one smallish double bed, and an enamel pitcher and basin standing on a washstand.

"This is fine, Sally."

"We got some big bath towels in the bathroom. It doesn't look like we're going to have anybody else here tonight, so you can use all you want."

She was standing just in front of me, her face tilted up as she spoke.

I can't truly say it was an impulse. I had been thinking about this ever since the first time I had seen her. I wasn't sure, but it was now or never.

I leaned over and kissed her full on the lips.

I didn't know what to expect and was prepared to duck a quick slap. Instead, I felt her lips part, and she put her arms around my neck. I held her in my arms, but not too closely. I didn't want her to know what was happening to me.

After a moment she dropped her arms and stepped back, looking at me with that enchanting smile.

"You're a pretty fast worker, aren't you, Russ?"

Fast worker. Jesus! I wasn't even sure how to kiss her, but I guess I'd done something right.

"Uh, no, not really. It's just that you're so pretty—" I finished rather lamely.

"How old are you, anyway?"

I gulped. Then I remembered my seaman's papers in my pack. If she decided to ask me, they were proof enough. "Nineteen."

"Nineteen. You seem older than that. Well, I'm twenty-one. I was just wondering."

"Is that okay, Sally?"

"Sure. Look, I've got to get back downstairs now to the restaurant. I close up at nine. Why don't you come down and get something to eat about eight-thirty?"

"That's great, sure."

She leaned forward, kissed me again lightly, and then left.

By nine we were alone in the Good Eats Cafe, and I had finished eating. Sally stared at me.

"I've been watching you move. Where did you fall when you went off that wagon?"

"I'm not sure, but the way my back feels on the left side, I think that's where I hit the ground."

"Stand up and let me take a look."

Carefully I edged out of the booth. Sally pulled my shirt up.
"Oh, Russ!"

"What's the matter?"

"You've got a bruise the whole length of your back." Gently, she touched me. Involuntarily, I jumped.

She became suddenly businesslike. "The boss has a big bottle of liniment in the kitchen. He's always complaining about his lumbago. You go upstairs and rest. Soon as I close up, I'll come upstairs and rub that liniment on you. It ought to help. I really feel like it's my fault, talking you into taking that job with those horses."

I stretched out on the bed and waited for her. My back was hurting so much that I really wasn't thinking of anything except the liniment. I was hoping it would help.

She opened the door, which I had left unbolted. "Okay, Russ, turn over and let me rub this on."

I rolled over on my stomach, and she pulled my shirt up to my shoulders. I winced at the pressure of her soft hands, but the heat from the liniment penetrated my aching body and I began to relax.

"Gee that feels good, Sally."

"I'm glad."

For a while neither of us said anything as she gently massaged my back. Soon I began to feel a warmth pervade me that had nothing to do with the liniment, and I was glad that I was lying on my stomach where my aroused condition was not visible.

I could feel the electricity in her hands, the heat from her very being, so close to me. By then the pain had disappeared from my consciousness, and Sally's lovely female presence was overwhelming me. I turned over and stared at her in the light cast by the bare bulb that dangled from a cord from the ceiling.

She stared back for an instant. Then she was in my arms and our bodies entwined on the bed. I could taste the sweetness of her mouth through her parted lips. She was breathing hard, and I knew that I should be doing more than merely kissing this lovely girl, but I just didn't dare. I felt her hand grasp mine and direct it downward. Oh, Lord, I thought, this can't be happening.

"Russ," she gasped, "please turn the light off." I could tell it was difficult for her to speak.

I got up and pulled the light cord, and my courage returned with the darkness.

I lay back on the bed, my hand seeking her. The bordellos of San Francisco had taught me nothing about foreplay. I doubt if I could have defined the word. But instinct took over. When I diffidently touched what I was feeling for, I involuntarily started. She was warm and wet and I wasn't sure that this was the way it was supposed to be. I didn't ask her if she was feeling all right, although it was on the tip of my tongue to do so.

As I started to pull down her panties she could barely speak.

"Russ—do you have anything—you know, to put on?"

I wasn't finding it all that easy to talk myself. "Sure," I murmured thickly.

For at least six months now I had two condoms that I carried in my wallet to meet just such a lovely emergency. But how in the hell could I fish one out and get it on—worried that Sally might change her mind. She quickly dismissed my concern.

"That's good, put it on." As she said this, she lifted herself on the bed and removed her panties.

I felt as if I had ten thumbs, but somehow I had the circular rolled rubber out of my wallet, and the metal buttons of my Levi's torn open. There was just no way I could do this romantically. For a moment I wondered if this instrument of love had survived six months in my wallet intact. Then, I thought, the hell with it! This die is cast.

I stalled for time by leaning over and kissing her again. Her lips were really parted now, her tongue darting into my mouth. I could feel her body twisting on the bed as I desperately tried to get that damn thing on. Try as I might, I couldn't get it unrolled, all the time fearing this beautiful dream would end.

"Russ, please, hurry up!"

It suddenly dawned on me that I was trying to get it on backwards—it just wouldn't unroll. I got up and sat on the edge of the bed and concentrated on the job at hand. Finally I was sheathed.

Then I was between her parted legs. I entered her and very shortly thereafter the world exploded for both of us.

Nothing in my rather specialized sexual experience had prepared me for this. Nor for her murmured question afterward. "I hope you don't think I'm cheap, do you?"

"Of course not. Why should I?"

"Well, it didn't exactly just happen, although I really didn't mean to make love to you. I felt so sorry for you with that terrible bruise. I don't know. When you turned over on your back and looked at me like that..." Her voice trailed off.

"I guess you can tell I haven't been around much, Sally. It just sort of happened to me too."

She chuckled softly. "You did seem to be having a time with that thing, getting it on."

I was too embarrassed to reply to that. We lay there drowsily for quite a while. After some time the warmth and scent of her nearness began to have its effect on me.

"Uh, Sally, I have another—"

She burst out laughing then, but pulled me to her and kissed me passionately.

"That's good, Russ. We can take it a little easier this time, okay?"

I simply nodded there in the darkness.

This time, untormented by doubts and my inexperience, it was even lovelier and, finally, more explosive than the first time.

We talked for quite a while after that. I learned that Sally had left Grand Forks to take the job in Rugby, North Dakota, after breaking off an engagement that had provided tremendous physical satisfaction but little else. She had the good sense and more than enough strength of character to realize that she had to go somewhere else. However, she had not reckoned on what it would be like for her in a small town like Rugby in terms of the constricted social life that would be forced upon her there.

I had come fairly close to the mark, as it turned out, in believing that it was not just me that had turned her on. The fact that I was a stranger who would soon be moving on was a strong factor in influencing her rather flirtatious behavior the first time we had met. She told me all this openly and with an air of good humor that made it impossible for me to resent anything she said.

It was getting fairly late when she finally got out of bed and stood up.

"Russ, that old lady who runs the boarding house where I live doesn't have any say over me, but how she talks. I've really got to get home now."

"Will I see you again?"

The light was still out in the room, and we were standing by the window with the moonlight pouring in. Her voice was gentle, and I could see the tenderness in her eyes.

"No, Russ. You told me you're heading for New York. If you didn't leave tomorrow you'd be going not too long after. This has been wonderful. Don't forget me!"

We kissed once more and then she was gone.
I never saw her again, and I have not forgotten her.

# 14

I was used to the early hours of the wheat harvest, and I opened my eyes at about five the next morning. Sleepily trying to remember just where I was, and puzzling over the unaccustomed feel of sheets and the sight of walls enclosing me, I finally came fully awake. It suddenly hit me that I didn't have anything I really had to do. With that realization going through my mind, I burrowed luxuriously into the sheets, turned the pillow to its cool side, and drifted off to sleep again.

It was full daylight when I awoke again—about seven-thirty. Practically the middle of the day, I thought somewhat sarcastically, remembering the long hours stooking on Fritz Hoffman's place and toiling on Oscar Peterson's threshing crew.

I caught a freight east about eleven in the morning, once again finding an empty box all to myself. My body still ached but I felt good. Sitting in my favorite spot at the open boxcar door, breathing deeply of the fresh, clean air as we rattled toward Grand Forks, I was content. My stomach was full, I had money in my pocket, and I was clean again. The soft wind blowing over my face was explicit evidence of the fact that I was traveling on—in the right direction— most comfortably.

I didn't have all of my money in my pocket. Finn had warned me about secreting money—if and when *that* ever became a problem.

I thought of his words now, remembering his experience and sense of humor.

"Ve ever get that stake, Russ, put most of it inside your sock. It's okay to carry a few bucks in your pocket, but best put the rest vhere I tell you. May not smell too good vhen you need it, but that's better than getting rolled for it in a boxcar or a yungle somevhere."

Before I left the hotel that morning I had smoothed out eight dollar bills, and tried to keep them flat as I pulled my left sock on over my small hoard. That left me three dollars in bills and loose change, amounting to almost another dollar, which I carried in the right front pocket of my Levi's.

Probably too much to suit Finn, I thought. On the other hand, if I ever did get rolled, the probabilities were that the thief was likely to believe he had gotten all of my money.

Once again I was facing a tough world without the comfort of Finn's presence, but the circumstances sure looked better to me this bright and sunny morning than when I said good-bye to Finn Bering back in Portal.

The train wasn't setting any speed records but it didn't get switched off on any sidings, either, and we swayed and rattled steadily on. Occasionally the engine sounded a long, mournful *whohoohoo* as it crossed an infrequent road that stretched over the prairie like a black ribbon between the golden fields.

About four that afternoon we pulled into Grand Forks, North Dakota. As it happened there was another freight heading east, made up, the engine huffing impatiently, blowing steam, and awaiting the highball only a short distance from where I had gotten off. There was just the one main line of the Great Northern running east and west in this part of the country. If the engine was heading in the right direction I couldn't make any mistakes. Fifteen minutes after arriving in Grand Forks I was riding east again.

We crossed the Minnesota border just a short time later. I supposed that it was my imagination—there really couldn't be too much difference in the terrain on either side of the North Dakota-Minnesota border—still there seemed to me to be a perceptible difference. Minnesota looked greener somehow, and there were more trees now.

It was midnight when we rolled into Bemidji, Minnesota, the division terminus of this particular train. I found a secluded spot in the jungle, rolled up in my blankets, and fell asleep almost immediately.

The next morning I walked into town, bought some cold meats and cheese to provision me for the next day's journey, and returned to the Bemidji railroad yard.

After checking my map, and making some inquiries in the jungle, I decided that I would stay on the Great Northern into Duluth. It was more a question of riding this easy line than anything else. It probably would have been better to start working southeast for Chicago, but it was practically like making passenger-train connections on the Great Northern—catching one freight after another with no problems. Then too I was interested in seeing the Great

Lakes seaport of Duluth. I had heard stories of the tremendous grain ships on the Lakes from some of my shipmates on the schooner, and I was looking forward to seeing some of these vessels myself.

My freight out of Bemidji would be rolling out of the yard about eight—the word being that it was a through train right on into Duluth.

The ride that morning was a sheer delight. We rolled by small blue lakes, stands of green forest scattered across the flat landscape and, in the distance, creamy-white clouds piled up in an azure sky. From time to time I dug into my brown paper bag of provisions for a piece of ham to roll around a slice of Swiss cheese. The beauty of the countryside, the feeling of accomplishment at traveling steadily in the right direction, and the good taste of my provisions combined to create a sense of enjoyment that was satisfying to my soul. I should have known it was too good to last.

The freight pulled off on a siding at Grand Rapids, a main division of the Great Northern railroad. I left my pack in the boxcar and jumped out to reconnoiter. Satisfied that we had simply pulled off to make way for a through passenger train on the main line, I returned to my boxcar.

When I climbed in, I was surprised to see two other men sitting on the floor, leaning back against the side wall. I was barely aboard when a passenger train came roaring through on the main line—confirming the fact that we had been switched off to make room for it. Just as the passenger train cleared the main switch I saw another hobo toss his pack onto the floor of the boxcar and climb in the left door. A moment later, as I felt the clanking jerk of the freight train getting under way, another pack was tossed in, and a fourth traveler climbed in the right door.

Despite the accommodating ways of the Great Northern railroad, I obviously was in no position to demand my privacy, and it was too late to get off and look for another empty boxcar anyway.

The four men didn't seem to know one another, and the last two who had climbed in the car were very close-mouthed.

One of the men whom I had found when I returned to the sidedoor Pullman was the friendliest of the four. He turned to me with a smile as I settled myself on my pack.

"Where you all headin'?"

"Duluth." He was friendly enough, with a soft southern accent, and there wasn't anything about him that I disliked, but I was just naturally terse and noncommittal under these circumstances.

After this brief exchange we bounced and swayed along the track with no conversation among us.

The other of the first two arrivals was dressed in hickory-striped bib overalls. He was rather squat, and there was something about him that I didn't like. After a while he pulled a deck of cards out of his hip pocket, cleaned off a piece of cardboard which he put in front of him, and sat with his legs crossed Indian-style. He began a desultory game of solitaire.

The Southerner watched him with some interest, the solitaire player seemingly oblivious to his stare. Then he looked up at the man watching him.

"You care to play a little three-card monte, friend?"

I was sitting with my back against the wall of the boxcar near them, watching the landscape roll by through the open door on the other side of the car.

I started when I heard the words "three-card monte", and my mind flashed back to an earlier encounter with this deceptively simple-looking game.

I heard the other man reply, "Don't rightly know that game, but why not?"

The card player wasn't looking at me, but when he looked up at the other man I got a good look at his face. He had a long, thin line of a mouth and hard-looking brown eyes. The way he looked and talked made me think of a toad sitting somnolent in the sun, snapping flies into its mouth with a rapid darting of its tongue. For some reason I had the feeling that the Southerner was about to be snapped up like an unwary fly.

"It's pretty simple." His voice had an unpleasant nasal twang that was in marked contrast to the soft cadences of the Southerner's speech. "I'll lay out three cards—king, queen and jack. You take a good look, then I'll flip them over, move them around a bit, and you try to guess which card you bet on."

"Bet?"

"Why, sure. We want to make it interesting, don't we?"

The other's tone was doubtful. "Well, I sho'ly don't have much money to gamble with, but I reckon I can try a dime or two to see how it goes. Go ahead."

Laboriously he selected the three cards from the deck and placed them in a row face up in front of him. Then he leaned back, "Which one you want?"

"I'll take the queen. Here's my dime."

Very much as I had expected, the cards were moved around rather inexpertly and the Southerner won three bets in a row. I never saw anyone more inept than the owner of the deck of cards, and I knew that he was setting up his mark. I also knew, or should have, that it's an excellent idea to mind one's own business when a couple of other men are gambling. I kept my mouth shut for a long time as the charade went on. Every once in a while, when he had picked the right card and collected another dime, the Southerner would look at me with a quick glance and a wink.

Finally, the dealer leaned back on his haunches.

"You goin' to clean me out. Tell you what, let's make this next one for a dollar."

"That sounds good to me." As the mark was digging into his pocket for the money, I could stand it no longer.

"For Christ's sake, mister, don't bet on another man's game!"

I knew as soon as the words were out of my mouth that I had made a mistake.

The man with the cards gave me a cold stare. "You so god-damned smart, why don't you put some of your money up!"

His tone was calculated to irritate me, and it did. Also, I had just had an inspiration. I knew this card sharp was about to clean out the Southerner. I would join the game with my three dollars and bet on all three of the cards. The odds were still with the dealer, but I had to win something.

"All right," I said, fishing the three dollar bills from my pocket. "I'm putting a buck on each one of the cards."

He just looked at me, shook his head, and replied, "You got to know, Mac, I make the rules for my game." His voice was soft but menacing. "You just go ahead now and place them three dollars on *one* of the cards."

I had already laid the three dollar bills near each one of the cards. I started to pick them up again.

"Wouldn't do that if I was you." His tone was hard. At just that instant I realized that the last two men who had climbed into the boxcar separately were staring, equally cold-eyed, at our small tableau. Then it hit me. The four of them were working the eastbound freights together, picking off damn fools like me who were fresh from the harvest.

Without a word I stacked my three dollars, representing more than twelve hours of backbreaking toil, near the jack.

The card sharp moved the cards with a deliberate, mocking dexterity that was totally different from his prior card handling.

"Go ahead, Mac, which one's the jack?"

I pointed to one of the cards, not giving a damn whether it was the king or queen, but knowing full well it would never be the jack. He flipped it over, and I stared at the queen of hearts.

The mark who had motivated my ill-advised intervention murmured sympathetically—he was playing his role to the end. "That's sho' too bad."

I just stared at him.

"Wanna try your luck again? You look like you just came out of the harvest. You can afford it." The brown eyes stared at me, a touch of amused contempt showing in his look.

Suddenly a chill ran down my back. I was alone in the boxcar with these four bastards. I didn't doubt that they would cut off my foot to get the other eight dollars if they knew it was there. For whatever reason, they preferred to work their flimflam game on unsuspecting hoboes, and I was certain they were capable of violence if the need arose.

I was feeling bitter enough at my own stupidity and at these vultures. It wasn't hard to sound convincing.

"You got all of it, mister. I worked a day and half before I got laid off."

He continued to look appraisingly at me—as did his three sidekicks.

I studiously avoided looking at any of them, keeping my gaze fixed on the green woods of Minnesota rolling by. Then I realized that the train was starting to slow. One thing for sure, I wanted to get out of that boxcar and away from these bastards.

I caught a glimpse of a milepost marker—"Floodwood". Casually I stood up and looked forward from the open door on my side of the car. I felt them tense up at my movement, and I knew that I hadn't convinced them that three dollars was all I had. They were not about to turn me loose now. The train had slowed as it approached the Floodwood railroad yard, but it was apparent that it wasn't going to stop there, and it wasn't going to slow down any more than it had already—which was still too damn fast to get off safely. At the same time, I knew that if I leaped off now they wouldn't risk their necks coming after me.

With one quick movement I grabbed the sling of my pack, balanced for a split second on the edge of the boxcar opening, and jumped. I heard a startled yell from one of them as I hit the cinders trying to run, but my forward momentum was just too much. I hit once with my right foot, a gigantic stride with my left, and then I went flying through the air. The only thing that saved me from killing myself was a gently sloping grassy bank running up to the railroad tracks. I had aimed myself away from the side of the boxcar when I jumped, and when I finally hit the earth, it was on my right side this time on the down slope. Over and over I rolled, still hanging on to my pack for dear life. Finally, I came to rest at the bottom of the slope and heard the banging clatter of the freight rolling by above me. By the time I could sit up, I could see all four standing in the open car looking back at me. I waited until the running lights on the caboose disappeared from sight. Nothing seemed to be broken. I was off my through train to Duluth, but at least I had escaped from those predators.

# 15

My head was aching and I felt as if my body had gone through a threshing machine, but once again I had escaped with no broken bones. The jungle near the Floodwood railroad yard wasn't too far from where I had leaped off the train. It bordered a small lake in a stand of cottonwood trees.

I hobbled painfully into a clearing near the water. There was only one other person in sight. He was squatting by a campfire, heating a can of water. He looked up as I slowly approached.

"Howdy, friend, where ya come from?"

My mental state was bleak and antisocial, a combination of disgust at my own stupidity and rage at those vultures I had just escaped from. I was in no mood for conversation. I jerked a thumb west over my shoulder.

He looked to be a bit older than I. He was dressed in bib overalls and wore a jacket of the same material and a cap of the type I had seen some of the farmers wear. It was something like the railroad engineers wore, with a large bill and a fairly high crown, made of the same heavy blue-denim material as his jacket and overalls.

"Why don't you sit a spell?" He looked at me closely. "You look kinda beat up the way you're walkin'."

I really did not want company at that moment, but I didn't feel like moving on either. I could hear the Midwestern twang in his speech, and there was something totally open about him.

"I am hurting, to tell the truth. I jumped off that freight when it was moving too fast and really took a spill."

"Thought it was somethin' like that. I'm about ready to cook up a mulligan. You're welcome."

I dropped my pack, gingerly eased down into a sitting position, and carefully stretched out my legs.

It struck me that I couldn't treat every man on the road as an enemy, and I sure didn't feel like walking anywhere to find food.

"Thanks. My name's Russ." I stuck out my hand without rising.

"Glad to meet you, Russ. My name's Howard Schroeder." He leaned over and gripped my hand, hard. When he stood up to shake hands I realized that he was a large man. He was about six feet four inches tall, with a strong, muscular build.

There was something about his clothes and well-fed look that set him apart from most of the hoboes I had met in the jungles. It suddenly dawned on me that inviting me to share his camp with him on first sight, and including his last name when he introduced himself, bespoke an innocence I hadn't run into before. The least I could do was make conversation.

"You working the wheat harvest, Howard?"

"Nosirree! I finished the harvest four weeks ago on our place down near Ames, Iowa. Now I'm just travelin'. Never been out of Iowa before. Decided that this was the time to do it. I'm headin' for Chicago. Got me a roll that'll keep me eatin' good while I see some of the country."

"Howard, for Christ's sake don't ever tell anybody you got a roll!"

He gave me a puzzled look. "Well now, you look like an honest guy to me. Why shouldn't I tell you?"

"How old are you?"

"Twenty-one."

"You been on the road before?"

"Not really. Hopped some freights down home just for the hell of it, but can't say I really been hoboin'."

If I had been feeling better I probably would have enjoyed my role as seasoned traveler. After what I had just been through, I felt only an obligation to inform this innocent before he got himself killed talking so freely about his money.

He listened wide-eyed as I told him about my recent experience and relayed what I had heard about the road from other hoboes—particularly traveling east.

When I was through he just shook his head.

"Down home the boys on the road are just workin' stiffs. My dad hires them every harvest for the shockin'. He's got two sections of wheat. I never really hear tell of the sort of stuff you're talkin' about."

"Most of the guys I've met on the road been like that too. Hard workers, just trying to make an honest dollar. All I'm trying to tell you is be careful."

"I surely do appreciate it. Let's go to work on this mulligan now."

Howard was a good cook, and he was fascinated by my travels to date. For reasons inexplicable to me, he was far more interested in seeing Chicago than heading west for San Francisco. We had a companionable meal by ourselves in the hobo camp and then rolled up in our blankets by the fire.

I was awakened the next morning by the sounds of Howard getting the fire started.

Peering sleepily out of my blankets, I saw him looking at me and grinning.

"How'd ya like bacon and eggs for breakfast, Russ?"

"Bacon and eggs!"

"Yep. Got my grub and gear out—all ready to go."

Howard traveled with a compact set of cooking utensils in his roll, which included a frying pan and a spatula. I couldn't quite believe my good fortune in meeting this well-equipped traveler.

I had the feeling that he had planned on the half dozen eggs and goodly portion of bacon, purchased in Floodwood the day before, for his own breakfast, but he was as generous as he was friendly.

Relaxing over coffee after breakfast I began to learn more about my new-found friend.

He was the third son in a family of prosperous German farmers in Iowa. He was the only one who had the itch to wander, and the more I heard of his father, Otto Schroeder, the more impressed I was. He was a devout German Catholic, and the affection in

Howard's voice when he described his father, mother, brothers, and sisters, made it clear that Papa and Mama Schroeder had obviously done something right in raising their family.

He worked hard, as they all did, but Papa paid each one of the grown sons for their contribution to the family wheat crop. I gathered that the misfortunes which had so afflicted Fritz Hoffman up in Saskatchewan had thus far bypassed the Schroeder family, and they had enjoyed five successive good years. I could hardly believe it when Howard proudly told me that he was traveling with one hundred dollars in cash, safely tucked in a money belt, and had another five hundred on deposit in the First National Bank of Ames, Iowa, drawing three percent compound interest.

Howard had a natural intelligence, honed by what appeared to be a solid, fundamentals-type grade-school education. His to me unbelievable naiveté was simply a product of the honest, hard-working environment that he had grown up in. Neighbors didn't lock their doors down home, and a man's word was his bond.

I didn't consider myself a cynic but, compared with Howard Schroeder, I was a man of the world.

It also became apparent that morning that he was lonely, not quite homesick yet, but missing the companionship of his large family.

"Russ, why don't we hook up until Chicago anyway? I got plenty of money for both of us. After those skunks cleaned you out—"

Given my lecture to him the night before, it was inconsistent of me to open up the way I did, but I couldn't stop myself. He was just too good a person for me to mislead in any way.

"They didn't get it all, Howard, I got eight dollars in my sock and almost a dollar in change in my pocket. That's why I jumped off that freight when I did. I'm sure they smelled it, and they were going to get it one way or another."

"Well now, I'm pleased to hear that, but you did tell me you're headin' for New York. You goin' to need every cent of that money."

He was right, of course. I felt a little bit the way I did when I had been forced to beg for food. Then I thought of Finn Bering's words about making someone else feel good by accepting a handout. Finally, there was the matter of my friend's incredible wealth and his wholehearted generosity. It didn't take me too long to decide.

"You're on, Howard! It'll sure be a help. Let's get a line on the freights into Duluth."

It took us two days to make Duluth on a series of short-run way freights but, in a way, it was as relaxed a time as I had experienced thus far on the road. Howard was good company and, despite his age, size, and wealth, he looked to me for leadership as we made our way east. We ate well in pleasant jungles, usually on the bank of a small, quiet lake, and saw practically no other hoboes.

Howard's eyes widened when we finally stood at the edge of Lake Superior on the waterfront of downtown Duluth.

"Man, oh man, that's a lot of water!"

I was impressed myself. Somehow I couldn't get used to the idea that this was a freshwater lake, and I could not see the far side. It was a horizon of water much like the Pacific Ocean I knew.

I saw for the first time the long, low-hulled Great Lakes ore and grain ships with their superstructures, containing the crew's quarters aft, and the long expanse of deck with cargo hatches stretching to the bow, rising to the wheelhouse forward.

"You ever been on a ship before, Howard?" I knew the answer to that question for sure, but I asked it anyway.

"No way." There was excitement in his voice. "Do you think we can get on it and look at one?"

"I don't know, but let's give it a try."

We were standing on the dock looking at a white, well-painted, trim-looking vessel. A sailor was standing at the head of the gangplank aft about fifty feet from where we stood.

Without really knowing, it seemed to me that these Lakes vessels wouldn't be on guard against stowaways like the ships on the West Coast. Also, the man at the gangplank was wearing a watch cap, not an officer's hat.

We walked to the stern, and I called up to him. "Ahoy, mate, any chance of coming aboard? My friend here's never been on a ship."

He looked at me and hesitated for a moment. "You a sailor?"

"I've shipped on the West Coast, not here on the Lakes. Never saw a vessel like this before myself."

He glanced around the vessel briefly, then motioned us up the gangway.

"All the officers are ashore. I've got the watch." He looked at us sharply. "We got strict orders—no handouts."

"Don't worry, we been eating pretty good. I'm just interested in taking a look at your quarters, and Howard here wants to see what a ship looks like from the deck."

"Okay. Drop your packs here and take a looksee, but be back in fifteen minutes. I don't want to catch hell from the Old Man. He's due back aboard in about an hour.

Howard's eyes were wide as I led him through the maze of cabins and the galley in the aft superstructure. Through his eyes I could remember the thrill of excitement I had felt the first time I had gone aboard a ship on the Embarcadero in San Francisco.

The wheat fields of Iowa were vast and majestic, the farm equipment strong and large, but a ship like this, for a farm boy, was the largest moveable manmade thing he had ever experienced. The water was quiet there in the Duluth harbor, and the steel deck felt as steady and unmoving as the pier we had just left.

I tried not to be too salty, but with Howard Schroeder it wasn't easy.

"Russ, how come folks get seasick on boats like this? Feels solid as a rock to me."

"Well, I've never sailed here, but I've heard that it can really blow up in a hurry on the Great Lakes. Take my word for it, Howard, no matter how big and solid this vessel feels tied up to a pier here in the harbor, she can really move around in a storm."

We were back at the gangway in fifteen minutes, as promised, and then headed for the railroad yards at the far edge of Duluth.

It took us another few days to make Chicago, but this wasn't the relaxed travel that our last two days on the Great Northern into Duluth had been. The industrial sprawl of Chicago seemed to be exerting its thrust far north of that bustling metropolis. We seemed to make one short haul after another, moving from one railroad division to the next on the outskirts of still another industrial complex.

Finally, we dropped off an Illinois Central freight in the northern outskirts of the city. It was time for another good-bye.

Traveling with Howard, despite the wearing travel of the last couple of days, had been a real comfort to me. Having someone to talk to whom I could trust, not to mention that prodigious bankroll of his which kept us comfortably fed, I knew I was going to miss him badly.

"Well, Russ, guess this is the end of the line for us. Sure enjoyed travelin' with ya."

He thrust out his huge right hand. I could feel the hard work calluses as I gripped his hand hard in mine.

I tried to grin, but I don't think I did too good a job of it.

"Been good for me too, Howard. You take care now, and remember, don't ever talk about that roll of yours to anyone, *hear?*"

"Reckon I won't now, after what you told me." It seemed that Howard was feeling a bit the way I was. Abruptly, he turned and strode off across the tracks and finally out of the yard. As he crossed the last set of rails, I was still standing there watching him. He turned as he cleared the tracks, looked for me, and waved. I waved back, and then Howard Schroeder disappeared from my sight and my life.

# 16

There must have been an easier way to get through that tremendous maze of railroad tracks and yards girdling Chicago, but I couldn't find it.

Hour after hour I tramped along, sometimes bordering the perimeter of the tracks, sometimes directly across them, the sweat running down my body in the late summer heat. There was no way to be sure where the main line east left this complex tangle of steel rails until I could be certain there was but one set of double tracks running east and west. I just didn't want to risk a run-in with a railroad bull for no good reason.

I made a dry camp just outside the yards that night. I had nothing to cook, and I would not have risked a fire even if I had. I ate two Hershey chocolate bars that I had in my pack. They helped to still the pangs of hunger but left my mouth feeling drier than ever. I lay there on my blanket listening to the occasional yard engine making up a freight and staring up at the sky where the stars didn't seem as near and bright as they did out west. I found myself thinking of those cold, crystal-clear rushing streams in the Canadian Rockies. With no one to talk to and no company except my own thoughts, it suddenly struck me that *my* memory, at least, had a built-in selector process. Remembering that forty-four mile trek from Red Pass, British Columbia, to Jasper, Alberta, all I could think about was how good the cold mountain water had tasted. It required only a small effort to remember how close I had come to not surviving that journey. If Finn Bering hadn't driven me off the end of the trestle just before that passenger train came hurtling by, and if Finn had not forced me on I wondered if I would have made it. Of course those thoughts were there forevermore but, at the moment, it was the memory of that wonderful water that was uppermost in my mind.

I rolled my pack early the next morning, while it was still dark, skirted the yard, and pressed eastward.

Finally, late in the afternoon of the second day after I had said good-bye to Howard, I was sure I had found what I was looking for. There was a short grade that I figured ought to slow down the freight east that I was seeking. I had been waiting there a couple of hours and had seen two passenger trains highballing through, one heading east, one heading west. I slung my pack across my back, the sling across my chest, and waited some more.

Finally I saw my freight coming. My need to get moving again, which was desperate by now, eliminated my good judgment. As I had figured, the grade at this point did slow the line of cars some. I could see New York Central painted on the engine.

It looked as if I would be able to make it. Running as fast as I could I grabbed for the ladder on the front end of a boxcar. I seized the iron rung with a death grip, my feet now taking gigantic strides on the roadbed as the momentum of the train pulled me along. Then I tried to jump on the bottom rung of the iron ladder. For an instant my body was airborne, and then I was flung against the side of the boxcar.

It was just too much. I didn't have the strength in my arms to hang against my full body weight, and I was wrenched off the iron like a bug being plucked off a plant by a gigantic hand. I felt the double impact—first of being slammed against the wooden side of the car and, almost immediately, hitting the ground off the right-of-way. Fortunately, I landed on my back, and my pack absorbed most of the impact of the fall.

I lay there stunned, and a moment or two later watched the caboose rattle by as the freight train chugged east.

Despite my bitter disappointment, and a growing feeling of despair, I remembered what Finn had taught me—I had tried to board the train on the front end of a box, thank God! I shuddered when I thought of what would have happened if I had grabbed for the rear ladder. The force of the blow to my body when I was thrown against the side of the car was convincing evidence of exactly what Finn had warned me about—getting tossed between two railroad cars and under the wheels if this had happened at the back end of the car.

Sitting disconsolately at the edge of the right-of-way trying to figure out just what I was going to do, other than walk all the way to New York, I heard the long *whohoohoo* of another freight approaching. It was almost dark, and I could see the glow of the firebox in the engine as it slowly approached.

When I first heard the whistle I didn't even bother to stand up. I wasn't going to risk getting killed trying to board another freight on the fly at that location, grade or no grade.

It was a long freight, a New York Central locomotive on the head end with, it seemed, one or more boxcars from every railroad in the country. I saw the logos of the Southern Pacific, Chesapeake & Ohio, Texas Pacific, Baltimore & Ohio, Illinois Central, Santa Fe, and on and on. Toward the end of the train, which must have numbered almost a hundred cars, I saw the familiar Great Northern mountain goat, front feet boldly planted on a rock, the "See America First" slogan proclaimed in white against the faded red of the boxcar. At that moment it was like seeing an old friend. I don't know whether it was the sight of the Great Northern mountain goat, or what, but it suddenly struck me that this freight was in fact moving slowly—a good deal slower than the last one, slow enough for me to catch it.

I hesitated momentarily. The caboose was about six cars down the line. I made up my mind and started to run. With a feeling of relief I realized that I was easily keeping up with the speed of the train, and I decided to go for the front end of a gondola carrying gravel. Loaded or empty, I would have a better and safer ride than on the top of a boxcar. At last I was aboard, wedged between the front end of the gondola and the sloping load of gravel it carried. Once again, finally, I was heading east.

# 17

It was a long time before the train started to pick up speed. Whether it was the slight grade that slowed this long freight, or whether it had to bide its time until the main line cleared, I never knew. Whatever the reason, providentially, I was able to board it.

All that night, all the next day, and into the next night, I stayed aboard. Occasionally I would cautiously peer over the side of the car as we slowed at a division. Gary, Indiana, Toledo, Ohio—the midwestern cities went rolling by. Once in a while we got switched off on a siding to let a passenger train through on the main line. It was dark during two of these times when, after carefully searching for anyone who even looked like a railroad bull, I climbed off and found a water spigot. All I had to eat were my remaining two Hershey bars. I tried to ration myself to just a bite now and then, but it wasn't easy. I never saw another hobo on the train and only occasionally a man in a jungle near the roadbed as we went thundering through a particular division. Then, early in the morning of the second day, as dawn was breaking, I realized that the sun wasn't coming up in the right direction. Instead of our heading more or less due east into the dawn, we were heading north as the sun rose, a spectacular low-edged glory of crimsons and light blues, as I stood and faced the head end of the train. I didn't bother to break out my map. By then I had studied it so often that I was almost an authority on the geography of the northeastern United States. Thinking back a few hours, I knew that the slow, halting progress from one siding to another must have routed us completely around Cleveland, where I had tentatively planned on getting off in the hope of catching another freight due east into Pennsylvania. This train was bound for Buffalo, and Lake Erie had to be somewhere off to the west. I had hardly figured this out when I looked in that direction and saw the sun glinting off a large body of water in the distance.

I still had six dollars left, and I decided I was getting off at the next division wherever or whatever it was. We were probably a long way south of Buffalo still, and I was so hungry I literally thought I might pass out if I didn't get some food in my stomach soon.

I could feel the train start to slow. I studied the mileposts. Then I saw the division sign—Ashtabula, Ohio. I couldn't fix the location of this town from memory, but it didn't matter. I was getting off.

I slung my pack across my back, and I hung onto the ladder as the train slowed more and more. Suddenly my blood froze as I stared forward—a husky-looking man dressed in dark clothing was staring intently at each car as it passed. He was a railroad bull. I quickly scrambled back onto the gravel in the gondola. Now the train was moving very slowly. I had to get off, but I sure didn't want to jump off in front of this guardian of the New York Central. I had caught a glimpse of the cartridge belt and the holstered pistol he wore just as I ducked back onto my load of gravel. Very slowly I peered over the side; we were just drifting past him now. He was still studying each car intently as it passed his inspection point, but he hadn't seen me yet.

With a clanking, jolting winding down the freight train stopped. It was broad daylight now, and I had to move fast. I took one more look and clambered down the ladder. He had been looking in the other direction as I hit the roadbed, but I hadn't taken two steps when I heard a roar, "Hey, bum, stop where you are!"

I had heard too many stories about New York Central railroad bulls to obey that order. I thought about that holstered pistol for an instant and started to run. Luckily, I saw only one set of tracks between me and a stand of trees just off the right-of-way. My adversary was far enough into the middle of the complex of tracks behind me. I was running hard through the trees while he was still stumbling across railroad ties and tracks, and I was putting distance between us. I could hear him bellow at me a couple of times. Finally, I was sure I'd lost him.

I didn't know how far I had run. When I eventually collapsed on a grassy hummock, my legs were shaking violently. Finally I decided I could walk without falling down and started hiking into Ashtabula, Ohio, population fifteen-thousand.

I was trying to find a bakery where I could buy day-old breadstuffs for next to nothing and a grocery store where I could buy some cold meats.

My way took me through a residential section where the homes didn't look all that expensive, but the setting was unlike anything I had ever experienced. As I eventually learned, these broad streets with the elm trees arching overhead, and the neatly painted homes set back from spacious lawns were fairly characteristic of long-settled, smaller midwestern and eastern communities. Laid out at a time when land was inexpensive, the homes were maintained by hardworking people with a strong pride of ownership. This neighborhood reminded me of a *Saturday Evening Post* magazine cover painted by Norman Rockwell. As hungry as I was, and as spent by my flight from the New York Central law, I was thoroughly enjoying my walk through this quiet, pleasant neighborhood. Very occasionally I would pass another pedestrian—a mailman on his rounds, or a young mother pushing her infant in a baby buggy. The pack on my back identified me for what I was—a hobo. Yet I perceived no hostility in the curious looks, simply a rather strong interest. I did get the impression that drifters like me were a somewhat unusual sight in this town. Knight of the Road was definitely *not* how I thought of myself; the life was just too hard and dangerous for such romanticism. I had worked and intended to work some more. I was on the road—hobo, bindle stiff, or whatever, but I sure as hell was no bum. I was deeply grateful that I still had money and was not compelled to knock on any back doors to beg for food.

In an odd sort of way I felt a certain nostalgia for this town that I had never seen before in my life and would be unlikely to ever see again. It looked like the sort of place where they had Fourth of July fireworks and parades. They probably celebrated Memorial Day to honor a few surviving Union veterans of the Grand Army of the Republic who had fought in the Civil War. I saw many similar towns later, but this first one in my experience left an indelible impression.

I found a bakery on the edge of the downtown business section and a small grocery store nearby. With fifteen cents' worth of day-old bread and sweet rolls, and twenty cents' worth of Italian salami and liverwurst, I prepared a feast. I had seen a small park about two blocks away, and I decided that this was where I would eat. I was a bit selfconscious with that roll slung on my shoulder in this stable community, and I wanted to get someplace where I would be relatively inconspicuous.

I gobbled three of the sweet rolls in the short walk to the park, and they took the edge off my ravenous appetite.

It was a lovely place—the Ashtabula city park. It was not all that large, but the acres of green lawn were well-tended and it had soaring leafy oak trees. I saw a statue of an infantryman, World War I vintage, in a charging position, bayonet fixed. I stopped to read the bronze plaque—a tribute to the sons of Ashtabula who had fallen in the Argonne and at Château-Thierry some twenty years before.

Across the park from the monument the white shell and raised stage of a bandstand stood poised; silent now, almost like that suspended instant in time when the maestro raises his baton just before the downbeat that opens the floodgates of music. Neat rows of backed benches, complete with armrests, were lined up in shallow semicircles in front of the bandstand. It was about noon, on a weekday, and I hadn't seen a soul in the park. I could see a drinking fountain at the end of the last row of benches and I decided immediately to dine there.

Slowly and carefully I fashioned generous sandwiches of first salami, then liverwurst. Every once in a while I took a drink of the cool water from the fountain. Finally I was full and still had enough rations to hold me for another day or two.

The long trip in that gravel gondola had worn me down more than I realized. I had dozed intermittently, but I hadn't had much uninterrupted sleep. The constant concern about the New York Central bulls, the continual scanning of the right-of-way for them, culminating in that last frantic dash to escape arrest, had done me in. With my hunger at last satisfied, I found my eyes closing, my head nodding there on the bench. I hadn't seen any sign of the local police, but I didn't want to invite trouble. I found a secluded glade some distance from the bandstand, out of sight from anyone who wasn't specifically searching for an itinerant wanderer. I stretched out on the grass under one of the trees and went soundly and blissfully to sleep.

# 18

When I awoke it was still daylight but late in the afternoon.

It took me about fifteen minutes to reach the New York Central railroad yard. I approached it cautiously, thinking about the railroad bull who had tried to chase me down this morning.

I was walking through a grassy defile just outside the yard, and I was concentrating so hard on the track area that I almost stumbled over two hoboes sitting on the ground. The sweetish, penetrating smell of alcohol wafted toward me. The smaller of the two men was squeezing something through a dirty rag into a tin can. Sterno bums—I felt a sudden surge of fear. Those drifters who squeezed the alcohol out of a container of canned heat to produce a cheap but devastating drunk were the lowest of the low.

They were both unshaven and filthy and, from the sound of the speech of the larger one who clumsily got up when he saw me, they were well on their way.

"Why don'cha sit a spell, boy? We got some good stuff here."

I saw that he was a big man when he stood up. He must have been over six feet four. He completely blocked the narrow path where I was heading. I sure didn't want to socialize with these two, but I didn't want to show my fear by turning and running back the way I had come.

"No, thanks. I'm just looking for a freight out of here."

His next words sent a chill down my back.

"Well, now, we'd like for you to stick around with us. What d'ya think, Bill?" He glanced at his companion who had carefully set aside his rag and can. He was slightly behind me and to my left.

"Yeah, I think that's a good idea. He sure has a nice ass."

Jockers! I had heard of these aggressive sodomists. They were brutal and sometimes traveled with young boys whom they cowed and cruelly dominated.

For a second I just stood there as the big man took a long step toward me. I could sense, rather than see, his sidekick scrambling to his feet behind me.

At that moment my almost paralyzing fear was supplanted by a rage that was overwhelming. For the first time in my life I wanted to kill someone!

As he reached for my jacket I threw a right hand straight for his middle with all the force of my body behind it. It was a lucky punch. His stomach was exposed as he reached out his right hand, and I was half turned away from him. As I pivoted on my left foot and swung, I put all of my weight behind the punch. I could feel my fist sink into the flabby flesh, and I yelled, "You dirty bastard!"

As he bent almost double, gasping for breath with a half moan, choking, "Ohh", I instinctively drove my right knee into his face. The blow snapped him backwards. He fell and I heard a sharp crack as the back of his head struck a rock.

I whirled on the other one who had stopped in his tracks, staring at the big man stretched out on the ground.

"Jesus, I think ya killed him!"

I stared at him, breathing hard, not from exertion but from the sheer intensity of my feelings.

"I hope so." My rage was not yet spent, and I felt like I could tear the smaller bum apart—and exult doing it.

He saw the look on my face and scuttled away. He looked back once and shouted, "Geez, we was just jokin'!"

"Like hell you were! Now get lost."

He ran down the path. I took another look at the big man on the ground. His eyes were closed; a trickle of blood was seeping out from his head onto the ground. I had truly meant what I said. A moment ago I hoped that I had killed this worthless scum.

Then the rage slowly left me, and I stared closely at him. He appeared to be breathing. I wasn't worried about the law—there was no way these bums would willingly get near a police officer. Still, I had no way of knowing if these two were by themselves or part of a larger gang. I decided I'd better get out of there.

I stood quietly and listened, but heard nothing. I stepped over the prostrate body and moved quickly down the path.

I walked along and was just about sick to my stomach at what had almost happened to me. Soon I began to be tormented by thoughts of what I should or should not do. As low as he was, the son of a bitch was still a human being, and he might be dying. Going back there was out of the question. Reporting it to the police was almost as bad.

I hadn't gone more than five hundred yards when I saw a red-brick utility substation just off the right-of-way. Suddenly I knew what I would do.

I rang the bell at the heavy, locked door. A moment later a small hatch in the door opened and I heard a man's voice.

"What do you want?" The question was brusque but not too hostile. It was almost dark, but there was a bare overhead light illuminating the stoop on which I stood.

"I've got to tell someone about a guy back down the tracks. I think he's hurt."

"Move back aways so I can get a good look at you."

I moved back a few feet on the stoop and stood there.

A moment later the hatch clicked shut and the heavy door opened.

I saw a medium-sized, pleasant-looking man dressed in clean overalls over a hickory shirt. He looked to be in his midforties with intelligent eyes now looking inquiringly at me.

"Okay. Come on in."

I walked into the substation on the elevated floor. I could hear the quiet whirr of electric turbines. The place was spotless and projected efficiency.

He studied me. "You look all right, son, but this station is located near the tracks. I've got to be careful. Let's sit in my office."

He sat down behind his desk, and motioned me to a straightbacked chair that was the only other piece of furniture in that spartan office. I repeated what I had told him earlier.

He peered closely at me, and I could see this man was no fool.

Casually he said, "The police car that patrols this section is usually in this part of town about now. I know the boys well. I'll give the dispatcher a call." He reached for the phone.

When he said "police" I started involuntarily. "What's the matter, son?"

"I ... I just ... I'd rather not have to get involved with the local cops, being on the bum and all."

He put the receiver back on the hook, leaned back in his swivel chair, and stared hard at me. "Why don't you just tell me why you're trying to be so helpful to some hobo you never saw before in your life?"

I hesitated, praying he would understand. Then with a feeling of resignation I blurted out exactly what had happened.

When I was through he looked at me. "Those worthless scum! Why do you want to do anything for that bastard now?"

"God, I don't know, mister—"

He interrupted me and stuck out his hand. "My name's Joe, Joe Henderson. What's yours?"

"Russ."

"You got a last name?"

Again I hesitated, but I decided I had to trust him.

"Hofvendahl."

"Well, Russ, seems to me like you just don't feel right about letting that son of a bitch lay there bleeding."

I nodded dumbly.

"And you don't feel like making a full report to the Ashtabula police?"

"Guess that's about right, Mr. Henderson."

"Joe—call me Joe." He leaned back in his chair, put his feet on his desk, and stared at the ceiling. Abruptly he dropped his feet back to the floor.

"Russ, you look okay to me. I know what worthless types some of these bums are, and I sure don't blame you for what you did. I've got to be careful myself. I've got a good job here and a family to support.

"I'm going to call the dispatcher and cut off the report with you standing on the stoop—just a hobo telling me there's another hobo who seems to be sick or something down the tracks. I know just where that spot is off the main-line switch. I won't say another word about you."

He was as good as his word. About forty-five minutes later a peremptory ring sounded through the station.

Joe looked at me. "Get down to the lower level, Russ, and stay out of sight. That's probably the local law."

I scurried down the metal steps and crouched behind one of the turbines, taking my pack with me.

The hatch in the door clicked open, then shut, and I could hear the door being opened.

"Well, Joe, I didn't find any bodies. Just two bums getting drunk on sterno juice."

"What did they look like?"

"One was a big bastard. His face looked like he walked smack into a door. Had a lot of blood on his shirt. The other one was kinda a runt. Did that 'bo who told you about the body give you his name?"

Joe ignored the direct question. "He looked scared. When he told me about what he saw he said he thought the guy might be dead. Guess that's why he wanted to tell someone. Got time to have a cup of coffee with me, Bill?"

"No, thanks, got to get back on my beat. Thank Christ I didn't find a stiff out there tonight. I woulda been writing a report for three hours. Be seeing you."

I could hear the door close and a moment later Joe walked over to the edge of the upper level.

"Okay, Russ, come on up. Looks like you didn't kill him after all."

Joe Henderson had been born in Ashtabula and had lived here all of his life. The longest distance he had traveled from his hometown was Buffalo to the north and Cleveland to the south.

I could picture his home, when he described it to me, on one of those lovely tree-lined streets. He knew he was lucky, having a good job in a Depression year—making enough to support his wife and three children. He was a sociable man, but it was a lonely job on the swing shift. He was just as fascinated by what had happened to me as Fritz Hoffman had been back in Saskatchewan. That seemed like a lifetime ago now.

He was an adroit questioner, and early on that evening had learned where I was heading and why.

"I'll tell you. Where you are now, about the only shot at it you got is to stick with the New York Central to Buffalo. But from what I hear, you better get off there and stick to the highway after that. The State Police in Ohio are worse than the railroad police for guys on the road, but I hear it's easier in New York. On the road anyway, but not on the New York Central!"

Joe Henderson knew the local freight schedules as well as the Ashtabula trainmaster. He told me there would be a freight making up at midnight that would get me through Erie, Pennsylvania, and on to Buffalo, New York. The railroad police were not too vigilant this time of night. There weren't likely to be any empties, but if I could stick it out on the top of a boxcar, watch for the railroad police in Erie, and get off fast in Buffalo, I should make it. At least I wouldn't have to catch this freight on the fly.

Despite the emotional roller coaster I had been on, I was rested, and still full of my afternoon repast.

Joe made good coffee, and we talked the hours away. His duties were not demanding, but the job required a high degree of skill and knowledge when it came time for him to do something to that intricate maze of dials and machinery.

About eleven o'clock he looked at me quizzically.

"You ever figured out why you had to tell me about that guy? You were taking a hell of a chance, Russ, once you were inside this station. You probably didn't notice, but you've got to know how to get that door open. If I'd decided to turn you in you'd been stuck."

"I just don't know, Joe. I really wanted to kill him when I hit him. But after he went down, seemed like in no time at all that feeling was gone. I still don't give a damn about him, but somehow it didn't seem right to just leave him laying there like that."

Joe nodded. "Don't know quite how I figured it myself, son, but it seemed to me you were trying to do the right thing. That's why I decided to help you out."

We were silent for quite a while, both of us lost in our own thoughts. Then Joe glanced at the clock on the wall. It showed eleven-thirty.

"Think it's about time for you to be pushing on. Tell you one thing, you sure broke the monotony on this shift!"

I just shook my head. There were some bastards in this world, and then there were men like Joe Henderson.

We shook hands at the open door and said good-bye.

"Joe, it's likely I'll never see you again, but I'll never forget you, believe me!"

*Russ Hofvendahl—*
*photograph from seaman's papers, 1937*

*Post card from Fortuna, North Dakota,*
*August 5, 1938*

*Same penny post card, address side*

Dear Aunt Doris,                    8-5-38
How is everyone? Fine I
hope. I jumped the ship in
New Westminster B.C. with
another fellow and we rode
the freights about 1500 miles
through Canada to Estevan, Sask.
We got a job there and work
4 days. We left this morning
because there was no more
work. Got the creases out of
my belly now, and a little
money besides, so I am
going to New York to ship
out again, or maybe get a job
ashore if possible. I will write
a letter later and explain
things more fully. Say hello to
everybody for me. Love, Russ

R. Hofvendahl
Fortuna, N.D.

FORTUNA
AUG
5
4 PM
1938

THIS SIDE OF CARD IS FOR ADDRESS

Mrs. D. Phillips
85 Justin Dr.
San Francisco
California

*Freight train approaching foothills of Rocky Mountains* (D. Warren Johnson)

*Typical railroad right-of-way in the Rocky Mountains* (D. Warren Johnson)

*Canadian Pacific railroad depot, Saskatchewan, Canada, mid-1930's*
*(California State Railroad Museum, Sacramento, California)*

*Great Northern boxcar, circa 1938* *(California State Railroad Museum, Sacramento, California)*

*...and at San Jose State University in 1939, wearing freshman football numerals award sweater*

*Russ Hofvendahl—in valet uniform, St. Francis Hotel roof, May 1938*

*Wheat threshing machine* (Gerald R. Massie)

*Ellis Island, late 1920's* (Brown Brothers, Sterling, Pennsylvania)

Partial view of Ciudad Juarez, Mexico. Population 30,000; the largest and most important city on the Mexican border. The Rio Grande and one of the International Bridges in foreground.

7A-H2576

POST CARD
THIS SPACE FOR ADDRESS ONLY

Dear Aunt Doris,
    Everything swell. Had a little trouble getting across Texas. Heading for Arizona. In about two hours. Say Hello to everyone for me. Love, Russ

Mrs. I Phillips
85 Justin Drive
San Francisco
California
U.S.A.

Post card from Ciudad Juarez, Mexico

*Ciudad Juarez—the Rio Grande in the foreground*

Bird's-Eye View of Ciudad Juarez, Mexico

*Santa Fe railroad right-of-way near Kingman, Arizona* (D. Warren Johnson)

*California Coast Range near Niles Canyon* (D. Warren Johnson)

*Doris Phillips, circa 1938*

*The nickel ferry approaching San Francisco, circa 1938* (Moulin Photo, San Francisco)

# 19

It wasn't a long freight, about thirty boxcars, and not an empty in the line. There were some bright overhead arc lights as the main line left the Ashtabula yard, and I didn't want to be riding the top when we went under them. I knew I would have to be up there for the long haul, but I would hang on to the front-end ladder until the train was clear of the yard.

I peeled one of my blankets off my roll, retied it, and slung the blanket over my shoulder, with my pack carrying line holding it down. Then I waited, just off the roadbed, opposite the front end of a boxcar that was about in the middle of the train.

Sometime after midnight I heard the highball from the engine and could hear the couplings clank on down the line as the freight started to move. I climbed on, swung around to the ladder on the front end. I was finally leaving Ashtabula.

It was a long, miserable night, but my blanket gave me some protection from the cold night air and I kept thinking that I wouldn't be on the New York Central much longer.

I came down from the top as we approached the Erie, Pennsylvania, yard, dropped off on the fly, and followed my freight from a distance just outside the tracks to where it stood on a siding at the far end of the yard.

It wasn't a long layover, and again I did just as I had getting out of Ashtabula. I rode the front end until we were out from under the overhead lights, climbed to the top, and stretched out prone on the catwalk, my blanket clutched around me, giving me some protection from the whistling wind. It had taken about three hours to make Erie, Pennsylvania, and I figured another three to four hours should get me to Buffalo, New York, and finally off the New York Central.

As I was mentally working this out, I felt a chill of apprehension run down my spine. I realized it would be full daylight when we hit Buffalo.

It was a through run from Erie to Buffalo and, at daybreak, I began to get ready to jump off.

There was no way I could reroll my pack on top of that bouncing, swaying boxcar, but again I got my blanket slung over one shoulder and my carrying sling for my roll across my body. Both hands were free now and I hung on grimly. I studied the tops of the boxcars from the head end to the caboose. There was no other hobo riding this train. I was by myself.

I could tell we were reaching a major railroad division as the maze of tracks began to fan out at the outskirts of the Buffalo yard.

I decided it was time to climb down just as I saw a signal tower looming up ahead. Immediately I caught a glint of sunlight on a long rifle barrel resting on the sill of the tower window. I hadn't quite believed the stories I had heard out West about the New York Central railroad bulls using rifles to shoot hoboes off their trains, but that one flash of reflected light convinced me.

I had just swung down from the top on the side ladder when I heard the sharp crack of a rifle. For a second I froze to the ladder. I realized that I made a perfect target on the side of the boxcar. The freight was going too fast for me to jump off, and I was far too high on the ladder to jump without killing myself. The only chance I had was to scramble down and swing around on the short ladder on the front end.

I was going down that ladder as fast as I could when two more shots rang out. They hit the corner of the top of the boxcar where I had been a moment earlier. I reached the bottom and swung around to the front end as two more shots nicked the side of the car I had just left. I was absolutely terrified. I couldn't believe that these railroad bulls could be so vicious.

What saved me was the freight starting to round an outside curve just as I got on the front end. For the time being, at least, the mass of the boxcar protected me. If it had been an inside curve, I would have been a helpless target from the elevation of the tower.

The freight was really slowing now. I looked down and saw to my horror that the boxcar was slowly, ever more slowly, trundling across a trestle high over a deep culvert. There was no way I could get off here.

Cautiously I peered ahead. It was difficult to tell if this freight was going to stop with me trapped on that boxcar in the middle of the trestle, or if it would keep moving until we crossed it.

There were no other towers in sight, so I didn't think I would be a target again but I sure didn't want to hang on there until a railroad bull pulled me off.

It was a lifetime for me, but it probably didn't take more than fifteen seconds for my boxcar to inch along and finally cross the trestle. The front end, where I was clinging to the ladder, stopped just clear of the trestle at an embankment that appeared to my terrified eyes to be a vertical wall at least fifty feet high. It wasn't quite, and I really didn't have much choice. I dropped off, with my legs extended from my body as far out as I could hold them, and slid on my back to the bottom of the gully.

When I had tumbled, bounced and slid to the very bottom, I made myself as small as possible, cringing against the ground.

Every second I expected to hear rifle shots ring out, but they never did.

Finally the freight above me started to move again, and I studied where I was. I saw that there were weeds about two feet high growing in the bottom of the gully. If I squirmed along on my belly I had a chance to get out of there unseen.

It was a long hundred yards, but finally the gully intersected a narrow blacktop road, and I was free of the New York Central at last.

# 20

I trudged along the road that bore off to the east from the railroad yard. Once a Model A Ford passed me, but I didn't even try to hitchhike. I hadn't seen anyone on the road with a bedroll quite like mine since I had been west of Chicago. It began to dawn on me that the roll truly identified me as a hobo, and it probably wouldn't help any trying to make it on the New York highways.

After an hour or so I found myself walking through a residential suburb somewhere on the outskirts of Buffalo. It had the same pleasant look as the neighborhood in Ashtabula that had so impressed me.

I found a gas station and waited quietly until the owner had finished pumping gas into his customer's tank.

When he was through I walked over to the small office where he had just rung up the sale on his cash register.

"Excuse me, mister, can you tell me how to find Highway 20 going east?"

He stared at me a moment. "Sure you don't want the railroad yard?"

I shook my head. "No, I'm going to try hitchhiking for a while."

He was a smallish man in his late thirties and obviously wanted to be helpful.

"Tell you one thing, it's going to be tough for you carrying that bedroll slung on your shoulder."

I nodded. "I've already figured that out, but I don't know what to do about it."

"Well, if I were you I'd retie it so you can carry it more like a suitcase. Not much traffic through here but if you follow this street for about three miles you'll hit 20 heading east."

"What do you think my chances are?"

"Not too good the way you look. Why don't you clean up a little in the men's room and do something with that roll of yours? What I'd do if I was you is head down the highway about a half mile to Mac's Diner. He serves real good food, and a lot of the truck drivers have lunch there on their way east. Maybe if you hang around you can talk one of them into giving you a lift."

"I really appreciate that. Is it okay if I use your men's room now?"

"Sure. Take your time. Not much business these days anyway."

I cleaned up, retied my roll into a squarish sort of bundle I could carry like a suitcase, and hiked off.

The gas station was at the edge of a small business district. A movie house was featuring *Mutiny on the Bounty*. I had seen the film about six months earlier in San Francisco, and it was one of my all-time favorites. Seeing that title on the marquee brought back a flood of memories: the opening scene with that beautiful square-rigged ship standing out to sea, the stirring strains of "Rule Britannia" swelling to a crescendo, the magnificent performances of Charles Laughton as Captain Bligh, and of Clark Gable as Fletcher Christian. But more than anything else, the memories of my aunt's home back in San Francisco and her love and warmth came rushing back. I was suddenly assailed by a wave of homesickness.

I forced myself to think of what I had to do now and kept on walking.

I found Mac's Diner about one o'clock and, sure enough, there were a couple of trucks parked outside. I didn't want to go inside because I wasn't sure I could identify the truck drivers I was looking for. I placed my pack on the ground, sat down on it, leaned my back against the wall of the diner, and waited. Through the open windows this late August day, I could hear the music from the jukebox— "There's a Small Hotel," and "Whispering." Like the film playing at the movie house, these songs had been around awhile, but they sure sounded good.

I had been waiting about ten minutes when I saw a husky young fellow, about twenty-five, come out and head for one of the trucks.

I stood up, grabbed my pack, and walked over to him just as he put his foot up on the running board and started to climb in.

"Would you be heading east, mister?"

He looked at me for a moment, studying me. "Matter of fact I am, you want a lift?"

"I would really appreciate it."

"Okay. Climb in. I'm only going as far as Avon, but if it's on your way you're welcome."

It wasn't easy, and I got turned down once in a while, but I established my operating procedure there just outside of Buffalo, and made my way east basically on trucks.

There were not many long-haul truckers driving that highway, but the drivers who did give me rides were friendly and helpful.

It seemed as if every town had a diner on the outskirts where the truckers tended to eat. It is easy enough for a driver to pass someone on the road with his thumb out, but I began to realize it's harder to do when someone asks you in person for that which is so easy to give and costs you nothing.

Thus, mainly by short lifts, I made my way east through Canandaigua, then Waterloo, skirting the northern tip of the lovely Finger Lakes region of upstate New York. I enjoyed the scenery immensely and, as I rolled ever east on the two-lane highway, I was getting closer to my destination of New York City, although my cash was being steadily depleted.

It wasn't just that I hated begging so. As relatively slow as the traveling was, I wasn't having any problems with the police, and I didn't want to risk having any by causing some householder to report me as a vagrant beggar. By the time I reached the eastern part of New York State, I had less than three dollars left.

Studying my map, I went south of Albany and crossed into

Massachusetts, where that particular ride ended in Pittsfield. It may have been my imagination, but the scenery and the topography changed almost immediately when we crossed the state line into Massachusetts. I had noticed the same thing out West, but there the distances between state borders were so much greater that the changes in scenery weren't so obvious. The farms were smaller, and I began to see stone fences for the first time in my life.

For some reason, perhaps derived from grammar-school accounts of the terrible first winter the Pilgrims had endured, "New England" had always connoted a stony, bleak landscape in my mind. Instead, I found the small New England towns, the majestic trees, and the rolling hills absolutely lovely. Everything appeared to be scaled down, and clearly it was, as compared with the landscape of the western prairie, which rolled on to the horizon. Still, for me, the smaller scale did not detract from the peace and beauty of the New England countryside.

From Pittsfield I got on to Highway 7 and into Falls Village, Connecticut, late one afternoon. The main highway ran about a quarter mile from the town square. The only connection between Highway 7 and Falls Village was a beautiful tree-arched lane running at a right angle to the highway.

It was a fairly short lift from Pittsfield to Falls Village where that particular ride took me but, as I walked down the main street, I knew I would have visited this place on purpose if I had known it was here. Even though Highway 7 which was a major route to New York City, ran not too far outside the town, it did not disturb the tranquil life of the community. The falls that gave the village its name were only about twenty feet high, tumbling from a small, crystal-clear river that rose in the hills to the east. The falls powered the wheel of an old mill which, with its weathered gray exterior and stone foundation, looked as much a part of the landscape as the river and the trees.

The stately elms towered overhead, filtering the sunlight through a soft green covering. I heard a clock in the town hall tower, at the far side of the square, strike four as I reached the veranda of the general store. There was a large bulletin board just outside the entrance to the store. There were numerous pieces of paper thumbtacked to it, and there was a man, with his back toward me, who was carefully pressing a tack through still another notice.

He was a short man, and I could easily read over his shoulder. I could see the "Help Wanted" printed on the top of the slip of paper.

He turned suddenly to face me. The quickness of his move startled me, and I stumbled back a step.

"So, do ya vant ta vork?"

My Jewish friends at home, with whom I had worked at the Hotel St. Francis, had a way of ending a sentence with a rising inflection, and I thought I recognized the accent.

"I do. What kind of a job is it?" I stepped closer to the bulletin board and saw that Israel Cohen was seeking a hard worker for one dollar a day and food. My heart sank; I was really hitting bottom in the labor market. But then I sure didn't want to reach New York City broke, and I wasn't too far from that condition right at the moment.

"Farm vork, ya eva done any farm vork?" He looked up at me.

He was short and wiry. A fringe of curly dark hair surrounded a tanned pate. He had a most engaging grin, and his brown eyes fairly danced as he looked me in the eyes.

I was about to automatically answer with a "Yes" when I remembered the runaway team in North Dakota.

"Well, I worked in the wheat harvest out West. What kind of work do you have?"

"Haulin' stones for my fences. Doin' some scythin'. My back's not vhat it used to be. I can use a strong young guy like you for about five days. My Becky—she's a real good cook. Vhat about it?"

He stuck out his hand. "My name's Izzy Cohen. Call me Izzy. And yours?"

"Russ Hofvendahl. Nice to meet you, Izzy."

"Okay, so ve got a deal. Let's get goin'." He led the way off the veranda to a Model T flatbed truck parked down the street.

As we were walking toward his truck I saw a slender young woman walking across the street to a blue 1937 Chevy convertible. She waved to Izzy and he waved back.

Izzy gave me an amused look as he nudged me. I guess I was staring harder than I thought.

"Dat's our neighbor, Edie Matthews. Pretty lady, no?"

"Well, yea..." My voice trailed off.

We rattled down the main street and turned off onto a dirt road, the convertible pulling away ahead of us.

# 21

When we reached his farm Izzy led me to a small shed attached to the chicken coop. There was a single frame bed and a clean-smelling straw-filled mattress on it. A basin and large pitcher of water on a stand completed the furnishings.

"Vill your blankets do ya, Russ?"

"Sure, Izzy. This sure beats some of the places I've been sleeping lately."

"Dat's good. Ve'll be eatin' in half an hour."

It was then about five in the evening.

Rebecca Cohen took the same pride in her cooking that Margaret Hoffman did. The Cohens didn't cook kosher but the dishes she served were different from anything I had ever experienced and I found her meals delicious. There were liver dumplings, blintzes, and rich chicken soup, among a great variety of other dishes, all flavored distinctively.

I had managed to eat fairly regularly recently, so I was able to take my first meal with the Cohens in a somewhat more civilized fashion than that first unforgettable meal at the Hoffman's.

Rebecca Cohen was apparently concerned that I would die of malnutrition if she didn't press the food on me unremittingly.

Finally I heaved a deep sigh of contentment. "That was wonderful, Mrs. Cohen, but I've really had enough."

She was small and as bright-eyed as her husband. "Vell, if you're sure. My boys, they're gone now to the city, but vatching them eat..." Her voice trailed off, and I realized what a pleasure it was for her to have a young male at the table to force-feed.

I turned to Izzy. "This is really pretty country. I've never seen anything quite like it. Is it okay if I take a walk and look around?"

"Vhy not! Probably another hour or so of daylight. Don't get lost now! I got vork for ya to do tomorrow."

It was rolling country with low stone fences neatly defining hay pastures and small orchards.

I started up the road where the blue convertible had disappeared earlier. About a half mile from the Cohen farm I saw a rambling colonial house. I didn't really know anything about residential architecture, but this home seemed to fit into the landscape the same way the mill in Falls Village did. The weather was pleasantly warm, and the fresh scent of grass was mixed with a slight whiff of honeysuckle.

I stood there staring at the house, thinking that it was as comfortable and homey-looking as any place I had ever seen.

"Do you like it?" Her voice came from behind me so suddenly I jumped.

I turned quickly. This was the same lady we had seen in Falls Village.

"I sure do. Is this your place?"

She nodded. "My name is Edith Matthews." She held out a cool, firm hand, which I automatically shook as she looked at me with slightly raised eyebrows. She was about five feet two inches tall and her figure was petite and lovely.

"Nice to meet you, Miss Matthews. My name's Russ Hofvendahl. I'm new here, never been in this part of the country before. This really is a nice place. Never saw anything quite like it."

I rushed on. This lady up close was even prettier than I had thought when I had seen her earlier. I guessed that she was about thirty years old. I felt a need to justify my presence.

"I'm working for Izzy Cohen. I guess you're neighbors."

She had a slightly amused look on her face now. "That's right. They're very nice people." She paused briefly. "This place was built before the Revolutionary War. A lot has been done to it since, of course. Would you like to see the inside?"

"I sure would."

"Okay, come on."

She led the way across the veranda and into the living room. It was a large room, with a massive hearth and fireplace centered on one side. Extending along the wall from both sides were bookcases filled with books. I had never seen so many books in one place outside of a library. At the far corner of the room I saw a half-finished painting on an easel. Leaning against the wall were a series of landscapes that looked professional to my uneducated eye. A scripted "EM" appeared unobtrusively on the left corner of them.

"Do you own all those books?"

Again she looked amused. "My ex-husband is quite a reader. I love to read too, but I suppose you'd say they belong to him more than to me. He's living in the city now. Doesn't have room for them in a small apartment, so this seems like the right place for them."

By then I was making my way down the bookcases, studying the titles. It was truly a catholic selection—from Voltaire and Dickens to Jack London. From Plutarch's *Lives* to Gibbon's *Roman Empire* to Sinclair Lewis and Ernest Hemingway—there weren't many I had read, but I recognized the names of the authors.

She watched me looking at the books.

"Do you enjoy reading, Russ?"

"I really do, ma'am, haven't had much chance lately."

"My friends call me Edie." Her smile parted her lips, showing even white teeth. Her eyes were deep brown, fringed with long lashes. There was just the faint aura of a perfume about her.

"Okay, Edie." I saw Jack London's *Sea Wolf* just where I was standing. "Do you like Jack London?"

"As a matter of fact I do."

"Have you read *The Sea Wolf*?"

"Indeed I have. It's one of my favorites!"

Jack London died before I was born, but the father of one of my closest friends had been a founding member of the West Coast Teamsters Union and had known London well in the early, bloody days of the labor strife in California. Somehow or other I was finding this conversation as enjoyable as any I'd had in a long time, and I was anxious to keep it going.

"I never met Jack London, of course, but I know a man who knew…"

She interrupted me. "How would you like some coffee, Russ? I'd love to hear about it. Make yourself comfortable while I make us a pot."

She disappeared into the back of the house. I pulled *The Sea Wolf* off the shelf, stretched out in the leather armchair on one side of the fireplace, and started to skim the pages.

I was so engrossed in reading again, toward the end of the book, about the terrible paralysis that was clamping Wolf Larsen in its inexorable vice, that I started when Edie reappeared quietly.

She placed the tray with the coffee, cups, cream and sugar on the low table and sat down in the easy chair across from me. As she tucked her legs in, I caught a brief glimpse of white flesh above her stockings that caused me to catch my breath.

When I told her about my vicarious knowledge of Jack London, it led naturally to an inquiry about where I was from. As so often seemed to be the case, the mere mention of San Francisco kindled an interest that was unfeigned.

Before I knew it, we had been talking for over two hours. I glanced at the clock.

"I've really enjoyed talking with you, Edie, but I better be going. I don't know just what time Izzy Cohen wants me to get started tomorrow but I'll bet it's early!"

She smiled that lovely smile once more. "I've enjoyed it too, Russ. If you're not too worn out tomorrow night why don't you stop by, and I'll make you coffee again. Perhaps I'll show you the rest of the house."

We were standing at the front door, and I was looking down at her. That remark about showing me the rest of the house seemed to mean something, but I wasn't sure what. I could feel the blood rush to my face.

She held out her hand and I shook it, not knowing quite what else to do.

"I'd like that. I'll be here tomorrow night."

# 22

The work was simple and hard. I pushed a broad-wheeled barrow across the field, stopping to load it with good-sized boulders. Then I pushed it to the nearest stone fence and added my load to the structure. It was not highly skilled work, but Izzy had impressed on me the importance of fitting the stones carefully into the existing structure so that their weight would be likely to keep them in place.

I wasn't consciously making an effort to impress my employer, but what I got done obviously pleased him or, like Fritz Hoffman, he had an instinctive grasp of how to get the most out of me. Also, he was thoughtful. He had given me a heavy pair of work gloves that morning and insisted that I use them for this work.

About a quarter to twelve he came out to the field, seated himself on a low section of stone fence, and watched as I trundled my latest load up to a point near him. He looked at me in silence as I carefully fitted the stones onto the fence.

"Ya a good vorker, Russ. Time for dinner now."

Gratefully, I straightened up and we walked down the hill to the farmhouse.

Izzy continued, "Dis afternoon I take ya up to da apple orchard, show ya how to use a scythe. Dat's hard vork too but it's a change, von't be so hard on your back."

After another delicious meal we went to the barn and picked up the large two-handed scythe. The apple orchard was the highest point on the farm and about as high as any hill that I could see in the surrounding countryside.

After showing me how to scythe the high grass that was growing between the rows of perfectly aligned apple trees, and watching me work for a few minutes, Izzy prepared to leave.

"Ya know, Russ, I vish I could afford to pay ya more but cash is short dese days."

"Don't worry about it, Izzy. Sometimes I feel like I ought to be paying you for that food Mrs. Cohen puts out!"

He grinned appreciatively. "So anyvay ya got more done this morning dan most of da men I hire for dis sort of vork. Ve quit about four today. Nine hours da vay ya been going is plenty. And if ya vant to take a break vunce in a vhile, do it. I'm not vorried about ya being lazy."

Scything was hard work, but it was a change from the constant bending over to pick up the stones. The sweat was rolling down my torso, but it felt good, as if my muscles were being lubricated. Finally, I took Izzy at his word and stopped in mid-afternoon to take a break.

It was lovely there in that old orchard. I sat on the ground and leaned back against the trunk of one of the apple trees, looking idly off in the distance. The late summer air was balmy and seemed to intensify the colors of the lush green of the trees and the clear blue of the sky. The white clouds piling up in the distance looked like whipped cream beaten stiff by some heavenly baker, and strewn randomly across the sky. I looked for Falls Village, but all I could see was the town hall tower thrusting out of the green trees.

Traveling by myself for what seemed a long time now, I found I was ruminating and thinking more than I had since I had been on the schooner.

Izzy's remarks about what a good worker I was pleased me, and set me to thinking about all of the hard work I had done in my young life to date.

I remembered the box company on 16th Street in the industrial section of San Francisco, where I had occasionally worked in three- to five-day stretches. I couldn't stay out of school any longer than that at a time without getting into trouble. I made twenty-five cents an hour for eight hours a day, standing at a drilling machine. Hour after hour, with mind-numbing monotony, I pierced holes in the corner of the boxes to accept the wooden dowels for the lock-corner construction. The owner had no regard for child labor laws, his workers' safety, or any other social consideration. But two dollars a day was important money in 1935, far more than I could make selling papers, which was my normal employment at age thirteen. Then there were the occasional twelve-hour days—still a straight twenty-five cents an hour—but three dollars a day was the payoff. I really hadn't thought about it before, but the California Box Company had probably done more to inculcate a hardworking psyche in me than any experience in my life. Grimly I remembered my first day on the drilling machine. I had gone to the foul-smelling toilet about ten in the morning. At about eleven fifteen I felt the need to relieve myself again. When I returned to my machine the second time the foreman was waiting for me, a scowl on his face.

"You want this job, buddy?"

"Yeah, sure!"

"Okay, you want it, you do it our way. You piss once in the morning, once in the afternoon, understand?"

I nodded. The dollars were too important to me to argue with the bastard.

At age fourteen I got a good job at the Hotel St. Francis Valet Shop. I learned how to press clothes and ran the shop by myself on my short night shift between the ten-hour day and ten-hour night shifts. The weekends, when I worked days, sometimes involved long hours at a Hoffman pressing machine when a convention or a sudden influx of hotel guests required me to help out with the pressing. But I enjoyed the variety of the work, the ambience of a first-class hotel in a cosmopolitan city, and the men I worked with. Perhaps most of all I appreciated the fact that the Hotel St. Francis job had rescued me from that deadly drilling machine forever.

I thought of the ten thousand fish days on the schooner in the Bering Sea—how I would feel after twelve to fourteen hours of exhausting work, barely able to climb into my bunk. Still, the variety of my duties, the excitement and danger, and most of all being at sea, didn't seem all that bad as I looked back.

The work on the *Dagmar Salen* was also rather varied—it just never stopped, except for brief meal interludes, for fifteen hours a day.

I thought of those days stooking for Fritz Hoffman, under the hot sky of the Saskatchewan prairie, and I thought of pitching bundles onto the belt from the lee side of Oscar Peterson's threshing machine in North Dakota.

Now here I was picking up boulders from a field and scything tall grass, hour after hour, for a dollar a day again.

I had always planned on going to college, motivated in no small part by my Aunt Doris's reverence for a higher education. Born to immigrant parents, and having completed only the eighth grade herself, she was determined that my generation of the family would be college-educated.

One thing for sure, I thought, as my mind drifted over these experiences, I'm damned if I'm going to work with my hands and my back for the rest of my life. That brief period of rumination there on the Connecticut hillside probably had more to do with determining my future than any other single thing in my young life to date.

It was four in the afternoon when Izzy hollered up to me and beckoned me down to where he was waiting near my shed.

"Russ, vhere ya go las' night? Ya vasn't valkin' all dat time, vas ya?"

I could feel the blood rush to my face. "No, I had coffee with Mrs. Matthews. She's real nice."

He chuckled. "Ya vouldn't be seein' her again tonight, nu?"

I nodded.

"Vell, ya don't smell so good so I set up a bath for ya. Ya goin' to see a pretty lady like dat ya vant to smell clean."

"A bath?"

"Dat's right." He led me into the shed and gestured to an old sheet-iron portable tub. Next to it on the rough wooden floor sat a large bucket of steaming water, a large bath towel, and a bar of soap.

"Izzy, I really appreciate this. I can hardly remember the last time I had a hot bath."

"Vell, be careful. Dere's a lot of hot vater in dat bucket. Dump it in first and den cool it vith vater from the pump."

I had a change of clean clothes in my pack. Even though I couldn't stretch my legs out, I luxuriated in that old metal tub until the water began to cool on me. Then I climbed out, toweled myself dry, and felt practically reborn in my clean clothes.

Like the Hoffmans, the Cohens didn't indulge in mealtime small talk. Eating was a serious business and, other than Mrs. Cohen's constant admonitions to me to eat more, there was little conversation.

From time to time I caught Izzy's eyes. He was studying me rather appraisingly, I thought, with a somewhat amused look on his face. I could feel myself start to blush when he looked at me like that.

Finally we were done, and Izzy spoke to his wife. "Becky, Russ met Edie Matthews last night. She made him some coffee." He didn't quite leer when he said it but the effect was close to it.

Rebecca Cohen was oblivious to whatever was going through her husband's mind. "She's a good neighbor, dat lady. I think she's lonely out here by herself." She looked at me innocently. "Ya vant to see her tonight, Russ?"

I nodded, expressed my appreciation for another outstanding meal, and took off.

# 23

Just as I started to lift the old-fashioned knocker on the front door it swung open. I jumped. Edie Matthews sure had a knack for surprising me.

She smiled impishly at me. "Did I scare you again, Russ? I saw you coming."

"Yeah, sort of. How are you?" It wasn't what I considered a scintillating greeting but it was the best I could do at the moment.

Her white dress was cut rather low in front and the tops of her breasts were just visible. They were as tanned as her arms. It was a most effective and eye-rewarding contrast to the white of her dress. I was aware of her perfume, and she looked even more enchanting than when I had last seen her.

We sat in the comfortable leather chairs across from each other. It could have been my imagination, but it seemed as if it took her a little longer to tuck her legs in tonight, and I saw more than a glimpse of that lovely white flesh above her stockings.

I didn't know how much I was staring, until I heard her amused chuckle.

"You're kind of quiet tonight, Russ. What are you thinking about?"

I didn't dare tell her what I was really thinking about, and I could literally feel my face burning.

"Come on, if you won't talk to me you can at least see the rest of this place." She stood up and held out her hand. I took it and she led me into the kitchen.

She was well-informed about the history of this old house, the open cooking hearth in the kitchen, and everything else that pertained to its construction and use in colonial times. For a San Francisco boy, who regarded any structure that had survived the 1906 earthquake and fire as being ancient, it was fascinating. When I thought of the lives that had been lived in this home for almost two hundred years, it gave me a sense of being connected to the past in a way that I had never thought about before.

However, with Edith Matthews leading the way, it was difficult for me to keep my eyes off her lovely posterior, outlined so invitingly in the snug white dress.

"Well, that's the downstairs. Let me show you the bedrooms upstairs."

She ascended the rather steep stairs just ahead of me, and I literally had to clench my hands to keep from reaching out and touching the seductive curve of her bottom.

After looking at three rather smallish bedrooms, all furnished with high canopy beds, she led me into the master bedroom.

I looked around. It was built directly over the living room, and a small hearth opened off of the chimney that served the living-room fireplace. There was a large double bed, with no canopy, and a pair of comfortable-looking easy chairs faced the fireplace. There were bookcases filled with books in this room too, and I thought that I had never seen such a comfortable, inviting bedroom in my life. I walked over and looked out the window, framing the vista to the rolling green hills in the distance.

"Do you like it?"

She was standing at my shoulder then, looking out the window with me. I turned to face her.

"Edie, this is just great! You know, I've never been in a home like this before, but it makes me feel like I could spend the rest of my life here."

"You're a nice guy, Russ. That's the way I feel about it too, but it does get lonely living here by myself."

She looked up at me, I hesitated for a moment, and then I bent to kiss her parted lips. Her tongue lightly touched my lips and I pulled her to me. I could feel the whole length of her body against mine, and I knew she could feel me.

She pulled away slightly. "Do you want to make love to me, Russ?"

"Oh, God, Edie, do I!"

She turned away and, with a graceful movement, she pulled her dress up over her head and took it off. She stepped out of her shoes and said, "Help me with my bra." She gestured to where her brassiere was fastened.

With trembling fingers I finally managed to get it unhooked. I could not believe this was really happening. My most erotic dreams were but a pale imitation of this beautiful reality.

Then she slid out of her panties and stood there facing me in a garter belt and stockings. None of her movements were hurried, yet it was incredible how quickly she had disrobed.

"Well, aren't you going to take your clothes off?"

I began to unbutton my shirt. She watched me, a slight smile on her face, as she unsnapped the garter belt, peeled off her stockings, and stood there completely naked.

Despite the circumstances, I was unbelievably embarrassed at the thought of taking off all of my clothes and exposing the rigid symbol of my consuming desire.

I think she enjoyed my discomfiture, not saying a word as I finally stood there as naked as she was. She looked at me approvingly.

She threw back the covers. "Come on, let's get into bed."

At that instant I remembered. I had used the only condoms I had in Rugby, North Dakota. Even though a packet of three could be purchased for a quarter, it had seemed to me to be an absolute absurdity to spend my money to be prepared for something as improbable as this.

I hesitated at the edge of the bed. "Gee, I don't have anything with me, you know..." My voice trailed off.

She laughed then. "Russ, will you please get into bed. I've taken care of everything. But that is nice of you to think about it. Just don't worry. Come here."

She was in my arms, her firm body pressed against me. She murmured against my cheek. "You smell so nice and clean." Silently I blessed Izzy for that hot bath and the strong soap. We were kissing passionately now, and I groped for her between her parted legs. She was breathing heavily. She pulled away slightly.

"Russ, not so hard. Try to touch a girl so lightly she hardly knows it's happening. Like this."

Then she began to stroke me, and it truly was like the touch of a feather—but I knew it was happening! I tried to concentrate on caressing her the way I was supposed to. She gently pulled my face to her breasts and guided my mouth to each erect nipple. At the same time, as carefully as I could, I touched the warm, moist cleft between her legs.

I was so absorbed in doing all of this the way this beautiful lady wanted me to do it that I momentarily lost sight of what was happening to me. Suddenly, her constant stroking produced an eruption that had me gasping for breath. As I started to come, her strokes became more vigorous and rapid and continued until I was spent. I lay back on the pillow, chagrined, and apologetic.

"I'm sorry, Edie. You did that so good. I guess I just didn't realize. I . . ."

She kissed me. "How old are you, Russ?"

"Nineteen." The overstated age came naturally to my lips now, and I had my seaman's papers to prove it if anyone questioned me. At sixteen it seemed as if I had already lived those extra three years.

"I'll bet you haven't made love much, or at all, the way you've been living, have you?"

I thought about Sally, and instinctively concluded that I had better leave her out of *this* discussion.

"That's right."

"Well, I know what I enjoy, and I don't like it if you barely get it in and then start coming. It's not going to take you very long to get hard again and then it will be wonderful, okay?"

She was right. This time we continued just as we had before. I began to realize that she had deliberately maintained control before; now she was letting go.

She was writhing on the bed as, rather soon it seemed, I was as erect as I had been before.

Urgently she pulled me on top of her. For only a second I couldn't penetrate her, but she lifted her legs, spread them wide, and I drove deep into her.

She gasped. Then she was moving with me almost violently, her legs entwined around my torso. Suddenly her eyes opened wide, she gave a long, shuddering half cry, half moan, and for a moment lay still.

I continued to move in and out. Almost immediately she was

responding again, and once more she cried out. "My God, that's good!"

I could feel myself approaching a crescendo of overwhelming, pure physical pleasure.

Then the world exploded for both of us simultaneously, and finally I lay there on top of her exhausted, but with a wonderful sense of peace and tranquility.

"Do you see what I mean now?"

I could only nod as she gently caressed my face.

I didn't realize at the time how much this passionate and knowledgeable lady had taught me. I think one of the things about her that was so endearing was the total abandon with which she made love. She was obviously in control during the preliminaries and her usual intelligent and sophisticated self afterward. But she gave herself completely, without reservation, when we made love.

We lay in bed for a long time and talked, not about books, but about her life. She bore no ill will toward her former husband. She was independently wealthy, at least by my standards, and living comfortably on income from a trust established by her deceased grandparents. I gathered that her husband, Tom Matthews, had become more and more engrossed in his career in advertising at the expense of his marriage. The parting, when it came, was amicable enough. I couldn't truly believe that any man would want to end a marriage with this enchantress but I had to accept her word for it. Her financial independence, and the fact that they had no children, lessened the normal trauma of a divorce to which they had mutually agreed. Edie was too much of a lady to say so explicitly, but I had the definite impression that her husband simply did not have the sex drive that she obviously had.

Edie didn't say why she favored me with her attentions, either, but I got the feeling that a great deal of it had to do with the fact that I was just passing through. She had strong physical needs, but she was a lady, and she would not jeopardize her reputation by conducting an affair with one of the local men.

"Are you going to live here from now on, Edie?"

"I don't think so. When we first broke up I thought I could be happy with my painting and taking care of this place. I do love it here." She paused for a moment. "Now I don't know. I think I'll go back to Boston for a while—probably when the first snow comes."

She had learned all there was to know about me, of course,

including my reason for trying to get to New York as soon as possible to try to see Finn Bering at Ellis Island.

I looked at her. "You ever think about going to New York City? I may be there for a while."

She laughed softly and kissed me. "You're sweet, Russ, but no, Boston is home. I don't know what I'll be doing eventually, but that's the next stop." She smiled mischievously. "Besides, I'm a little old for you, honey. You realize I'm eleven years older than you are?"

"Maybe so, Edie, but it sure didn't make any difference tonight, did it?"

She shook her head, snuggled into my arms, and we lay there for a long time—not saying anything, at peace with the world.

Finally I got up and stared at the grandfather clock in the corner. "I really hate to go, but I've got a lot of rocks to haul and grass to scythe tomorrow. Can I see you tomorrow night?"

"Of course, Russ. About the same time?"

I pulled on my clothes, and started back toward my shed on Izzy Cohen's farm.

For three more days I labored in Izzy's fields. I worked hard, he continued to praise my efforts and, at the end of each day, the portable metal tub, the hot water, soap, and towel were waiting for me.

Mrs. Cohen's meals continued to be outstanding, my muscles were adapting to the work but, far more than anything else, Edie Matthews was waiting for me each evening in her warm and comfortable home.

It should not have been possible, but each time we made love it seemed better than the last.

That final day I couldn't get her out of my mind. I longed to see her but I knew this would be the last time.

Occasionally I told myself that it was most unlikely I would see Finn Bering at Ellis Island anyway, and there probably was other work I could get in Falls Village. Then I would feel guilty, thinking of the last time I saw Finn. I had made the commitment, he had not exacted it. Whether or not Finn had led us into that harrowing tramp through the Canadian Rockies didn't matter. He had literally saved my life twice. I thought back to Blue River and how desperately sick I had been. He stood by me then and, even if I didn't see him at Ellis Island, I knew I had to make the attempt and the sooner the better.

After that first wonderful evening with Edie, there was a subtle change in Izzy's attitude. Even before I had made love to her, he had expected it to happen.

But the next morning at breakfast he had simply asked me, "Enjoy yaself last night, Russ?"

I could feel the blood rush to my face, and I knew that he knew.

I was surprised and relieved when he merely remarked, "I told ya she is a nice lady. Probably good for ya both to talk about books and visit."

I began to realize that Izzy Cohen, in his own way, was a real gentleman. He could tease me before it happened but, when he was certain that it had, he treated the situation with respect. He was still active and healthy, and I am sure Edie must have affected him the way she did me. But he didn't question me about it, and the tone of his voice was altogether different—not at all as it had been the first time I had stared at her in Falls Village. Having sons of his own, I am sure he knew how torn up I was feeling about leaving as my time in Falls Village drew to an end.

The hours simply vanished that last lovely night. We were sitting in the easy chairs in the bedroom afterward, and my heart was so full, I was finding it difficult to talk.

She made conversation, again talking about books—Mark Twain's *Huckleberry Finn*, which was one of my favorites.

"Do you remember that wonderful scene, Russ, when Huck is agonizing over stealing a widow's property by helping her slave escape?"

"I sure do. When Huck has just about decided he's got to turn him in, and then Jim tells him he's the best friend he ever had."

"That's right. Huck figures he's damned if he does and damned if he doesn't, but he decides for friendship, doesn't he?"

I looked hard at her and nodded.

"Jesus, Edie, I feel just miserable about saying good-bye to you."

"I know, honey, I'm not feeling very good about it myself." Her voice was soft. "But you know I've learned a lot about you the last few days. It wouldn't be too hard for you to find another job around here, and I would love to go on seeing you. But sooner or later it's going to end anyway. I'm not all that optimistic about your finding Finn at Ellis Island, but you told him you were going to do it, didn't you?"

"I did promise," I said.

Thus Edith Matthews, gently and effectively, steered me in the direction I had to go.

I had worked through the Labor Day weekend. Tomorrow would be Wednesday, September 7, 1938. The only reason I had to rise at an early hour was to have breakfast with the Cohens. I didn't have to sleep to gather strength for another day of hard work.

So it was later than usual when I looked at the grandfather clock for the last time. It showed 11:00 P.M., and it began to strike the hour as I stood up.

"Edie,..." my voice choked. Tears were blinding me.

"I know, Russ. It's time for you to leave."

We stood at the open front door and breathed in the soft night air. I took one last look at that warm, inviting room where we had first discussed books and had truly become friends.

Then she was in my arms. I could feel the tears on her face too.

I crushed her to me, hard, forgetting in my anguish what this lovely lady had taught me about gentleness.

With a wrench that was so agonizing I could feel it in my stomach, I kissed her hard one last time and turned away.

"Good-bye, Russ."

"Good-bye, Edie."

# 24

The next morning for breakfast Rebecca Cohen outdid herself. There were scrambled eggs, hot cheese blintzes, and a delicious chicken liver pâté to be spread on the home-baked bread.

Izzy carefully counted out five dollar bills for me.

"Vish it vas more, Russ. Ya really earned it!"

"Like I told you, Izzy, I should pay you for Mrs. Cohen's cooking."

Rebecca Cohen beamed. I knew she was going to miss force-feeding the hired hand, but this last tribute to her cooking pleased her very much.

Considerate as always, Izzy drove me into Falls Village in the old Model T and then down the tree-lined road to Highway 7.

"Vell, Russ, I think dis a good place as any to try gettin' a ride."
He looked at me intently. "Ya know if ya ever get back dis vay, ya
velcome to stay vith us."

"Thanks a lot, Izzy, I appreciate that."

We both knew it was not going to happen but he meant it, and
I did appreciate it.

We shook hands, I climbed out of the truck, and Izzy Cohen
disappeared from my life, his truck heading back toward Falls
Village.

I had tied my pack suitcase-style again and sat on it by the side
of the road. There was not much traffic heading south this morning
but, whenever I saw a vehicle approaching in the distance, I stood up
and extended my right thumb, trying to look as pleasant and
congenial as I could.

An hour passed with no luck. When I stood up again I saw a
dusty, rather battered-looking 1931 Model A Ford approaching.

To my great relief it slowed down and braked to a halt. The
engine was noisy, and the Model A made a trembling sound, as if
catching its breath.

A large, friendly-looking man wearing a battered fedora hollered
out at me.

"Where ya bound for?"

"New York City."

"Okay, climb in. I'm headin' that way."

I climbed into the passenger seat and he turned toward me,
extending a huge right hand. "My name's Johnny Polany. What's
yours?"

He was really large with an open, friendly face and intelligent
brown eyes. The top of his fedora just touched the roof of the
high-topped old Ford. I got the feeling that Johnny was no stranger
to hobo jungles, but we weren't in a jungle now. He had done me
the great favor of stopping to give me a ride, and the courtesy of
stating his last name. I responded in kind.

"Russ Hofvendahl. I sure appreciate this, Johnny, I was beginning to think I would be stuck here forever."

"Haven't done much hitchhiking lately, but I know it's tough in
these parts. Where ya from?"

It was a three-hour drive to Manhattan, and Johnny was absolutely
fascinated by my journey to date—and envious. Not because he
hadn't done it all himself, other than the seagoing, but simply
because he loved hoboing and missed it.

He was in his early thirties and had crisscrossed the entire country at least three times. He had worked the wheat harvest on threshing outfits in the Dakotas, but always as a field pitcher, never driving a team. He was from Avenel, New Jersey, a small town on the main highway south from the Holland Tunnel about twenty miles from the city.

He laughed uproariously when I told him about my misadventures with the runaway team.

"Jesus Christ, Russ, a city boy should know better than to tell somebody ya can handle horses!"

"I know that now, believe me, but it worked for a while."

He had toiled in the harvesting of just about every agricultural crop in the country that required transient labor. The apple orchards of Washington were one of his favorites, and he felt the same warmth and affection for the Great Northern railroad that I had developed.

For several years he had been working the late summer, early fall potato harvest in Maine, which I gathered paid very well compared with most work of this type. He was driving home from Maine now to return to his part-time mechanical repair jobs in Avenel, which also paid him fairly well. He owned his own car and *that* really marked him as a man of means in my eyes. But I could tell from the way he reminisced about his days on the road that he had an incurable yen to go wandering.

We had a common frame of reference, and I enjoyed talking with Johnny Polany as much as he seemed to enjoy it.

It would have been simpler for Johnny to cross the Hudson north of Manhattan and go into Jersey on the west side of the river but, when he learned that New York City was my destination and why, he insisted on driving me right into Manhattan.

He had a fund of practical knowledge.

"If ya do get a job in the Big Town ya can't be sleepin' in the park every night. Ever hear of the Mills Hotel?"

I shook my head.

"It's down on Bleecker Street in the Village. Thirty-five cents a night. Known on the road as the "Hobo Hotel." The rooms ain't much but the place is clean; ya won't get lousy there. They got a great big washroom in the basement. Ya can wash your clothes there, hang 'em on the pipes, and they'll damn near be dry by the time you finish showering."

I did some quick mental arithmetic. If I could earn even

twenty-five cents an hour pressing clothes somewhere, I could afford it. Johnny was right of course. If I did get a job I more or less had to have a fixed abode.

"That sounds good, Johnny. This has really been a break for me—the ride into the city and your advice."

"Don't forget what I told ya, Russ. Those rooms ain't much, but ya'll have a place to light."

We had been talking steadily for more than two hours. By unspoken agreement, we fell into a companionable silence. I think Johnny was lost in reveries of his earlier wanderings. As for me, I could feel the excitement building. I would soon be in New York City, where I had been aiming to be for what seemed a lifetime now.

# 25

Johnny's old Model A bounced along over the bridge from the Bronx crossing the Harlem River, and I caught my breath as the magical spires of Manhattan came into sight.

"Ya may like it here, Russ, but it's too big for my taste. Remember what I told ya, I live in Avenel, over in Jersey, just about twenty miles down the line from the Holland Tunnel. If ya change your mind, or if ya have to make a stake, look me up. It's a small town and everybody knows Johnny Polany."

"That's good of you, Johnny, but I told you what I have to do here, about seeing Finn. Then I'm going to try to get a job. I won't forget, believe me, if I change my mind."

Johnny nodded. "One thing ya better do is stash that bedroll of yours somewhere, no matter how you got it lashed up now. It's okay out West, but these harness bulls in the city ain't used to seeing a bindle stiff walkin' along the street. I don't know if they'll jug ya or not, but I wouldn't take a chance on it."

"What do you think I ought to do?"

"How much dough ya got?"

"About seven bucks."

"Well, ya could stop over in the Mills Hotel like I told ya."

"I'll keep it in mind, Johnny, but I'll need my dough to get around and eat on first. What else can I do?"

"We'll be going down Riverside Drive, and I can swing over and drop ya on the west side of Central Park. It's still nice and warm this time of year. I think ya can probably find a good place to sack out in the park and stash your roll while ya do what ya have to do about seein' Finn. For Christ's sake don't make a fire or wander around with that bedroll slung on your back. If ya don't run across any bulls I think you'll be okay. Most of the hoboes that hit this town end up down in the Village or in the Bowery. I don't think the cops will bother ya up in Central Park if ya keep out of sight as much as ya can."

It was September 8, 1938, just after the Labor Day weekend. The oppressive city heat of the long summer had broken early, but the air was warm and balmy.

Like other men I had met on my travels, Johnny went out of his way to be helpful. He was a good-hearted individual who enjoyed helping out someone else. In addition, however, was the brother-hood of the road. Having hoboed from one end of the country to the other himself, he knew what it was like to hit a strange town not knowing anyone. The sheer immensity of New York City magnified the importance of his giving me all the help he could.

He turned off Riverside Drive at West 72nd Street and eventu-ally into Central Park. There was very little traffic, and Johnny surveyed the landscape with a practiced eye.

"Ya see that stand of trees over there? There's some pretty heavy bushes right near it. I don't see any bridle paths or anything near it. Looks like a can over there beyond that road where ya can wash up in the morning. When ya leave the park ya can stash your roll way back in the bushes, and I don't think anyone will bother ya. Just remember what I tell ya, don't start any fires or anything. Just kinda keep out of sight here in the park, y'unnerstan?"

"I understand, Johnny, and I really appreciate it—the lift down from Connecticut—and all the good advice."

Johnny shoved out his hand. "Ya know, Russ, I kinda envy you. This town's not my cup of tea, but ya never seen it before—it's something else!"

I gripped his hand hard, and then I was out of the two-door Model A. I stood and watched, my pack at my feet, as Johnny Polany briskly executed a U-turn, and then, with a last friendly wave, he was gone.

I looked around. There wasn't a soul in sight. So far so good. I walked over to the stand of trees Johnny had pointed out and saw that it was even better than it had looked from the road. There was a slight, grassy declivity on the far side of the trees from the road, which would make a great place to spread my blankets. I knew that he was right; it would only be asking for trouble to start a fire here, but it sure would make a great camp. I felt a sudden surge of sheer loneliness when I thought of Finn Bering and the hobo jungles of western Canada. I missed his company. Tomorrow maybe I would see him. The thought raised my spirits, but now I had to deal with my present circumstances.

Having decided where I would spread my blankets that night, I concentrated hard on fixing this location in my mind. One thing I did not need was to conceal my pack in Central Park and not be able to find it again! Satisfied that the road, the public lavatory, and the juxtaposition of the trees and the bushes were sufficiently impressed on my memory, I shoved my pack well into the bushes and stood back. From even a few feet away it was practically invisible.

I walked the short distance out of the park to the same road we had driven in on, and came out on Central Park West, a continuation of Eighth Avenue bordering Central Park on the west side. Finn had told me about the remarkable subway system that linked four of the five boroughs. You could travel just about anywhere for a nickel, except to Staten Island, and the Staten Island Ferry cost only another five cents to reach the most southerly of the five boroughs.

Now I was bound for Times Square. I had seen the famous building at the center of Times Square many times in movies and newsreels, with the moving messages flashing continuously across the squared end of the triangular building. This was the first place in New York City that I wanted to visit.

It was about seven in the evening, still warm and pleasant, and I felt a thrill of excitement as I emerged from the park.

There were a few pedestrians on the sidewalk—all in a hurry. Finally I caught up to a man standing on the corner of Central Park West and 73rd Street, waiting for a green light.

"Excuse me,—"

"Yeah, what-d'ya want?" His tone was brusque.

"I'm a stranger here, I wonder if you could tell me where to get the subway to Times Square?" I spoke rapidly, trying to get my questions out before he disappeared on me.

With what seemed to me an odd combination of impatience and

helpfulness, he replied, "Okay. C'mon. I'll show ya." He hurried across the street as soon as the light changed. I walked quickly to keep up with him. He didn't say another word, and I wondered if he had understood my question.

At 72nd Street he stopped and jerked a thumb in the direction of Broadway to the west. "Down there at 72nd and Broadway. The sub'll have 'Times Square' on the front."

He was gone before I could thank him. It was my first introduction to the psyche of the New York City resident—unique in the world, I came to believe.

My first overwhelming impression of the New York subway system came as I was standing on that platform as the train rolled in. There was nothing to prevent a person from falling over the edge of the platform and in front of an onrushing train. At that particular time of the evening there weren't too many people either getting off the subway when it arrived or getting on to go downtown. Perhaps it was the subconscious memory of some of the close calls I had had traveling on freight trains that made me think in those terms. Still, I stood well back from the edge of the platform, and wondered what it would be like with a good-sized crowd jostling each other. As often as I later rode the subway, I never got over this phobia of mine, although I never saw, or heard of, anyone even coming close to going over the edge.

It was a fast smooth ride to the Times Square station. When I emerged onto 42nd Street, I couldn't believe the surge of hustling, moving people. Everyone was in a hurry, brushing by me as if I were an inanimate object. I soon forgot them when I saw the moving news spelled out across the front of the building: "Chamberlain Proposes Meeting with Hitler Over Czechoslovakia." I was reasonably well-informed about current affairs, but far from informed enough to read into the news the prelude to disaster that the infamous Munich Agreement later that month would become. "Peace In Our Time" was perhaps the bitterest irony of all that last pre-World War II year, but none of these considerations affected me this balmy evening.

New York was an exciting and fascinating place for me. Having been born and reared in a city like San Francisco, I felt at home and ready to explore all that there was to see and do—limited only by my financial condition. However, with a cost-free, comfortable place to sleep in Central Park, and travel to and from my arboreal bedroom costing me only five cents, I felt downright independent.

I hadn't eaten since morning, and I remembered the automats that Finn had told me about. He hadn't described them in any great detail, and I suppose I had imagined some kind of automated food-conveyor chain. Moving along the crowded sidewalks, elbowing my way through the throng like a native, I found the nearest one on 43rd Street near Fifth Avenue and went in with high expectations. I was somewhat disappointed to learn that the process consisted of placing a nickel in the slot of the door of a compartment and removing the plate of food behind the glass. The food was constantly being replenished by the help in white uniforms working behind the scenes. Still, I had never seen anything quite like this in my life and it *was* a different way to get fed.

I blew thirty cents on two different meat dishes, costing two nickels each, a generous slice of apple pie, and a good-sized carton of milk.

Thoroughly refreshed by my repast, I went out into the warm night to continue exploring the Times Square area. People were everywhere and everyone was in a hurry.

I walked down Fifth Avenue to 42nd Street, and for the first time saw the imposing structure of the New York Public Library. A library, since shortly after I had learned to read, had been a sanctuary. For me it had the same effect, I suppose, that churches have for others. This library, with its broad esplanade of steps leading to the front entrance reminded me very much of the main library at the Civic Center back home in San Francisco. The main library at home had its long marble stairway inside the front doors, with a large leaded-pane window at the top of the stairs at the rear of the entry room, but the cathedral-like effect was much the same. I couldn't resist going in and looking around. The main reading room with its high windows, suffused now with the fading light from the west, thousands and thousands of books lining the walls, and the long rows of tables, all reminded me even more of the main library at home. I felt a sense of peace and relaxation in this quiet room that a library invariably produced in me.

I didn't stay long, but left with a feeling of satisfaction and security at having found this place in the heart of the bustling metropolis. I knew I would feel welcome and at home whenever I chose to come here.

I had always been an avid fight fan, and I had read that Jack Dempsey owned a successful bar and restaurant in this general area of New York City. What I didn't know was that a number of other former ring greats also owned bars in this mid-section of Manhattan. In order to capitalize on their names and keep the business coming in, they spent a good deal of time in their particular establishments. I learned this to my delight when I saw Jim Braddock's bar and ventured in. All of these watering holes, as I eventually learned, followed a certain pattern of decor. They were fairly narrow places in this high-rent area of the city, dark-paneled, furnished with leather-cushioned barstools, and patronized almost exclusively by male customers. The walls were just about covered with fight pictures—action shots mainly—showing the proprietor putting someone away. Jim Braddock, the "Cinderella Man," was a particular favorite of mine. I had been selling papers in San Francisco when he won the decision over Max Baer more than three years earlier on June 13, 1935. I remembered how this tremendous upset victory over Baer had sold a lot of papers for me the next day.

I was about a third of the way down the bar, looking at the photos, when the bartender called from behind the bar.

"What-d'ya need, buddy?"

"Nothing, really. Is it okay if I look at these pictures?"

I think the bartender was about to tell me to get lost when I heard a voice form the back corner. "Make y'self at home, kid. Look all ya want."

It was Jim Braddock himself! He was sitting at a table with some friends. I was just about speechless at this development but managed to stammer out my thanks as he genially waved them off and returned to his conversation.

I was torn between looking at the fight pictures and surreptitiously trying to watch the ex-champ in the flesh. On June 22, 1937 he had taken a fearful beating when Joe Louis knocked him out in eight rounds to become the new heavyweight champion. Jim Braddock certainly looked like an ex-pug, but I was relieved to see that he didn't seem to be particularly marked up as a result of the Louis fight. I remembered that occasion as being one of the few times the radio operator ever put out a news bulletin when I was on the schooner *William H. Smith* the year before. I also remembered it because, as much as I admired Jim Braddock, I was convinced that Joe Louis was going to beat him, and I won five codfish on that fight.

I finally decided that I better leave, in case I had a problem catching the subway back to Central Park, and reluctantly left the bar. I wanted to be down at the Battery early the next morning to take the ferry to Ellis Island. I had no way of knowing if Finn was still there, but I was hoping, and I did want to get there the first chance I could.

I caught the subway back uptown with no problem and got off at the 72nd Street station, where I had caught the downtown train earlier. I found the same street into the park, but at night it was looking a lot different. I started to panic. Then I told myself that even if I couldn't find my bedroll tonight I could certainly find it the next morning. I didn't relish the idea of sleeping out with no cover at all, but it wouldn't kill me in this weather. Steadied by this train of thought, I concentrated on how far into the park I should walk. When I figured out that I was about where I should be, I began to look for the landmarks I remembered. To my great relief I saw the dull gleam of the white-painted public lavatory. I soon located the stand of trees, and found my pack in the bushes.

It probably was due, in part, to the comfort that I felt at locating my gear, but I was well-content with my initial sightseeing venture into the big city. I rolled up, with a blanket around me and another under me, and slipped off to sleep as the distant sounds of the city drifted into the park.

# 26

The unmistakable clip-clop sound of a horse moving at a slow trot awakened me the next morning. For a moment I felt disoriented. A small sparrow was chirping merrily, perched on a branch above my head. These bucolic sounds in the middle of one of the largest cities in the world were a bit too much for me to readily comprehend. The sound of those hooves on the pavement probably meant one of the mounted policemen of New York's finest. Cautiously I peered over the edge of the small hollow in which I had bedded down. I could see the mounted officer approaching. He made a fine figure with his dark-blue, double-breasted uniform jacket buttoned to his neck, looking alertly from one direction to another as he patrolled, mounted on a magnificent black horse—its coat gleaming from a recent grooming. The policeman was looking in the opposite direction as I raised my head and I quickly ducked out of sight. In another moment I could hear the rhythmic jogging sound of the horse's hooves on the road moving past me, and I breathed a sigh of relief. I waited until the sound had completely disappeared into the center of the park before I got up. Then I washed in the public lavatory, rolled my pack, stowed it in the bushes, and left Central Park.

I was heading for the Battery to catch a ferry to Ellis Island and, God willing, talk to Finn Bering once more before he was deported. There simply was no way to guess whether Finn would still be there, but this I had to do.

It was about eight in the morning when I caught the same subway downtown. This time there was a large jostling crowd on the platform and I stood far back from the edge. Almost too far because, when the train rolled in and the doors slid open, there was an immediate surge of people pushing into the cars. I struggled in just as the door slid shut behind me. I managed to get off the train and make the right connection at the Times Square station for the Battery. At about a quarter to nine I emerged into the bright sunshine of Battery Park at the southernmost end of Manhattan Island. The wind blew off the Hudson River, there were countless sea gulls circling in the blue sky, squawking raucously, and I took a deep breath of the fresh maritime air.

The ferry ride to Ellis Island cost five cents and took about ten minutes. I would have enjoyed it more if I hadn't been so concerned about whether my friend was still there.

In 1924 the United States immigration laws were changed to require processing of immigrants at American consulates abroad. Ellis Island ceased to be the first bewildering way station for the hordes of hopeful immigrants arriving in this country. Now its basic function was as the main East Coast deportation center, and it was a certainty that Finn Bering would be processed through here for deportation to Denmark.

As we disembarked at the Island I saw a group of red buildings dominated by a huge structure at the top of a slate staircase. I climbed the stairs to the Great Hall—170 feet long, 102 feet wide, the ceiling towering 58 feet above. I inquired at the first desk I saw near the top of the staircase.

"Excuse me, I'm looking for Finn Bering. I think he's here."

The immigration officer behind the desk looked at me rather pugnaciously.

"Ya *tink* he's here! Ya know how many people we got on dis island? Ya gotta do betta dan dat."

I had long since learned to approach an authoritarian figure with hat in hand, figuratively speaking.

"I'm sorry. All I can tell you is he's a Danish citizen and I think he's going to be deported."

As seemed so characteristic of most New Yorkers I had met, the initial suspiciousness was followed by a reluctant sort of helpfulness—as if the particular individual was somewhat ashamed to show a better side of his nature.

"Dat oughtta make it easier. See dat door on de udda side of de room?"

I nodded.

"Dat's de chief deportation section. Dey'll let ya know, one way or de udda."

I thanked him and made my way to the first desk in the other office. A stocky balding man of about fifty greeted me in the matter with which I was becoming familiar.

"Yeah?"

"I have a friend here by the name of Finn Bering. I believe he's going to be deported to Denmark. The man in the other office said you could help me find him."

"You a relative?"

"No. Just a friend."

"Well, people held for deportation don't usually have visiting privileges."

"Please, sir, he's a very good friend."

He eyed me narrowly for a moment. Then he sighed, turned around in his swivel chair, pulled a rather large volume from a rack behind him and opened it on the top of the desk. I watched breathlessly as he opened the alphabetized book to the B section.

"What's yer friend's name again?"

"Finn Bering."

It seemed an eternity as he painstakingly went down the columns of names. "Yep, here he is—Bering, Finn, Danish national."

My heart leaped. "Where is he?"

The excitement in my voice penetrated his tough New York veneer. He looked up from the book and shook his head. "He's on de Atlantic now, son, headin' for Denmark."

I could have wept, and I am sure the expression on my face showed it. I swallowed the lump in my throat. "How—how long ago did he shove off?"

The immigration officer studied the book again. "Eight days ago. We shipped him on de S. S. *Visingham*. She's a Danish vessel."

I managed to get out a thank you before I turned and left the office.

I walked blindly toward the ferry landing. I knew it was a long shot—the possibility of my getting to New York City and seeing Finn before he was deported. But the realization of just how close I had come, that surge of elation when the immigration officer found his name, followed by the shattering news that he was already gone—it was just too much for me to handle. I tried to be rational about it. Even if I had had a chance to visit Finn at Ellis Island, that's all it would have been—a brief visit. But it did no good. Finn Bering had been such a significant figure in my life, however brief our friendship, that it was monumentally important to me to let him know that I had made it to New York City on my own, and that I had kept the faith by finding him at Ellis Island. Given the state of international affairs in Europe in 1938, the probability of my ever seeing Finn Bering again was minimal. I knew that and it added to my despair.

Eight days—I thought back over my odyssey from the North Dakota prairie to New York City. If I hadn't worked on the threshing crew, if I hadn't worked for Izzy Cohen, would I have made it in time? I might have, and then again I might have literally starved to death, or been jailed on a vagrancy charge for begging food. I had traveled as hard and as steadily as my circumstances permitted. It was small comfort, but I had done the best I could.

When I returned to Battery Park it was the same sunny pleasant day. The light sparkled off the waves where the East River surged to meet the Hudson at the tip of Manhattan, the sea gulls soared gracefully above, and the wind was fresh and invigorating. I sat on a bench, staring out over the water, and I was oblivious to it all. I simply had not realized what a blow this would be.

I forced myself to think of my immediate future. As badly as I felt just then, it was not the fault of this large, impersonal, and fascinating city. It was just that I was in no mood to enjoy anything at that moment.

As devastated as I felt, I decided that I had better familiarize myself with the job market. At least it might take my mind off my present misery.

I took the subway north and, after many questions and two

transfers, finally got off at Sixth Avenue and 30th Street where the employment agencies were clustered.

Sixth Avenue under the elevated railway was a cacophony of sound. Hordes of people—hot dog vendors, sidewalk salesmen peddling merchandise of every description, shouted themselves hoarse to make themselves heard over the crashing rumble of the elevated as it roared by on the tracks above every five minutes or so. The employment agencies, "slave shops" in hobo lingo, had blackboards propped against their street fronts advertising every type of unskilled labor, from dishwashing, rather ceremoniously called "pearl-diving" in hoboese, to pick-and-shovel labor to farm work out on Long Island. The top wage seemed to be a dollar a day, and I had an accurate idea of how many hours of hard labor would be necessary to collect that buck.

I had become a proficient clothes presser working at the Valet Shop at the St. Francis Hotel back home in San Francisco. Many of the men I had worked with were not hoboes, but they tended to be drifters, moving from place to place and job to job. Beating a Hoffman steam press wasn't the greatest work in the world they said, but a good presser could always find a job. I decided that now was the time to find out.

After studying the blackboards of the first six agencies and not seeing anything about pressing, I finally went into the next one and spoke to the owner.

"You got anything for a Hoffman presser?"

He was a Jewish gentleman, of whom there were many in New York City, and he spoke with the Yiddish inflection in his speech so characteristic of the European Jews who formed a significant portion of the city population in those years.

"So—" he peered at me closely. "You an honest-to-God presser yet?"

"That's right. You got any openings?"

"Do I haff openings! Pay's good too, forty cents an hour."

This was a relief. The way things were going, I wondered if I'd ever make a decent wage again.

"What kind of pressing?"

"Dry-cleaning plants, mainly. Ve charge you ten percent first veek. You gotta advance three bucks for the job. Vun veek guaranteed. You ready to go to vork?"

I hadn't realized that the agencies required some advance payment for the higher-paying jobs. I did some rapid figuring. A night at the Mills Hotel, subway fare, at least something for food would cost me about a dollar a day. I would have less than three dollars left after paying the three dollars.

It was then Thursday, early afternoon. If I went to work the next day and worked through Saturday, I would earn six dollars and forty cents. I could then make it through the next week, but I'd better get paid on Saturday.

"When's payday?"

"De end of de veek. Pays ya in cash if ya vant it."

"Well, by the time I pay you, I've got to be sure I can get paid Saturday, because I'll be cleaned out good by then."

"You'll get paid. I guarantee it!"

I didn't quite have the guts to ask him how I could be certain he had the job for me. And three dollars was quite a bit more than ten percent of an eight-hour, six-day job at forty cents an hour.

It was as if he read my mind.

"Look, schlemiel, ve licensed by the city. Dat job not dere, you could turn me in, unnerstan?"

I nodded, still working with the arithmetic.

"Three bucks is more dan ten percent de first veek, but ve permitted to charge dat for guaranteein' vun full veek. You any good, you probably vork longer."

With all of his tough Yiddish manner I intuitively felt that I could trust him.

"Okay, you got a deal. Here's my three bucks."

Carefully he wrote out a receipt and a placement slip.

"Remember, kid, you told me you were a Hoffman presser. If you can't cut it in dis plant, dat's yer problem."

"I understand. Where's the plant?"

"Up in Harlem. 135th and Lenox. I'll call 'em now and tell 'em you'll be in tomorrow 8 A.M."

I waited while he placed the call, satisfied now that this slave shop was legitimate, and left with the placement slip and the receipt tucked in my pocket.

The excitement I felt at the prospect of finally working at a trade I knew, and at a decent wage, had momentarily diverted me from the overwhelming loss I felt at having missed Finn.

As I left the employment agency, I thought of the Public Library at 42nd and Fifth Avenue. It didn't seem at the time that there was anything that could cheer me up, but maybe just browsing in the reading room would make me feel better.

I bought a foot-long hot dog for five cents and a large bottle of orange soda for another nickel. I climbed the steps to the Sixth Avenue elevated station platform, found an unoccupied bench, and ate my lunch.

It wouldn't have been a long walk to the library but, as I watched the elevated trains come rushing noisily into the platform where I sat, and then go rolling out, it occurred to me that a ride on the El would provide a different view of the city.

It did indeed provide a changed perspective. In that part of Manhattan the elevated seemed to run past the back sides of tenements mainly, clothing drying on lines strung from one back door to another, but it was definitely more interesting than rolling through the black tunnels of the subway system.

I got off the elevated at the 42nd Street station and walked to the library. I spent a couple of hours in the reading room, mainly skimming through old favorites—Jack London's *Call of the Wild* and *The Sea Wolf*, Percival Wren's *Beau Geste*, and others.

It was like visiting with old friends—and being comforted by them. The ache was still there but I did feel better.

Finally I thought of what I had yet to do today and reluctantly left the library.

I took the subway up to Central Park, retrieved my pack, and then took the subway back downtown to Greenwich Village. It was almost dusk when I emerged from the Bleecker Street station and almost immediately I could see the blue neon sign of the Mills Hotel a block away.

There was an entirely different feel to this part of Manhattan. It was a warm evening, and men in their undershirts were sitting on the stoops of the brick tenements. They were talking with one another amiably, and I saw some young boys playing street hockey with a battered tin can and broom sticks. There seemed to be Italian restaurants at least two to the block, and the delicious smell of pasta, tomato sauce, and veal came wafting out of them.

I didn't know enough about the city then to realize it was a long way to Harlem from the Village, but I felt more at home here than I had in any other part of this overwhelming metropolis. The pace didn't seem as intense, or frantic, as it was uptown, and I was glad that the Mills Hotel was located here in the Village.

Johnny Polany had described it accurately. The showers and washroom were everything he said they would be, and my room sure as hell wasn't much. A monk's cell would have been luxurious compared with my narrow cubicle, just barely wide enough for the cot with the straw tick on it, and a small window facing on a large inner courtyard. Still, I reminded myself, for thirty-five cents a night I could hardly expect accommodations like the St. Francis Hotel at home.

It was great to be totally clean again and with all of my clothes washed and dried.

After stowing my gear in my room I left to find a place to eat.

I found a small Italian restaurant around the corner from the Mills Hotel and, for twenty-five cents, had a ravioli dinner that was as good as anything I had eaten in North Beach in San Francisco.

As I was wiping up the last bit of delicious sauce from my plate with a crusty piece of Italian bread, I felt my head nodding. The events of the day had worn me out.

I walked back to the Mills Hotel and, after leaving word at the desk to be sure to wake me at six the next morning, I turned in and was asleep as soon as my head hit that straw-filled tick of a pillow.

# 27

The crash on the thin wooden door of my cell-like room all but jolted me off the cot.

"Rise and shine, 6 A.M.!" I could hear the raucous shout just outside my room.

There were no room telephones at the Mills Hotel, but the management recognized its obligation to its working guests to roust them out in the morning if a call had been requested.

A burly night clerk marched down the corridors with a list of room numbers in one hand and a battered police baton in the other. He took a sadistic delight in pounding a door as hard as he could to generate maximum sound. 6 A.M was the earliest wake-up call, then again half an hour later, and finally 7 A.M. That was the last wake-up service the hotel provided. Since the pounding on the doors oc-curred on every floor at random locations, the noise never seemed to stop.

I swung my legs over to the edge of the cot and sat there

sleepily. I could hear the curses and threats of men who still wanted to sleep roll down the hall. I decided that my request for a wake-up call had been a bit superfluous. I didn't need the shock waves of sound that pounding baton produced. Under the circumstances it was just about impossible to sleep anywhere in the Mills Hotel after 6 A.M anyway, and that was the last morning I ever requested a wake-up call.

The morning air in Greenwich Village wasn't quite like a day in the country but, compared with the heavy disinfectant-laden atmosphere of the Mills Hotel, it smelled good to me, and I took deep breaths as I walked to the platform for the Sixth Avenue El that would take me up to Harlem.

The Elite Cleaners was located on 135th Street, about half a block east of Lenox. It was owned and operated by Jewish businessmen. Most of the skilled help, spotters and pressers, were white.

I walked in, sniffing the familiar, but difficult to describe, smell created by the steam from a battery of Hoffman presses.

The shop foreman watched me press a double breasted man's suit and hang it carefully on the hanger on the rack just behind me.

"Ya know what yer doin' kid. Just don't dog it. We pay good here, but we expect ya to turn out the work."

My machine was just to the left of a press operated by a slender, good-looking black man. I had arrived well before eight to demonstrate my proficiency for the shop foreman. My neighbor arrived about five minutes to eight.

"Y'all de new pressuh?" He spoke with a soft Southern drawl.

"Sure am, my name's Russ Hofvendahl." I extended my hand.

He seemed to hesitate for a minute, then shoved out his hand and grasped mine firmly, giving me a warm smile at the same time. "Gawge Adams, Russ. Nice to meet ya."

It was hard, demanding work and, like all dry-cleaning plants, hot and noisy. The owners were downright enlightened—they voluntarily gave all of the pressers a ten-minute break in the morning and another in mid-afternoon.

During the morning break George Adams pulled a couple of heavy wooden boxes out from behind his machine.

"Bettah set awhile and rest yo feet, Russ."

Gratefully I sat down. It had been a long time since I had beat a Hoffman press hour after hour. It was tiring, and hard on the feet. George Adams looked at me.

"Y'all don' sound lak a New Yawka to me. Where ya from?"

"San Francisco."

His eyes lit up and a broad smile lightened his face. "What a libuty town! Ah was dere once when ah was in de Navy."

There was a small but clearly defined black neighborhood in San Francisco—the Fillmore District—but I had never spent any time there.

As we sat resting, and talking quietly, it dawned on me that this was the first black man I had ever socialized with.

He was a hard worker but was essentially ignored by the other whites working in the plant. He had not expected me, a white man, to shake hands with him. But this small, reasonable gesture established our friendship.

By the following Tuesday afternoon I had learned a good deal about George Adams, and he had learned much about me.

He was then thirty-eight years of age, the youngest of ten siblings reared on a Georgia plantation. During our afternoon break on Friday, he told me that his father had been born into slavery. We talked mostly during the morning and afternoon rest periods. He looked at me intently and nodded, almost imperceptibly, when he saw the effect this information had on me.

"Dat's right, Russ. Sho ain't dat fah behin' us, is it?"

I didn't know what to say or do. We went back to work, and the noise of the hissing steam, the pounding of the heads on the pads, made conversation impossible. All that afternoon I kept thinking about George's family and slavery. Mark Twain had illuminated the dreadful institution for me with his immortal characterization of Huck Finn's faithful friend Jim, a slave. Still, I had to admit to myself, somewhat guiltily, that Huck Finn's trip down the Mississippi on the raft had so captivated me that I hadn't thought about the anguish of Jim's plight as much as I should have.

By the time five o'clock finally rolled around, I had made up my mind. George would not have mentioned the subject if he wasn't willing to talk about it. I hung up my last pressed suit for the day, turned off the steam valves to my machine, opened the drain, and looked at George. He was busy securing his machine for the night and didn't notice me at first. Then he saw me staring at him and broke into a wide grin.

"What's eatin' ya, Russ?"

"I can't get that out of my mind, what you told me about your dad being born a slave." The words started to rush out. "How did he feel about that? Did he talk about it much?" We had walked out of the plant together and were standing in front of 135th Street.

George put up a protesting hand. "My daddy jes a little kid when Fathuh Abe done freed 'em. He don' member much, but *his* daddy sho talked to him about it, and he passed de stories on to us young'uns." George stopped talking and looked at me appraisingly for a moment.

"Ya'll got any plans for tonight?"

I thought of my cell at the Mills Hotel. I stayed out of it as long as I could every night. Sometimes in a branch library I had located near the Village, sometimes just strolling slowly along the sidewalks enjoying the sights and sounds of the humanity teeming all about me.

"I sure don't, George. Why?"

"Y'all like Southern cookin'?"

"Don't believe I've ever had any. Why?"

"Mama's Cafe jes two blocks from here on 133rd. Bes' fried chicken y'all evah gonna have. Gravy, biscuits, black-eyed peas, chitlins, umm umph!"

He lost me with the black-eyed peas and chitlins but I was interested.

"Sure sounds good, George, but I've only got a buck and a half. Got to get down to the Village and back here tomorrow plus some eating. What does it cost?"

"All ya can eat fo a quawtuh. Come on."

A few minutes later we were seated in the rear of Mama's Cafe at an oilcloth-covered table. It was a bit early for the dinner trade, and we had that part of the place to ourselves. The table, the utensils, everything was spotless, and the aroma wafting out of the kitchen had me salivating.

It was a fixed menu, no choices, but I had never tasted fried chicken like that. This was indeed Southern cooking at its best.

Once we were seated George started talking and only stopped while he was devouring more of that delicious food.

He spoke eloquently about his daddy's place, the red earth of Georgia, and the huge shade trees.

"How come you're working in New York if you like that country so much?"

"Russ, dat country is purty, but..." His expression became somber. "It's bad fo us cullid sometimes. Dat's why I jined de Navy to get away durin' de war. Didn't get treated too good den eithah, but bettah den havin' some of dose Gawgia crackahs runnin' 'round evah once in de while with a lynchin' rope." He shook his head. "Nope, far as I'se concerned, Halam is de gawden spot of de world! Ain't nevah goin' back South."

It was an awakening experience for me. I was the only white in Mama's Cafe and I did draw some curious stares. But I was so fascinated by what I was learning about a large part of this country of mine that I didn't mind. It seemed as if George Adams had a lot he wanted to say and, for whatever reason, he wanted to say it to a white. He was no Uncle Tom but he was far too conditioned by a Southern childhood, and a steward's job in the U.S. Navy, to be asserting himself unwisely either. For him, with its overwhelmingly black population, Harlem was indeed a safe and comfortable refuge. He planned to spend the rest of his life here for just that reason.

I could feel my temper rise when he told me about the mores of the South, what it meant for a black to "keep yo place" in Georgia; stepping off the wooden sidewalk, in the small town near his daddy's acreage, just to let the white folks pass.

"Jesus, George, did you *have* to do that?"

"Y'all bettah, ain't wuth gettin' lynched fer."

I had never felt so indignant in my life—or so helpless and frustrated. George Adams wasn't about to start any revolutions, but it seemed important to him to let his white friend know what he had been through in his life—just because his skin was darker than mine.

It was a sobering and enlightening experience for me, listening to George Adams. In addition to what I was learning, I liked him as a person. He was hardworking, courteous, and always cheerful.

We finally said good-night and I caught the El down to the Village.

I was looking forward to more talks with George and more dinners at Mama's Cafe, but it was not to be.

The next afternoon the plant foreman told me one of the owners wanted to talk to me. My heart sank. I really believed I was doing the job but this must mean, for whatever reason, I was being fired.

Meyer Levin was a short, heavy-set man in his early fifties. He was chewing on an unlit cigar as I walked into his office.

"Yes, sir?"

"Da foreman tells me ya got a nice touch vith de gahments."

I stared at him in surprise. "Well, thanks..." My voice trailed off.

"My brothuh Moe has a sport gahment operation downtown. He's been askin' me to keep an eye out for a pressuh who'll do a good job on new merchandise. Ya innerested?"

"Sure, I guess so."

"Don' vorry. He'll pay ya da same. Forty cents an hour. Prob'ly a bit easiuh vork den dis plant. He's got deliveries for ya to make. Vhat ya think?"

The idea of working farther downtown, maybe getting to see something of the city, and getting paid for it, appealed to me. Escaping from the hour-after-hour drudgery of this dry-cleaning plant was no small part of it. It didn't take me long to make up my mind.

"When does he want me?"

"Monday mornin'. I got de address here. It's a loft, 314 Fifth Avenue. Okay? Ve'll pay you off tonight. Ya repawt to Moe, Monday 8 A.M."

"Thanks a lot, Mr. Levin, that sounds good."

He waved off my thanks. "Don' mention it. Vouldn't send ya ta Moe unless I figgered ya could cut it."

When I returned to my press George looked concerned.

I raised my voice above the noise of the plant and smiled. "It's okay, George, I didn't get canned."

During our afternoon break I told him about this surprising development.

George was, as always, the gentleman.

"Dat sounds good, Russ, but I'm gonna miss y'all. Was sorta hopin' we could hit Mama's agin sometime."

"I'll miss you too, George. I'll try to get up to see you. Whether I do or I don't I won't forget what you've told me."

That seemed to please him. That night I shut down my press for the last time at the Elite Cleaners and said good-bye to George Adams.

# 28

On Monday morning I walked through the wooden door that opened onto Fifth Avenue, up a long narrow flight of stairs, and into a large high-ceilinged loft. There were rows of sewing machines but, at 7:45 A.M., no one was working yet.

There was an office in the far corner with "DeLuxe Sportswear" neatly lettered on the clear glass door.

I knocked once and Moe Levin looked up from his desk, "Come in, come in!"

He was a younger version of his brother, Meyer.

"Ya de new pressuh Meyuh sent me?"

"That's right."

"Okay, let's see vhat ya can do."

He got up from his desk and led me to another narrow stairway at the far side of the loft. There was a freight-elevator shaft barred by a waist-high wooden-slatted gate next to the stairway.

We walked up the stairs, Moe Levin talking quickly. "I vant somevun who von't ruin my gahments. Dere soft material, don't need much pressin', but I keep gettin' dese schlemiels, hit dem vit dat head, damn near ruin 'em."

I saw a Hoffman press at the far side of this rather low-ceilinged room. Next to it was a canvas-sided four-wheel cart much like the ones used in a dry-cleaning plant. It was filled to the top with tan sports jackets.

Without waiting for instructions, I went over to the press and stepped on the bottom steam pedal. The machine had already been turned on and the steam hissed up through the buck. There was a clothing rack on wheels with hangers on it on the other side of the machine. I pulled one of the jackets out of the cart and looked at it. The material was nice, soft, almost like cashmere. The jacket was not badly wrinkled, but it obviously needed pressing to be ready to sell.

I had become used to working with expensive clothing at the Valet Shop at the St. Francis, and we were taught to use a lot of bottom steam whenever possible. We also tried to avoid causing a shine on the particular garment by not coming down too hard on it with the head. Instinctively I knew that these jackets were near and dear to Moe Levin's heart, and he wanted them treated tenderly.

I pulled the back of the jacket over the buck, hit the bottom steam, and lightly stretched it. As I had thought, the wrinkles steamed out of the soft material very readily. Quickly, I basically steamed out the whole garment, using the head very lightly, with a good deal of top steam on the two front sections. As soon as I had finished I hung it very carefully on a hanger on the rack.

Moe Levin had been watching me intently the entire time. "Dat's good. Vhat did ya say yer name was—Russ? Okay, Russ, ya on. I like da vay ya vork. Vhen ya get dat load pressed come down to my office, I got an errand fah ya."

Just before 8:00 A.M. Sheila Lessin and Abe Biederman came in. As I was to learn, the three of us were the sole occupants of the upper story of DeLuxe Sportswear.

Sheila was bright-eyed, quick-moving, and dressed in a blouse and skirt, which fit very snugly across her well-shaped posterior. Her blouse was buttoned at the neck but it stretched taut across her bosom, defining two very well-shaped, voluptuous breasts.

She stopped at my machine. "Hi, you the new pressuh? I'm Sheila Lessin."

I stopped working for a minute, stepped away from the machine, and extended my hand.

"Nice to meet you, Sheila. My name's Russ Hofvendahl."

She had a mischievous smile and dimples.

"Hofvendahl! What's a goy like you doin' workin' for Moe?"

"Goy?" It was the first time I had heard the term.

"Yeah. You know, non-Yid. You're the first one I've seen in this place and I been here three years." She obviously was not an immigrant. She didn't have the accent of many of the older Jewish people in New York City, but she had a staccato manner of speech and ended many of her statements on a rising inflection.

The middle-aged man who had walked in with her gave me one rather dour look and walked by without saying a word.

I looked questioningly at him across the large low-ceilinged room, and then at Sheila.

"That's Abe Biederman. He's a real bundle of laughs. Don't let it get ya down. He don't like no one."

Sheila did the packing of the finished sports jackets in the cardboard boxes on our floor. Abe worked on both floors, delivering the bolts of cloth to the cutters and sewers in the loft below, bringing the carts of jackets up on the freight elevator, loading the boxes with the finished jackets in the same carts and taking them down for shipment or, as I was to learn, for me to deliver to various retail outlets throughout Manhattan, Brooklyn, the Bronx, and Queens.

It took me about an hour and a half to get the cartload of jackets pressed. When I had hung the last of them on the rack I said to Sheila, "The boss told me to go to his office when I had this load done."

"Do what he told ya, Russ. He's the boss. I'm just workin' here like you."

"I know, I just thought, . . ." my voice trailed off. Sheila kept up a rather constant chatter as she worked very efficiently and quickly at the packing table, assembling the flattened cardboard boxes into three-dimensional containers, placing the white tissue paper in them before carefully folding the jackets and putting them into the boxes. Every once in a while she would direct Abe to bring her more boxes, or tissue paper, and I had simply assumed she was in charge up here.

It was a different experience for me to be working on a job like this basically on an unsupervised basis. I realized that it was a pleasant change.

Moe Levin had two sets of five boxes each, tied together with stout cord, standing in the corner of his office.

"Ya know dis town, Russ?"

My heart sank. Part of my duties was to act as a deliveryman, and I was really enjoying the work here, but I was immediately fearful that my lack of familiarity with Greater New York City could cost me this job. I started to say yes, and then I remembered the horses in North Dakota and my assurance to Oscar Peterson that I could handle them. There was no one to teach me here, and I had hoped that this would be a regular job. I decided I had better be truthful with the boss.

"Not really, Mr. Levin, I know how to get around Manhattan fairly well, but I honestly can't say I know the city."

"Dat's good, Russ. Rathuh have ya level vith me. Ya seem purty smaht. Most of de drops are here in Manhattan. Ya goin' somevhere else ya ask directions. It'll be okay. Here's de list."

Thus began what turned out to be a most interesting and satisfying job. Moe Levin was a hustler, and he was trying to break into a highly competitive market with his new sports jackets in the Greater New York City area. He spent a lot of time on the telephone, I later learned, placing his sports jackets on consignment in some of the better, more expensive retail outlets. When he got the consent of a merchant to give his merchandise a try, he didn't waste any time, and I made the same-day deliveries.

As it turned out, in the seven weeks I worked for Moe Levin, there were not more than eight days total that I was pressing all day. My usual pattern was to press for a couple of hours at the beginning of the day, make deliveries for two to four hours in the middle, and finish the day at the machine.

My boss was conscientious in reimbursing me for every nickel I spent on the New York subway system. I was so enraptured with this fascinating city, and the opportunity to get paid for seeing it, that I hardly ever took as much as thirty minutes for a lunch break. Moe Levin *did* know this city, and I believe he appreciated my efficient deliveries. I would buy a foot-long hot dog and a soft drink wherever I happened to be at lunchtime, devour the food and drink, and keep on my rounds. I discovered knishes in one of the Jewish neighborhoods in Brooklyn, absolutely loved them, and went out of my way to lunch on the piping-hot chopped-liver stuffed pies whenever I could. Sometimes they were stuffed with only a cheese-flavored, mashed-potato filling. They were all delicious.

One noon in Brooklyn I was biting into a particularly delicious knish and the smell and the taste transported me back to Rebecca Cohen's kitchen in Connecticut. A moment later I felt guilty when I thought about what a wonderful cook my Aunt Doris was. I knew that I should be remembering her delicious meals and not these foreign delicacies. But my beloved aunt was open-minded and receptive to new ideas. She would be so relieved to have me safely home again that she would probably bake grasshoppers for me if that's what I wanted. It would be fun to tell her about some of this Yiddish food. I was sure she would be willing to give it a try and, with her cooking expertise, I was confident she would bring it off.

The weather was consistently pleasant that fall, and I was enjoying every day of it.

I saw the sphere and the pylon of the projected 1939 World's Fair in Queens, and the Yankee Stadium in the Bronx when the subway emerged from the underground tunnel and onto the elevated tracks. I was traveling about the city so consistently on a day-in, day-out basis that in a week I knew how to get around. This was not O. Henry's city of *The Four Million*. He had written about this metropolis at the turn of the century. Yet somehow the flavor of the distinctive neighborhoods was still there. From the Lower East Side to Columbia University off Riverside Drive to the north, from Greenwich Village to Harlem—it was all fascinating.

As I made my deliveries I also picked up on the transfer points for other places I wanted to see—Coney Island, the Staten Island terminal where the ferry took you for a nickel to a borough that was part of the city but had working farms only a short streetcar ride from where the ferry docked. It was for me a never-ending kaleido-scope of sights and sounds.

Battery Park at the southernmost tip of Manhattan Island was my favorite place. There were only a couple of retail stores in the Wall Street area where I made deliveries but, when I figured I was ahead of schedule and everything worked right on the subway connections, I would go down to Battery Park, eat my mid-day repast sitting on one of the massive bollards, and breathe deeply of the sea air. The white gulls circling over the water, the ship traffic moving through the distant narrows made me ache to go to sea again. But it had not taken me long to realize that shipping was very tight on the East Coast. There was no way I could find a berth. I had resigned myself to this, but it didn't keep me from dreaming about it in Battery Park.

Every night after work I walked somewhere in Manhattan, eating at small Italian or Polish restaurants, sometimes at Jewish delis, sometimes at the Automat. Occasionally I would go to the movies. My main objective was to avoid my cell at the Mills Hotel for as long as possible. It continued to be a convenient, practical place to live, and I had learned that I was not going to beat the price of thirty-five cents a night anywhere in Manhattan. However, that narrow cubicle, with the dim light that wasn't even bright enough for comfortable reading, wasn't a place to do anything but sleep.

My daily expenses, including the room, round-trip fare on the elevated to my job, and three meals a day, were running about a dollar and a half. A minuscule deduction for Social Security, which had become law in 1936, came out of my weekly check, but that was all. I was saving about a dollar and a half a day out of my daily wage of three dollars and twenty cents. Having given up on the possibility of shipping out on the East Coast, I had definitely decided to return home. I planned to start during the second week in November to allow plenty of time to hobo south to New Orleans and then west through Texas, New Mexico, Arizona, and finally to California. Even saving about nine dollars a week would not permit me to ride the cushions home, but it sure would eliminate the possibility that I would ever have to beg for my food again.

It had not been all that long since I had dropped off the freight in Buffalo, but the bad memories were already fading. Even if I had the money I doubt that I would have paid for a ride home. Sometimes at night I would drift off to sleep remembering the lonesome whistle of a freight train chugging across the western prairie. I would think about the camaraderie of the hobos sitting around a jungle campfire swapping stories. The Big Rock Candy Mountains were beckoning. As much as I was enjoying myself in Manhattan, my feet were starting to itch again.

Sheila Lessin and Abe Biederman, in entirely different ways, began to assume more importance in my life than merely as coworkers.

Dale Carnegie would have been surprised, if not astounded, to learn what a direct impact his book *How to Win Friends and Influence People* had on my sex life, but it was indeed the case.

The Thursday evening of my first week at DeLuxe Sportswear I took a stroll past the Waldorf-Astoria Hotel. I had already dined at the Automat, it was about eight o'clock, and I had absolutely nothing else to do.

I stopped to glance at the outside announcement board and saw that Dale Carnegie was speaking in the Oak Room at the hotel. He had written a phenomenal best-seller a year or two earlier, and on the spur of the moment I decided that it would be very interesting to learn just how one did win friends and influence people.

I was dressed neatly, and the uniformed doorman merely glanced at me as I walked through the entrance to this magnificent old hotel.

Mr. Carnegie's talk was under way in a large conference room on the mezzanine floor when I arrived. I saw the sign on the table outside the entrance—"By Invitation Only," but no one was sitting there at the time so I eased quietly into the room and unobtrusively took one of the few remaining seats at the rear.

Dale Carnegie was a plain, rather meek-looking man, with wire-rimmed spectacles but, imbued with the message he was bringing to the world, he was a dynamic speaker.

I had missed the early part of his lecture which, on this particular evening, was devoted to two rules stated in his book. The first was: If you want to have people like you, smile. One part of this presentation went, "Nobody needs a smile so much as those who have none left to give." As I sat there I thought of Abe Biederman. I didn't know why Abe was so unpleasant and morose, but he certainly acted as if he had no smiles left to give. The second rule was: A man's name is to him the sweetest and most important sound in any language. Once again, as I sat there listening attentively, I thought of Abe. In all of the hours we had worked together he had never addressed one word to me and, after one abortive attempt to talk to him, I had given up and simply ignored him. Everything Mr. Carnegie was saying made sense, but what excited me was the thought that I had the perfect subject to test these rules on. I could hardly wait.

The next morning Sheila and I arrived first, and a few minutes later Abe Biederman walked in.

I was standing at Sheila's packing table, talking to her, when I heard his footsteps at the top of the stairway. I turned away from Sheila, put on my friendliest smile, and called across the room, "Morning, Abe, how are you?"

He gave me one dark look, said not a word, and walked across the room to start work. As for Sheila, she looked at me as if I had suddenly lost my mind.

"So, what's that all about, Russ? Abe is suddenly a good friend of yours?"

My overture had been so totally rebuffed that I felt a bit foolish, and I was not about to tell Sheila that I was conducting a Great Experiment. Still, I felt as if I had to say something.

"It's nothing, Sheila. Just seems to me like Abe's a pretty lonely guy. Won't hurt anything to be friendly to him."

She sniffed. "The way he acts he deserves to be lonely!"

That morning when I left the third floor to make my deliveries I went out of my way to wave to Abe Biederman, give him a friendly smile, and say, "See you when I get back, Abe."

This time Sheila looked at me with an ironically amused look on her face and shook her head.

For the two remaining workdays of that week, and for the first four days of the next week, I repeated my greetings, my farewells, the smiles, and always the use of his name. I was getting absolutely no response, not even a grunt, but Sheila was a very bright girl and I sure was getting her attention. What I was doing looked like an exercise in absolute futility, but she deduced that I was trying to prove something. She just wasn't sure what.

On the following Wednesday, as I was shutting down my machine for the night, Abe actually stopped and looked me full in the face when I called out a cheery good night to him, again as always, using his name. This time I saw a puzzled look in his eyes, which at least was better than the cold disregard he had so far shown me. He still didn't say a word as he left, but Sheila, who didn't miss a thing, saw that look too.

We usually got to work before Abe Biederman, and he invariably left before we did. Part of Sheila's duties were to lock up the entire premises, since she usually worked a half-hour later, packing garments for the next day's shipment.

In the far corner of our third floor, there were bolts of cloth stacked about three feet high and covered with a light cloth. This was the inventory that was carted down to the seamstresses on the floor below, and constantly replenished by incoming shipments from New England clothing mills.

Sheila crooked a finger at me.

"Russ, let's rest our feet awhile, I gotta talk to you!" She walked across the room to the stacks of cloth. I didn't get to see her walk very often, but when I did I appreciated the seductive motion of her hips in the tight-fitting skirt. I hesitated a moment then joined her where she was sitting on the bolts.

"So what's this with Abe?"

"Nothing."

"Come on. I never seen a more unfriendly guy, and for the last week you been treatin' him like a long-lost uncle. What gives?"

"Well, there's just the three of us working up here, Sheila. I just thought it would be nicer for all of us if Abe was friendlier."

"I'll give you that all right, but there's something else goin' on. What is it?"

I didn't know if I should tell her. On the one hand, as I thought about it, it did seem a bit cold-blooded to use Abe Biederman as a human guinea pig. On the other hand, if I could get him to loosen up it would make it pleasanter for all of us, and maybe it would make him feel better also. I made up my mind.

"You ever hear of Dale Carnegie?"

"Yeah, I think so. He write a book or something?"

"*How to Win Friends and Influence People*. Ever hear of it?"

"Yeah, but I never read it."

"Well neither have I, but I heard him lecture one night last week."

Then I told her about the two rules and my perception that Abe Biederman had to be the acid test.

She looked at me with more interest than I had previously noticed. "You're a funny sort of guy, Russ. I'm glad you told me about that. I was beginning to think you had a screw loose. Maybe you're right. It would be nicer around here if Abe would lighten up." Then she shook her head. "Still, I don't think you're going to make it with him. I don't know much about him, but the boss told me a couple of years ago that he's widowed. No family at all that anyone knows about."

"Well, maybe if I can make him feel a little bit better, it'll be worth it, won't it?"

We were sitting side by side at the edge of the stack of bolts, our feet dangling. She reached over and kissed me lightly, then dropped down to the floor.

I was so surprised that I just sat there for a moment.

She turned back and looked at me. "Don't get any ideas, buddy. That's just because I think you're a nice guy."

"I won't get any ideas, Sheila."

The next morning it happened. When Abe Biederman walked in I greeted him with my usual smile and the use of his name.

To my astonishment he replied, "Goot mornin', Russ, how're tings vith ya?" It wasn't the brightest smile I had ever seen but it was undeniably a smile. On him it was like the dawn breaking.

Then he turned to Sheila.

"So, how ya dis mornin', Sheila?"

She was so surprised she almost stammered. "Fine, fine, Abe."

Dale Carnegie was vindicated. It was a more pleasant environment on the third floor of DeLuxe Sportswear, and I caught Sheila Lessin looking at me from time to time with a certain look in her eyes.

It was fascinating to realize that it was no longer an effort to greet Abe cheerfully, and even more interesting to see how he occasionally talked to Sheila. He did not smile often, but when he did it was heartwarming.

The following Wednesday evening, Sheila and I were alone on the third floor. Abe had already left. It was later than usual and the place was deserted. I had just turned off the steam on my Hoffman press, and as I stepped away from the machine I almost bumped into Sheila.

She stood there looking at me, her breasts invitingly thrust forward. While I was far from being a man of the world, I wasn't quite that dense either. I had fantasized about taking Sheila on that stack of cloth bolts enough times. Her lips were parted slightly, her eyes were sparkling, and I bent down to kiss her. She responded with a passion that took me completely by surprise.

"You got any rubbers?"

It was quite obvious that if anyone was being seduced it was not Sheila Lessin.

With my current financial liquidity I had purchased a packet of

Trojans with no real hope that I would ever get to use them. But I carried them with me just in case, in the small tin container—not in my wallet.

She took me by the hand and led me over to the stack of material. It was a firm surface but not unyielding, and we stretched out on the top, groping wildly at each other.

I was trying to get her panties off when she pulled away and, in one swift movement, had stripped them off herself. I looked at her lying there, her skirt pulled up, and her legs spread. I thought I saw a flicker of amusement in her eyes as I turned away to sheath myself.

Then I penetrated her and she went absolutely wild. She arched her back and moved at me as I thrust harder and faster. We came simultaneously and explosively. It could not have been five minutes since she had stood by my machine.

As I lay there on top of her, breathing hard, she looked up at me. She was breathing hard too, but now she was in control.

"That was good, Russ. I want to do it again but I'll let you know, okay?"

"Whatever you say, Sheila."

"I just don't want you grabbin' a feel or actin' like you own me. We both gotta work here, and I don't want anyone to tumble to this. Y'unnerstan?"

At that moment I would have promised her anything.

It seemed to be my good fortune to encounter women with sexual needs that were as urgent as my own, as improbable as that seemed to me at the time.

In the weeks that followed we made love at least two times a week on the bolts of cloth. Sometimes more when Sheila was in the mood.

I learned that she lived with a fairly large family in a walk-up on the Lower East Side. She had learned about sex at an early age and realized how much she needed and enjoyed it. Her living quarters were so restricted, and her life in Manhattan in 1938 was so circumscribed by her environment, that she simply did not have any good opportunity to satisfy her needs—except on the third floor of DeLuxe Sportswear.

We talked a lot after we made love, and we learned a great deal about each other. I suspected, but never asked, that I was not the first one to enjoy the pleasures of her vibrant, passionate body there on the bolts of cloth.

She learned about my planned departure for home, and I told

myself she was going to miss me as I would truly miss her. But always, after making love, it was a much quicker journey for her back to reality than it was for me.

Occasionally she would tease me about how quick and compelling our lovemaking was.

"Geez, ya a regla rabbit tonight, Russ, ya know it?"

"I'm sorry Sheila, you okay?"

Then she would hug me and smile up at me. "If I wasn't okay, believe me, buddy, I'd let ya know!"

# 29

The weather continued to be mild and comfortable until the third week in September when the terrible hurricane of 1938 struck. It decimated much of New England, but by some providential fate effectively bypassed Manhattan. It was enough, however, to start me planning seriously for my trip home. I really had to get south before the cold weather started, and I began to provision myself.

I bought a cylindrical canvas valise large enough to contain my two blankets, a change of clothes, and personal effects. It avoided the bindle-stiff look generated by my bedroll, but it was of a size that I could conveniently sling it with carrying lines, leaving my hands free to catch the ladder of a moving freight car. Everything else I would ship home to San Francisco. I remembered the diary I had kept on the schooner. It occurred to me that this might be an interesting journey south and then west to California. I had written letters and post cards home to Aunt Doris with some frequency, and I was relatively sure she would have saved them, although I had not asked her to do so. Still, a day-to-day account of this trip would be a convenient way to inform her and the rest of the family about my experiences on the road. A serviceable blue-covered notebook cost me ten cents, and it went into my valise.

I truly had never enjoyed a job as much as I did working for Moe Levin at DeLuxe Sportswear. No small part of the pleasure derived from my frequent passionate encounters with Sheila, and I reflected from time to time on just how lucky I was.

Even though I had started the business with Abe Biederman to satisfy my own curiosity about Dale Carnegie's rules, it was particularly gratifying to observe the continuing change in his behavior. He was opening up in a way I would not have believed possible.

I still wasn't used to the New York City persona of just about everyone I met on my daily rounds, or the crowds bustling along the thronged sidewalks. It wasn't that these folks were unfriendly. They just appeared to be so wrapped up in their own concerns that it was as if nothing else affected their collective consciousness.

One day, as I was emerging from the subway on 48th Street, I tripped over the last step and went sprawling, my load of boxed jackets flying in all directions. I hadn't hurt myself badly but I was stunned. As I lay there on my stomach I became aware of a small crowd gathering. I could hear the voices as I shook my head to clear it.

"Ya awright, buddy?"

"Pick up dose boxes fer him."

Then I felt the strong arms of two men gently raising me up. By the time I was on my feet I was downright embarrassed but, more than that, touched by the genuine solicitude and concern I could see in the eyes of these strangers.

"I'll be okay. Thanks a lot." I restacked the boxes and, as soon as they were sure I was not seriously hurt, the crowd hurried off at the usual quick pace of the New York City denizens.

My left knee was hurting, but I felt a glow inside. I realized that, despite their outward demeanor, these people were as decent and as caring as so many others I had met on my travels.

October 30, 1938, I walked through the front doors of the Mills Hotel to find the place in a turmoil. Men were rushing out of the place, and there was a large knot of men gathered around the small radio on the counter by the desk clerk.

I could hear him muttering, "Jesus Christ, dere landin' in Joisey. We'll be next!"

I pushed my way into the group.

"What's going on?"

The clerk's voice was tense. "Just listen!" I leaned over and I could hear a frightened male voice announcing that even more space ships were landing. The announcement had all of the authenticity of a conventional news broadcast.

I was absolutely nonplussed. Space ships! But it sure was scaring everyone.

I decided there wasn't anything else to be done anyway, so I stayed as close to the radio as I could, listening as the minutes ticked by with ever-increasing urgency in the periodic newsflashes.

Suddenly, at nine o'clock, Orson Welles' memorable *The War of the Worlds* broadcast ended, and just about an entire nation had been taken in by one of the greatest entertainment hoaxes of all time.

I had aimed to shove off during the second week in November, and I decided to leave on Tuesday morning, November 8, 1938.

I had given notice to Moe Levin the week before, and I worked the last Saturday, November 5th, at DeLuxe Sportswear.

As usual Sheila and I were the last ones in the place. The boss had given me my check, I would be able to cash it Monday, and I was just about packed and ready to go.

The word that I was leaving had filtered out, of course, and I was genuinely moved when Abe Biederman stopped at my machine that Saturday evening.

"Ve'll miss ya, Russ. Me 'specially."

He shoved out his hand and I grasped it hard. Then he turned and disappeared down the stairway.

Sheila had been sitting at her table watching us. She stood up and walked over to me.

She put her arms around my neck and I lightly caressed her breasts. I could feel the erect nipples under her blouse. I had kept the faith. I had never in any way taken liberties when there was any chance of someone seeing us. When we were by ourselves, and I knew she was in the mood, that was something else.

"Ya know, Russ, I'd never believed what you did with Abe. He seems like a different guy. Me, I'm gonna miss ya too!"

We began kissing passionately and we moved together to our couch of love, the bolts of cloth on the third floor of DeLuxe Sportswear.

It had always been particularly urgent, it seemed, every time we had made love. I had learned that Sheila was going steady with a nice Jewish boy. Whether or not she loved him I wasn't sure, but it had gradually dawned on me that releasing her sex drive with me was one means of keeping herself under control when she was with her young man—which was what the conventions of her family and her particular society required.

We took it much more slowly than usual. I stripped off all of her clothes and removed all of mine. I gently stroked her and could feel her about to climax.

"Oh, Russ, I will miss you!" Then with a long shuddering moan she came and lay there quietly in my arms.

This time I was able to keep myself under better control than usual. Probably the fact that we had made love the evening before had something to do with it.

I penetrated her gently, and then ever more vigorously, until we came together in one final shattering climax.

I stroked her forehead. "Sheila, you know how much I'll miss you too, don't you?"

She looked up at me, moved her hand slightly across my cheek, and nodded.

Neither of us said anything more. When we had our clothes on again I held her in my arms one last time, kissed her hard, and then I was gone.

That Sunday I took the subway out to Coney Island for a final visit. The weather was brisk and there wasn't anyone on the beach, but some of the concession stands were still operating. I bought a piping-hot knish and munched on it as I strolled along the boardwalk. It felt lonely then, with the wind scattering some papers along the beach, and I was saddened thinking about how much I had come to know and appreciate this great city.

On Monday I cashed my paycheck, shipped a small box of belongings home, and finished my packing. I paid a final visit to the great library at 42nd Street and Fifth Avenue. I stayed there until after dark, skimming through favorite books. I thought about how low I had been the day I learned that Finn Bering was on the way home to Denmark.

Looking back over my stay in New York City, I took some satisfaction in the way I had adapted. It wasn't that tough compared with some of what I had gone through on the way east. Still, to feel as knowledgeable as I did now, about this city, to have experienced all that I had, and to be ready to start for home with money to sustain myself, gave me a sense of quiet satisfaction. I sure as hell was better organized than when Finn and I had jumped the S.S. *Dagmar Salen*. It seemed a lifetime ago.

The next morning I was up early. The last thing I did in Manhattan was mail a letter to my Aunt Doris. She did in fact save it as she did all of my post cards and letters. The letter is written in pencil, dated November 8, 1938. The postmark on the envelope bears the same date and is stamped "New York, N.Y. Sta A." The letter concludes, "Please don't worry. I hope you will pardon the brevity of this letter, but I'm slightly excited this morning and I'll be seeing you soon anyway." "Slightly excited" was no overstatement as I left New York City on my way home.

# 30

I took the subway to the Spring Street Station, caught a bus, rode through the Holland Tunnel, through Jersey City and finally out to U.S. Highway 1. It was the busiest and one of the most important highways in the country. It had two lanes in each direction and the traffic was heavy as I started hitchhiking.

By a stroke of luck a young naval pilot picked me up and drove me all the way to Baltimore. He was justly proud of the wings he had recently earned in Pensacola and, although he was dressed in civies, he made it a point to show me his gold flyer's wings and his U.S. Navy I.D. card. The scenery was pleasant and, having gotten off to such a good start, I decided that I would do some sightseeing on my way south.

The pilot dropped me in Baltimore amid seemingly endless rows of "houses exactly duplicating each other" as my diary entry notes. It did not occur to me that the same thing could well have been said about certain sections of the Richmond and Sunset districts in San Francisco.

My ride with the naval officer had given me an interest in visiting the Naval Academy in Annapolis. I should have found a place to bed down in Baltimore but, overly optimistic about my efficient trip to Baltimore, I found myself on the outskirts of the city just as it was growing dark.

According to my map, it was a short distance to Annapolis. A vintage 1927 Chevrolet stopped and an elderly gentleman beckoned me into his car.

"How far you goin', son?"

"Annapolis."

"That's fine, 'taint very far and this is the right road."

I sat back to enjoy the ride, but about twenty minutes later, to my complete dismay, he stopped at a road intersecting the highway.

"Well, I turn off fer home here. Good luck!"

I thanked him, trying to keep the disappointment out of my voice. On the highway, as the taillight of the Chevrolet disappeared into the darkness, I realized that I had no idea where I was, other than on the road to Annapolis, and this was dark and rural country.

There was no point in trying to hitch a ride in the darkness, so I studied the surrounding terrain. It looked like recently harvested row-crop country, and I comforted myself with the fact that the earth in these fields would be relatively soft.

I had planned to eat in Annapolis, and having had only a light lunch in Baltimore, I was hungry. Still, there had been times when I had been a hell of a lot hungrier.

I scuffed out a level place in the nearby field, rolled myself in my blankets, and was soon peacefully asleep, even though my empty stomach was rumbling.

I awoke about 3 A.M, momentarily unable to figure out what had happened. I was freezing and my chattering teeth had awakened me. Bitterly, I remembered the immutable law of the road: Count your blessings when you have them because it's going to get worse!

I tried for an hour to get back to sleep, but it was no use. It was just too damn cold. All of a sudden I had a real fear of something bad happening to me if I didn't get moving. With numbed fingers I got my blankets stowed in my valise and started hiking down the highway on feet that felt like two blocks of ice. It was pitch-dark, and I couldn't even see a light in the distant farmhouses that dotted the landscape.

Dawn was just breaking as I trudged miserably on. I heard the sputtering engine of an old Model T truck behind me. I turned around, stuck my thumb out, and tried to look as beseeching and hopeful as I could.

The flatbed farm truck rattled to a halt and a burly farmer, bundled up in a sheepskin jacket, hollered out, "Where ya bound fer?"

My teeth were chattering so I could hardly speak. "An... Annapolis."

"Get in!"

He looked at me as I climbed in.

"What in the name of God you doin' in this weather, this time of day?"

I explained that I had been stranded the night before by a well-meaning, but unthinking driver.

He shook his head.

"You know what the temperature is this morning?" It was a rhetorical question. "Thirty degrees. That's how it comes in these parts this time of year. Dropped twenty-five degrees last night."

By then the heat of the old engine had begun to thaw me out a little and I could speak with some coherence.

"I thought it got pretty cold last night. It was okay when I rolled up in my blankets, but when I woke up I really thought I was going to freeze to death."

"Good thing you did wake up, son. You really could have frozen to death if you didn't get moving. Well, you'll be okay by the time we get to Annapolis."

In half an hour we were rolling into Annapolis and I thought, rather bitterly, of what a miserable night I had spent such a relatively short distance from my destination.

"Where can I drop you, son?"

"Anywhere that suits you, mister; I want to take a look at the Naval Academy."

He had a rather amused look on his face. "Yer a real tourist, ain't ya? Well, it's right on my way. I'll drop you off at the main gate."

Just a few minutes later I climbed down from the truck and stared at the beautifully manicured lawns and grounds of the United States Naval Academy.

There was no particular part of the academy that I wanted to see, although I was sure that a visitor could spend days there. I simply wandered through the grounds, impressed by the clean-cut athletic-looking young midshipmen in their trim blue uniforms.

I found a quiet corner and studied my map. I figured it was about twenty miles to Washington, D.C., and I estimated that I should be able to ride a bus there for about fifteen cents.

I located the bus depot downtown and was soon rolling through the lovely countryside, bound for our nation's capital. After being caught between Baltimore and Annapolis, I decided that I could afford to pay for some public transportation and not risk wasting my time, and a possible run-in with the local police.

The main thing I was interested in was seeing the sights, and I figured that the less I left to the vagaries of the road, the more time I would have to spend visiting Washington, D.C. I had seen pictures of the Capitol, but the reality of the Washington Monument thrusting into the sky took my breath away.

It was a fairly long walk from the downtown bus depot but the great white obelisk was like a beacon guiding me. After walking to the Monument I took the elevator to the top. The view was breathtaking. I could see the broad thoroughfares laid out with geometric precision, the dome of the Capitol at one end of Pennsylvania Avenue and the White House at the other. I thought that Washington, D.C., must be one of the most beautiful cities in the world. Of course, it did not have the hills and bay of my beloved San Francisco but, on the other hand, it seemed so much more spacious and open than New York City that it was truly impressive for that reason alone.

It was about a mile from the Washington Monument to the Capitol. I walked along Constitution Avenue and a short distance up Pennsylvania Avenue to the Hill. Standing in the rotunda, the dome soaring above me, I was overwhelmed. We had learned all the verses of "America the Beautiful" in third grade, and I remembered all of the words. For some reason, the line "from sea to shining sea" kept ringing through my mind. Having been born in San Francisco, it wasn't too remarkable that I had seen *that* shining sea and had indeed sailed on the Pacific. That other shining sea I had at least seen from a distance. The words of that beautiful song, the majesty of the rotunda, and all that I had seen of these United States inspired a sudden surge of pride and patriotism, a love for my country that brought tears to my eyes.

I could have spent days exploring this beautiful city, but I knew that winter was coming on and I could not linger. I made one more stop, at the nearby Library of Congress. While I enjoyed the peaceful atmosphere, I soon found that it was a much more specialized repository than the usual library, and I could not locate the reading rooms stacked with books that I loved so much in the library at home and in Manhattan. What I did find, to my delight, was a section of local newspapers from every major city in the United States. I had kept up fairly well with current events but reading a newspaper published in my hometown for the first time in more than four months was like getting a letter from home. I quickly scanned the sports pages since it was a particular annoyance to me that the eastern press and radio stations paid little or no attention to West Coast football, even though the California Golden Bears would be playing in the Rose Bowl next New Year's Day.

The *San Francisco News* was the afternoon paper I had hustled not too many years before, and that was the paper I read most avidly. I also took a look at the *Chronicle*, one of the morning newspapers, and noticed that there was a new columnist in town by the name of Herb Caen. I started to scan his column and then began to read every word. He had a breezy and fascinating style that kept me reading.

It was about two in the afternoon and time for me to be moving on. It cost me five cents for a trolley ride out to Arlington, which wasn't too far from Highway 66. I intended to stay on it until it intersected U.S. Highway 11, which would take me in a southwesterly direction through the Shenandoah Valley, the Blue Ridge Mountains, through Roanoke, Virginia, and to Knoxville, Tennessee. As nearly as I could tell from my battered map, U.S. Highway 11 bore south and eventually ended at New Orleans, which was my first major destination.

By a series of short rides I made it out to the intersection of Highway 66 and U.S. Highway 11 south. From that point it looked to me to be about 125 miles to Roanoke. The rides seemed to be getting shorter and shorter, but the Virginians who picked me up were uniformly friendly and gracious, and I was fascinated by their soft Southern drawl.

I was let off in Harrisonburg late in the day. I made up my mind that I was not going to get caught out in the cold again and started to explore the town. Walking down a side street, I noticed a door that opened onto the sidewalk; one pane of glass was missing from the upper two-pane section. It must have been below freezing and there was a brisk wind blowing. It didn't take me long to make up my mind. Looking carefully in both directions to make sure I was unobserved, I managed to squirm my way through the missing section of the door, pull my valise in after me, and make up my bed on the wooden floor. It was dark by then, and I couldn't tell whether I was in some sort of abandoned store or what. I did know that I was out of that freezing wind and soon drifted off to sleep.

# 31

The Shenandoah Valley and the Blue Ridge Mountains were beautiful, the people I met were friendly, and I was enjoying my journey thoroughly. The fall colors still painted some of the trees scarlet and yellow, the small towns were clean and neat, and Virginia seemed to me to be a clearly defined state with great natural beauty.

I reached the stately community of Lexington, home of the Virginia Military Institute, and decided to take some time to attend to my personal appearance. I had stayed a good deal cleaner hitchhiking than riding the rails, but I still needed a shower. The local YMCA provided me with a hot shower for ten cents, and I was back on the highway out of Lexington when the greatest good luck I had ever experienced on the road appeared in the guise of a shiny, new, blue 1939 Buick. Sometimes, despite an occasional mishap, it seemed as if my personal guardian angel was really watching over me.

As the car pulled over, I could see a man at the wheel and a lady on the passenger side of the front seat. He gestured toward the back seat and I hurriedly climbed in.

"Where you bound for?"

I hesitated for a second and then answered, "Knoxville."

This was literally the truth; it was about two hundred miles from Lexington, but I did not want my benefactor to find out at first acquaintance that he had picked up a real long-distance traveler.

"We're planning to spend the night in Knoxville ourselves, so settle down." The man glanced around at me and gave me a friendly smile.

"This sure is a nice car." I had the feeling it was an important part of his life and I was right.

"Yep. Just picked her up from the dealer last week. This is the first trip—"

I didn't see his wife nudge him, but I was rather sure some such gesture had cut him off in mid-sentence.

I thought gratefully of that hot shower and knew that I looked and smelled clean.

Part of the skill in effective hitchhiking was to make a determination as to just how much the driver wanted to talk.

I had the feeling this particular man was a gregarious sort, but I wasn't too sure about his wife. I decided to press ahead.

"My name's Russ Hofvendahl. Where you folks from?"

He answered the question first. "Rahway, in Jersey. I'm George Mitchell—this is my wife, Mary."

I was politeness personified. "Nice to meet you Mrs. Mitchell, Mr. Mitchell."

She turned and gave me a brief smile.

George kept his eyes on the road but I was right. He was a talker, and it did not seem to me that his wife was all that much company for him.

I guessed they were in their mid-forties. He was a pleasant-looking man with a shock of brown hair. His hands on the wheel looked strong and capable. His wife was rather attractive, with what appeared to be a good figure, as much as I could tell from the back seat.

I decided to follow up on the new Buick again. It wasn't difficult; the back seat was roomy and comfortable, and the car had the distinctive smell of a new automobile.

"Man, this is sure a great car. I don't usually get to ride in a brand-new one like this."

George nodded with satisfaction. "Yep, we're pretty lucky. Got myself a good machine shop in Rahway, just got a long-term production contract well under way. Got an honest foreman to run things for me so we decided to take a little trip and celebrate."

In 1938 people traveling for sheer pleasure were not that usual. George Mitchell took a justifiable pride in his business success, and now I had another avenue to explore.

He answered my questions very readily and I learned just how he had become a journeyman machinist, borrowed money to start his own business some ten years ago, had somehow survived the bitterest early years of the Depression, and had finally achieved a substantial measure of success. I also learned that they were childless. He did not quite say so but my very definite impression was that, like many couples in those years, the sheer struggle for economic survival had ruled out a family as a luxury they simply could not afford. It also occurred to me that George Mitchell would have made a wonderful father, and maybe Mary Mitchell felt some lingering unhappiness over the fact that their economic success arrived a bit too late for them to have a family.

After a while George Mitchell fell silent and I was surprised when his wife turned to me and said, "Where are you from, Russ?"

"San Francisco."

"My, you're a long way from home. How did you get to these parts?"

"It's kind of a long story, Mrs. Mitchell."

She gave me a pleasant smile. "I wouldn't ask if I didn't want to know. Tell us about it."

At that point I decided to give them the full story as long as they looked as if they were interested. They were bright people and, if they did figure out that they had picked up a real long-distance traveler, that was the chance I had to take.

They both were truly fascinated, and I did not spare any of the details—good and bad. I found that I was enjoying being the focus of their attention, and they both interrupted me with frequent questions.

"You mean they were really trying to shoot you on that freight train into Buffalo?" George Mitchell's tone was incredulous.

"It sure seemed like it to me, Mr. Mitchell. I know I got off as quick as I could."

They both shook their heads in wonderment.

The time flew by, and we stopped for lunch in a small town south of Roanoke. We ate at a diner on the highway, and I really had to argue to pay for my own meal.

Mary Mitchell walked in ahead of us, and I touched George Mitchell's arm.

"Mr. Mitchell, I want to pay for my own lunch."

"Come on, Russ. I can afford it. Let me buy."

"I'm sure you can, you folks have been so good to me already that I'd just feel better if I was paying for myself."

"Okay, Russ, if that's the way you want it. I kinda admire you for it."

I felt a bit guilty at that point, thinking about my ulterior motive. I simply wanted to be as unobtrusive and inexpensive for them as possible. I had learned by then that they were in fact driving all the way to New Orleans and I desperately wanted to ride with them to the end. It wasn't just the sheer luxury of riding in the comfortable back seat of that new Buick. I had heard enough stories about chain gangs in the South, and about what a hard time someone on the road could encounter to be very wary of this leg of my journey. As long as I was traveling with the Mitchells, I was not only making remarkable time on my way home, but I was traveling in a completely protected environment.

It worked out as I had hoped. I excused myself to go to the men's room when we were just about through lunch. When I returned to our booth, Mary Mitchell was particularly kind and friendly, and I had a hunch that her husband had told her about my insisting on paying my own way. Also I had a feeling that somehow or other I had aroused her latent maternal instincts.

When we were on our way again, she turned and asked me directly, "Are you heading for New Orleans, Russ?"

I hesitated briefly. "Well, as a matter of fact..."

"My Lord, why didn't you say so! George and I are going to get a good night's sleep in Knoxville, then we're driving straight through tomorrow to New Orleans. You're surely welcome to ride with us."

I could scarcely believe it, and I was a bit choked up by their generous good will. After all, this was a vacation trip they had planned for a long time and having a stranger travel with them for such a long part of the trip sure was *not* part of their vacation plans.

"Gee, Mrs. Mitchell, I really appreciate it. I guess you know from what I've told you that I don't usually get to travel like this."

George Mitchell gave me a broad grin in the rear-view mirror. "Couldn't be easier for us, Russ, and it makes us feel good to be able to help you out."

I remembered what Finn Bering had told me a long time ago about people feeling good giving something. How easy it was to contribute to that feeling by accepting what was offered—Finn was so right.

We reached Knoxville just as it was growing dark. George Mitchell located the downtown hotel where they would be staying and then drove to a nearby parking lot.

As we got out of the car Mary Mitchell looked at me, a worried look in her eyes.

"Where are you going to spend the night, Russ?"

"I'll find some place. Don't worry about me."

"Well, if you say so..."

I knew she was aching to invite me to stay with them at the hotel, but I also figured that her husband had impressed on her my determination not to impose. I guessed that she was remembering some of the places I had told them about where I had bedded down during my travels.

George came around to where we were standing on the passenger side of the Buick.

"You know, Russ, you're welcome to have dinner with us."

"I really do appreciate it, Mr. Mitchell, but I think you've had enough of me for one day. What time you getting under way tomorrow?"

He smiled. "About eight o'clock. You be here now!"

I smiled back. "I'll be here."

Then I walked off carrying my valise. I had a place in mind, but

I did not want to upset my friends by telling them about my plan for the night. As we drove down the main street into town I had seen what was unmistakably the local county jail, and I suddenly remembered something I had heard from one of the well-traveled Knights of the Road out West. According to him, the police officers in the South could be brutally aggressive in seeking out wanderers, arresting them on general principles as vagrants, and a hobo could find himself doing thirty days' hard time for no reason other than being in the wrong place at the wrong time. On the other hand, he said that he had found a good night's lodging in more than one Southern local jail simply by walking in and asking. It was something of a grasping of the nettle approach and it sure beat sleeping out in this weather.

With my first-class travel set now, all the way to New Orleans, I did not want to risk getting arrested in Knoxville and missing the ride tomorrow morning.

So, after a dinner that cost me twenty cents in a local coffee shop, I walked into the Knoxville county jail about nine o'clock that night.

There was only one uniformed officer sitting at a desk directly opposite the entrance. He looked up as I walked in.

"What y'all doin' heah, boy?"

I was as respectful and deferential as I could manage. "Sir, I'm just passing through and it's really cold tonight. Could I sleep in here?"

He was a muscular, blond man in his mid-thirties. He looked tough but suddenly, to my surprise, he looked amused too.

"Don't get many calls like that round heah. Why the hell not? Want me to lock you up?"

I hadn't counted on this possibility, and I felt a sudden surge of panic remembering the physical impact of those steel doors clanging shut behind me in the federal jail in Portal, North Dakota.

"Well, sir, I'd rather not if there's just some place I can be out of the way."

He grinned at me then in a friendly way and stood up. "Okay, buddy, y'all jes follow me." He led me down a corridor, opened a door to a small room containing only a bare wooden table and two chairs, and gestured inside.

I guessed that it probably was used for interrogating suspects.

"Y'all unnerstan' we don't have room service but it's all yours."

"Officer, I really appreciate it."

He turned on his heel, and went back down the corridor.

I could smell the institutional air of close quarters, strong soap, and disinfectant. From somewhere in that maze of cells I heard a drunken shout and the sound of scuffling. Then I shut the door to my quarters, spread out my blankets on the floor, and went sound asleep.

Once in a while during the night I was awakened by the sound of a yell, and curses, but I soon went back to sleep. The small steam heater in one corner kept me warm and comfortable.

I awoke about five-thirty in the morning momentarily disoriented. I remembered where I was and stretched out in my blankets, feeling some satisfaction at having vindicated the theory I had heard about a long time before.

I realized that I had to get out of this jail too, and I didn't think that would present any real problem. Still, I sure didn't want to upset things now.

As I stowed my blankets in my valise I was suddenly hit by a powerful urge to relieve myself. I decided to return to the front desk and ask permission to use the lavatory before I left.

There was a different officer sitting at the desk now, but he was very much the same type as the one who had given me permission to stay there last night.

He looked at me as I approached the desk. "Bille Joe done told me we had a guest down the hall. Sleep well?" The question was sarcastic but his tone was friendly.

"Yes, sir. You got a men's room I could use?"

He didn't reply, merely jerked his thumb over his shoulder where I could see a door with "Men" painted on it in a faded white.

I moved gratefully toward the door, had it half open, when I was stopped in my tracks by a bellow from the desk. "Boy!" That one word seemed to have at least three syllables. "What in the hell y'all doin' goin' into the nigger can?"

I stopped short and stared at the door I had pushed half open. Well above the "Men" was another faded set of letters—"Colored."

I had traveled through the South so rapidly that I really had not been too exposed to the racial mores of this part of the country. However, I had seen the segregated public lavatories starting at about Baltimore all the way south, George Adams had informed me about the lot of his people down here, and I really did know better.

In the urgency of my need, I simply had not noticed the "Colored" sign on the door. Now I stood transfixed for a second. I knew I had almost committed a mortal sin in this part of the country. Quickly I turned away from the door and faced the officer.

"I'm sorry, sir, I had to go real bad and just didn't notice..."

He shook his head disgustedly. "Goddamned Yankees—jes' don' know no bettuh! That's the toilet I pointed at." This time he stabbed an index finger at another door just five feet away.

The signs on this door were equally faded but I was really concentrating now. "White" was painted on that door above the "Men" and I darted through it.

As I stood there I thought about how a hobo could be locked up in this part of the country for doing nothing, and I wondered what was going to happen to me now. I decided that maybe the longer I took in the lavatory the more time it would give him to cool off. I was sure there was no way I could get out that front door unobserved. So I took my time brushing my teeth, washing myself, and getting squared away.

Finally I braced myself and walked out of the men's room carrying my valise. I was prepared to see the officer standing there with his weapon drawn, a set of handcuffs dangling from his other hand.

Instead, as I walked out he was busy on the telephone. The earpiece was jammed against his left ear, propped against his shoulder, and he was writing rapidly on a note pad on the desk.

I stopped at his desk. "Sir, I'm really sorry..."

He simply shook his head, gestured impatiently at the telephone, and went on writing.

I didn't linger. I was through the front entrance of the jail a moment later on my way to meet the Mitchells.

My diary entry for November 11, 1938, is quite simple. "Spent last night in the Knoxville county jail. Steam heat and even a place to wash."

# 32

I had coffee and grits at the same small coffee shop where I had eaten last night. I made it a point of eating food that was new to me and "grits" certainly fit that category. It appeared to be a staple on every restaurant menu I ever saw in the South, but I wasn't too impressed. It was filling, but it wasn't in the same class with the southern fried chicken George Adams had introduced me to in Harlem. Sitting there thinking about George focused my thoughts on what I had almost done at the Knoxville county jail this morning.

I felt a surge of the same sort of indignation I had felt when George Adams told me about the life of a black in the South. All I had really done was almost use some segregated toilet facilities. What in the hell was so wrong about that, I asked myself. Still, I remembered that officer's tone of voice when he bellowed at me. As far as *he* was concerned that was about as wrong as a person could get.

I thought of all of the Southerners I had met thus far. It seemed that, without exception, they were warmer and friendlier by far than any New Yorker I had ever met. The combination of their soft drawl, so gentle on the ears, and their courteous way with strangers, made it impossible for me not to respond in kind. Still, they had this deep-seated prejudice against black people—a somber misanthropic streak in their makeup that I had never encountered before. It was a puzzle for me and I finally decided it was a puzzle I did not have to solve just then.

As if to validate my general feelings about Southerners, the waitress appeared at my seat at the counter. She smiled in a very friendly way, "Mo coffee, suh?"

"Yeah, sure," I replied absently, inwardly shaking my head over the moral enigma these folks were to me.

I met the Mitchells in the parking lot and we were soon on our way out of Knoxville. Mary Mitchell turned in the front seat to look at me.

"Where did you spend the night, Russ? I was so worried about you."

"I had a good night's sleep, Mrs. Mitchell."

"That's *not* what I asked you! Where did you spend the night?"

"As a matter of fact in the Knoxville county jail."

They both exclaimed, practically in unison, "The jail!"

"Yeah, I really got a good night's sleep. It was okay."

Mary Mitchell pursed her lips and shook her head at me. I could see George Mitchell grinning in the rear-view mirror.

From Knoxville we drove southwesterly to Chattanooga and on into Alabama. We had left the Great Smoky Mountains behind us in

Tennessee and now, in Alabama, the topography and the environment seemed to change rapidly as we crossed the state line, a phenomenon I had noticed before. Rural shanties were scattered across the red-earth fields. Occasionally, we saw a team of mules straining against a plough—most often driven by a powerful-looking black man.

U.S. Highway 11 was a good road, but only two lanes wide and it seemed as if we became a part of the landscape as we rolled along.

One of the real pleasures of traveling with the Mitchells was their unabashed delight in seeing a part of the country they had never visited before. There wasn't much conversation, I rather assumed we had talked ourselves out yesterday, but when one or the other did say something it was very much to the point of what we were then observing.

The farther south we drove the softer the air seemed to become, and we were driving with the windows down now, breathing deeply of the smell of freshly turned earth and occasionally the sharp, clear scent of newly cut hay.

Through Birmingham, we drove, then through Tuscaloosa and finally into Mississippi, still on U.S. Highway 11.

As soon as we crossed into Mississippi, once again the countryside assumed a separate, clearly marked identity. White clouds piled up against the distant horizon, etched against a bright-blue sky. The land was flat in all directions and the earth, where it was freshly ploughed, was a deep, rich black. Occasionally, we passed a cotton gin and I was inordinately pleased to see the fluffy white cotton balls. I had never seen cotton in this form before.

We stopped for a late lunch in Meridian, Mississippi, not far from the Alabama state line. Once again I paid for my meal—this time with no argument from the Mitchells.

We all had fried chicken, biscuits and gravy, and black-eyed peas. It was just about the same bill of fare I had enjoyed with George Adams at Mama's Cafe in Harlem, and the black-eyed peas were sure an improvement on grits. As far as the southern fried chicken with biscuits and gravy were concerned, I decided I could dine on them every day the rest of my life and be quite content.

The men's room was at the back of the restaurant, and as I left it I could hear our pretty, young, blond waitress talking to a huge black cook, attired in white chef's cap and white apron.

I paused momentarily to listen. I really had to concentrate to understand what she was saying because of her accent.

"Them folks ah jes waited on, Moses, they tawk so funny ah cain't hawdly unndestan' them. And they do tawk so fas'."

Moses just grinned at her, then noticed me standing behind the waitress. He kept on looking at me, smiling, until she turned around to see what he was looking at.

When she saw me standing there she clapped her hand to her mouth and blushed furiously. "Lawd, mistuh, ah nevuh...."

"That's okay," I said, talking with very exaggerated slowness, drawing out every word, "You folks are so nice down here that we really do want you to understand what we're saying."

She fled into the kitchen.

It was just getting dark as we crossed the Mississippi state line into Louisiana. A beautiful full moon was rising and I saw an occasional live oak tree festooned with Spanish moss. As we started over the long bridge across Lake Pontchartrain the moon traced a silver path across the water, the trees with their descending tendrils of moss were silhouetted on the edge of the lake, the air was soft and balmy.

As we rolled across the bridge it struck me that I was about to complete the fastest, most comfortable segment of my long journey in the company of two of the nicest people I had ever met.

I knew that there would be a sudden sense of loss at the prospect of parting with the Mitchells. I didn't realize how quiet I had been until Mary Mitchell turned around and looked at me.

"You haven't said a word for a long time, Russ. What's the matter?"

My reply came from the heart. "I been thinking about how much I'm going to miss you folks, Mrs. Mitchell, guess I'm feeling a little blue."

"Oh, Russ! We're going to miss you too."

George interrupted to put an end to all of this sentimentality.

"Tell you one thing, son, I sure learned a lot more than I ever thought I would when we picked you up back in Lexington."

One of the things I had told the Mitchells about life on the road was the inevitable endings of short, meaningful friendships with good people. Now, as my time with them was coming to an end, I thought of the kaleidoscope of experiences so like this, at least in terms of the emotional impact. Fritz Hoffman in Saskatchewan, Finn Bering, of course, Howard Schroeder in the railroad yards of Chicago, Izzy Cohen in Connecticut—I would never forget any of them. The ladies, of course; Sally, Edie, and Sheila—in a way saying good-bye to them had hurt the most. I wondered why I wasn't getting used to this. It sure seemed to happen often enough!

Mary Mitchell was the type of traveler who read all she could find about a place she was going to visit and she had certainly informed herself about New Orleans. In the course of our swift, smooth passage south I had learned from her about the French Quarter, the history of the Crescent City, and its general layout.

I knew that I wanted to spend at least a short time exploring the French Quarter, and the weather was so balmy that I wasn't too concerned about finding a place to bed down for the night.

Their hotel was on Canal Street, not far from the French Quarter, and I decided that I might as well ride with them to their hotel and say good-bye there.

George Mitchell turned over the Buick to a valet after their bags were unloaded, and the three of us stood there at the front entrance to the hotel.

He shoved out his hand and I grasped it hard. "Russ, I know what you've said about good-byes and maybe we won't ever see you again. But remember, we're in the telephone book in Rahway—if you ever do get back...."

"I'll remember, Mr. Mitchell, I won't even try to tell you what this has meant to me." I shook my head. "Guess you know from what I've told you, I've never made distance like this so fast—and with such nice people!"

Then Mary Mitchell was standing there, tears in her eyes, and I was really embarrassed. She couldn't say anything, so she hugged me hard, kissed me on the cheek, and turned quickly to go into the hotel with her husband.

I watched them disappear into the hotel and walked off down Canal Street. I found a place to sleep on some packing cases under the overhanging roof of a warehouse on the waterfront.

My diary for November 12, 1938, commences: "Arrived in New Orleans last night. Just four days and three nights from New York. I doubt if I could have made any better time on the train or bus."

I was awakened by a blinding light in my eyes and a peremptory growl. "What in the hell y'all think you're doin' heah?"

I sat up on the large packing case, blinking. I'm sure I sounded as scared as I felt. "Just trying to get some sleep, sir."

"Well get yer ass down! That's expensive goods y'all picked to sleep on."

By this time I was on my feet, and I could see a uniformed police officer with his flashlight no longer blinding me.

"I'm sorry, it just looked like a good place to sleep."

"Where y'll from?"

"San Francisco. I'm heading home."

"May take y'all awhile to get there if I book ya for trespassing."

"Please, officer, I didn't mean no harm. These cases were under the overhang of the warehouse in case it started to rain."

He suddenly came back to the subject of my hometown. "San Francisco, huh. I've heard tell it's a lot like New Awleans. That right?"

I was finally beginning to function. "Yes, sir. But I sure like what I've seen here so far."

"How old are ya, kid?"

This time I decided to state my true age. "Sixteen."

He stared at me for a moment. "Don' make much sense to lock up a kid like you. Sure y'all didn't know what was in those crates?"

"No, sir!"

"Well, it's one hell of a lot of expensive booze waitin' to be shipped up river. Probably the worst place y'all could have picked. Come on."

My heart sank. "Can I get my gear together?" I was sure I was heading for a Southern jail and this sounded serious.

"Hell, yes. There's an empty boxcar spotted out on the dock. Make a good place for ya to bed down the rest of the night. Then I'd get the hell off this dock."

I could hardly believe my ears. Not only was I not heading for jail, this officer was finding me a place to sleep the rest of the night.

"I promise you, officer, I'll be out of here before daylight."

He shined his flashlight in the direction of the boxcar, turned and strode away. It was then about two in the morning, and it took me awhile to get back to sleep inside the boxcar, but I finally did so.

True to my word, I was off the dock well before daybreak and walking toward the French Quarter, which was about a mile away.

It was about five in the morning when I heard the sound of a jazz piano in the morning stillness. I pushed the door to the cafe open and saw a shirt-sleeved black pianist pounding the keys on a platform behind the bar. There were not many patrons left, but he was playing "When the Saints Go Marching in" as if the place were still jam-packed.

I stood there at the entrance, just inside, until he finished with a rollicking flourish. Then I applauded with the half-dozen patrons who were still there. The pianist flashed me an appreciative grin, and waved.

By late morning I had completed my tour of the French Quarter and had taken a trolley to the western edge of the city and was heading west on Highway 10.

I didn't know much about Cajun country, but I learned a lot that day as I gradually made my way west, being picked up by one exuberant Cajun after another.

It was slow going, with a series of short rides. Just as it was becoming dusk, a large cargo truck slammed to a halt where I stood by the side of the road with my thumb out.

The driver was a black-haired man about twenty-eight. His white teeth flashed in a pleasant smile as I reached the side of the truck.

"Where y'all headin?" I could tell from some undefinable inflection in his speech that he was Cajun too.

"California."

He laughed uproariously. "Can't get you dat far. How's Houston?"

This was in a class with my ride with the Mitchells. A lift to Houston would sure get me well on my way into Texas.

"That's great!" I climbed in and we went roaring down the highway.

"My name's Joe Laflonde. What's yours?" He shouted over the engine noise.

"Russ Hofvendahl."

"Man, nevair heard a name lik' dat in dese parts. California, huh?"

"That's right."

Joe drove with verve and I began to feel a mild concern at the way he rolled that truck of his along. There were not too many curves in the highway, but he never slowed for any of them and I found myself hanging on to the door handle and anything else I could grab as we roared along.

Just east of Lake Charles, Joe swung his truck off the highway with a screech of tires and into a grove of trees covered with Spanish moss. I saw a neon light about fifty yards away.

"Russ, y'all evuh heah Cajun music?"

"Not that I know of, Joe. Why?"

"Man. Ya got a treat waitin'. This a great Cajun roadhouse. Come on!"

He was out of the truck ahead of me and I followed along. Then I made out the sign—"Henri's Café."

I could hear the sound of really lively music and, as Joe shoved through the front door, it engulfed us.

The place was low-ceilinged, smoky and jam-packed. There were plenty of girls there, and the liveliest dancing I had ever seen on the small dance floor in front of the bandstand. The music was produced by a diminutive accordion and a fiddle—the beat as fast as I had ever heard, and in a class by itself.

Joe was obviously well-known and a favorite here. There were shouts of greeting as he pushed his way to a small table at the edge of the dance floor. He literally bounced on his chair keeping time to the music, watching the dancers doing intricate and rapid two-steps and whirls. A waiter arrived.

"Joe, mon ami! What'll it be?"

"Two beers and some Cajun popcorn for my fren' and me."

A moment later there was a huge platter of crayfish, a dish of some type of liquid, and two mugs of beer slammed down on our table.

"Joe, what's Cajun popcorn?"

"Crayfish, man, where y'all been?"

He showed me how to snap off the delicious morsel of this fresh-water delicacy, dip it into the liquid, and toss it into one's mouth.

I only dipped it once, and I thought my mouth had caught fire. Joe laughed when he saw the tears streaming down my face as I frantically gulped my beer.

He was on the floor as the music stopped, took possession of a striking girl in a tight-fitting skirt, and went spinning off with her as the music began again, almost immediately, just as fast as the last tune.

Gradually my mouth returned to normal and I tried the crayfish without that dynamite dip. They were delicious, and I was thoroughly enjoying myself watching the dancing, feeling the vigorous life of this country roadhouse.

From time to time, as the hours wore on, Joe returned to our table to rest for a minute, quaff another beer, munch on the crayfish—always dipped in that fiery sauce—and then he was off for more dancing.

I figured that Houston was about two hundred miles west, and I began to wonder when Joe Laflonde would decide it was time to push on. Given his friendly hospitality, and the way he was obviously having the time of his life, it didn't seem fitting for me to bring up the subject of how far we had to go. Joe had earlier told me that he was picking up a cargo in Houston for a return haul to New Orleans. He owned his own rig, and I knew it was important for him to be at the loading dock in Houston at nine the next morning.

I remembered the wild ride with him to Henri's Café, and I began to wonder what it was going to be like with all that beer he had aboard.

"How ya like dis place, Russ?"

"It's great Joe..." There was an unspoken question in my voice.

"Don' worry, Russ. I dance off dat beer. Time to go now, yes?"

I felt an odd mixture of relief and apprehension. At least we would be on our way again, and he did seem relatively sober. Still, the memory of the earlier ride here was still on my mind.

We left Henri's Café with many raucous good-byes, a kiss from three of Joe's dance partners, and then he was gunning his truck west on Highway 10 again.

There was no apparent change in his driving habits and I was determined to stay awake to keep him company, and to keep this truck on the road by the sheer force of my will.

But it was no use. I had not had as much beer as Joe, but then I hadn't danced it off either. Finally, about 4 A.M. I could keep my eyes open no longer. I saw Joe grinning at me from time to time as my head nodded and I snapped back awake. Then I said the hell with it, slid down slightly in my seat, rested my head on the back of it, and went sound asleep.

At eight-thirty that morning I blinked awake in time to see a highway sign announcing that Houston was five miles away.

"Y'all sleep okay, Russ?" It was a genuine question, no sarcasm, no resentment.

"Yeah, I really did, Joe, but I feel guilty not staying awake and keeping you company."

"Dat's okay. We be dere soon."

He really was amazing. He looked just as fresh as when he had picked me up yesterday evening.

He rolled into the loading dock at eight-fifty and I was relatively sure he would be heading back to New Orleans as soon as he was loaded, but I was afraid to ask.

I climbed down from the cab of the truck rather stiffly and walked around to where Joe was standing at the driver's side.

"This has been a great ride for me, Joe, not to mention that Cajun popcorn and music."

He flashed that smile at me again. "Glad y'all liked it, Russ. Us Cajuns try to be friendly."

Then we shook hands and I was on my way again, out of Houston.

# 33

Leaving Houston I miscalculated. Instead of finding the main highway west to San Antonio, I found myself heading southwesterly toward Victoria. Still, the rides were coming pretty regularly, the Texans were friendly, and at least I was moving in a generally westerly direction.

Outside of Victoria I got on Texas Highway 87 to head back northerly and intersect the main road west. Then a short lift out of Victoria left me stranded with no logical stopping place for a driver to pick up a hitchhiker, and the Texas highway bearing off northwesterly, straight as an arrow, into the far distance.

I comforted myself with the thought that I was only six days out of New York City, set my valise down by the side of the road, leaned against it, and caught up in my diary. I had been eating fairly regularly, this *was* a highway and, sooner or later, someone would give me a lift.

It was just growing dusk when an old Model A Ford came rattling up. I had seen it approaching from a distance, across that Texas plain and I had plenty of time to get on my feet and get my thumb out.

There was an older couple in the car and they both gave me friendly smiles as their ancient vehicle wheezed to a halt where I stood.

"Want a lift, son?" the old gentleman called out. I guessed they were in their mid-seventies.

"Sure do!"

"Well, climb in, we can take you to Cuero."

"That'll be great!" At least I would make it to a town for the night.

They were not a talkative pair, but they had one foible that absolutely fascinated me. The old gent rolled his own smokes, very skillfully, spilling hardly a grain of the tobacco from his Bull Durham sack as we bounced along. Then, after dragging it down to where he could just barely handle it, he passed the butt to his lady who took two more satisfying drags, and then tossed the tiny remnant out the window.

None of the women in my family smoked, and I really didn't know many outside my family who did. One thing for sure, I had never seen a woman smoke the remnant of a homemade cigarette before.

The scene is preserved in my diary: "I got a bit of a shock when the old gent, who rolled his own, would pass the slightly soggy short to the old lady who nonchalantly took a few puffs and then tossed it away."

We were rattling along, probably just a couple of miles from Cuero, when suddenly I saw him. I couldn't stop myself. "Look! A cowboy!"

He was jogging along, just off to the side of the dusty road. He wasn't wearing a six-gun and holster, but he was mounted on a beautiful well-groomed sorrel horse, and in every way, including his battered Stetson, he was the image of every cowboy I had ever seen in the movies. I could see some silver flashing off the large Western saddle with a lariat cinched to the left side of his saddle horn.

The old gent looked puzzled at first, then faintly amused. "We call 'em cowhands in these parts, ain't ya ever seen one before?"

Now I was embarrassed by my excitement, but there was no point in trying to act salty with these folks.

"No, sir. I've seen a lot of them in movies, but that's the first cowboy I've ever seen up close."

"Wal, now, this is cow country. Y'all gonna see quite a few hands in town. They ride in fer a night out ever' so often."

Then we were in town. There were three horses standing in front of an old saloon that looked as if it had been removed from a Western movie set and placed here for my pleasure.

"How come those horses don't run off? They're not tied to anything?" My excitement was still charging.

Again, the old gent looked amused. "Them's cow ponies. They

ground tied. They not gonna move with them reins dropped. Well, son, this as far as we go." He had pulled off on a side street.

"Thanks a lot, mister, ma'am—" I climbed out. They both gave me friendly smiles.

In its own way, Cuero was a small town unlike any in my experience, but vaguely familiar to me from all of the western movies I had seen. There was lots of space out here and the streets were wide and dusty. There weren't too many trees, but here and there I saw stands of cottonwood.

I found a diner and enjoyed a T-bone steak dinner for twenty cents. Suddenly I felt tired. I hadn't slept all that much, or that well, last night, and I had been traveling steadily for what seemed to be a long time now.

By the time I finished dinner it was dark, which suited me fine. All I wanted to find now was a place to bed down for the night.

I finally found a schoolyard, deserted this time of night, and spread my blankets on the ground behind the single one-story building away from the front entrance. The weather wasn't as balmy as it had been in Louisiana but it was still comfortable. It was about eight o'clock when I stretched out in my blankets, staring up at the star-canopied, velvet-blue sky and tried to remember some of the constellations Finn Bering had described to me. That must have lasted all of two minutes, and then I was sound asleep.

# 34

It took me two arduous days of hitchhiking to reach the town of Junction, Texas. It seemed that the traffic was getting lighter all the time, and the distance between towns longer.

On the day I left Cuero I wrote in my diary: "I'm really getting into the wide open spaces now. This is cattle country and in many of the small towns you can see cowboys hanging around. Their horses are darned good-looking animals."

That last ride on the freight into Buffalo had left a mark on me. This was getting to be west rather than south, but I remembered hearing about hoboes being fired on in this part of the country also.

The sound of that rifle fire in Buffalo was still seared into my consciousness, and I didn't relish the thought of catching the freights again. Still, if I wanted to make it home in time to start college in January, I didn't have much choice.

The Llano River ran through Junction and gave this town a different feel. The sight of that water seemed to freshen and brighten the very look of the town. The streets were tree-lined, and there was a sense of peace and serenity here.

It was just getting dark and I was walking rather slowly down the main street, more or less reconnoitering for a place to sleep, when I heard a voice behind me.

"Howdy, Mac, Ya lookin' for a place to light?"

I was startled and whirled around quickly.

I faced a medium-sized man, close to sixty. He wore rather battered-looking Levi's and a work shirt, but his clothes were clean and he was obviously sober.

"As a matter of fact, I am."

"Got me a good camp under the bridge down by the river. Yer welcome."

I hesitated briefly. "Sounds fine to me. I appreciate it." I shoved out my hand. "My name's Russ."

He grasped my hand firmly. "Glad to know you, Russ, my name's Jeff. Come on."

We turned off the main street and walked a couple of blocks to an embankment leading down to a sandy beach at the river's edge. The bridge over the Llano River was about ten feet above the bank and covered the campsite, which had an air of permanence about it. A circle of rocks surrounded the ashes of a fire. A metal tripod on each side supported a rod going across from which was suspended a blackened gallon can. Off to one side I could see blankets spread on the sand. Near the stone circle was a neat pile of firewood and a frying pan with several clean empty cans next to it.

"This is okay, Jeff. How long you been here?"

"Three months. Yer right, it *is* a good camp, but damn it gets lonely. Yer the first 'bo I've seen in a month."

"How come you lit here?"

"Well, Russ, I'm almost sixty now. The road's gettin' pretty rough fer me. I don't know how long I'll stay here, but at least through the winter. I'm told it doesn't get too cold down here. Nice folks in this town and I pick up odd jobs enough to keep me in food without bummin'. I work reglar for the wife of the chief of police. That helps because the local bulls don't give me no trouble."

"Looks to me like you really got it made, Jeff."

By then Jeff was starting a fire and I stretched out my legs, using my valise as a backrest.

"Spose ya could say that. Not too many hoboes come through this town. The Texas Pacific main line runs some north of here. So that makes it good—got no competition really for jobs. But I got no one to yarn with either."

It struck me then that Jeff was really lonely. I learned that he had lost his job in an industrial plant in Akron, Ohio, six years earlier when the Depression was at its worst. His three adult children were gone from home by then, when the sudden death of his wife delivered a final blow. There was nothing to hold him in Akron, and he had taken to the road. He had worked the apple harvests in Washington and the wheat harvests on the Great Plains, among other seasonal jobs. But the backbreaking work was getting to be too much for him. With more forethought than many of his brethren on the road, he had looked for a town like Junction where he could make some kind of niche for himself. It was far enough off the main rail line east and west that not many itinerant travelers wandered through. That made it easier for him to fit in here. The river water was clean and drinkable, he did have a comfortable camp, he was eating regularly, and he wasn't being harassed by railroad bulls. Still and all it was lonely for him, and I could tell how much he welcomed my company.

Like many other hoboes I had met in my travels, Jeff was a wealth of practical information. He had not traveled in the eastern United States but he knew the rest of the country well.

"I hitchhiked down here from the main line, Russ. Think that's about the only way yer goin' to get north. But you should be able to catch a Texas Pacific freight from San Angelo right into El Paso. After that, the way you want to go, it's goin' to get rough on the Santa Fe. That line's about as tough as what ya tole me about the New York Central."

"I'm really not looking forward to that, Jeff. I enjoyed riding the Great Northern, up in Dakota and Minnesota, but I'm not looking forward to dodging railroad bulls again. Guess I don't have much choice now."

"That's right, son, but you'll make it okay. Let's have some grub."

Jeff's larder was stowed in a covered wooden crate, buried in the sand and covered with a couple of large river boulders to keep stray animals out.

He took some potatoes and chunks of beef from the crate, and proceeded to cook us a delicious mulligan in the can suspended over the fire.

After dinner we stretched out on our blankets, talking, and staring at the starry sky visible above from both sides of the narrow bridge.

I thought about Jeff and it suddenly struck me that he was a man to be admired. Life had been no bed of roses for him ever—not in that factory back in Akron, and certainly not working as an itinerant harvest hand. But I heard not a word of complaint from him other than his mild regret at the loneliness of his life here in Junction.

He was not a Communist, and there were many hoboes who were, understandably enough—bitterly condemning the system that had reduced them to the lowest economic level in what was still one of the richest countries in the world.

Somehow or other, on the road, I found it easy to ask rather personal questions of men I had known only briefly.

"Jeff, how come you're not a Commie? I've run into a lot of them on the road. Seems like you've got plenty to bitch about, losing your job and all."

He stared into the fire for a moment before answering.

"Dunno, Russ. Couple of things, I guess. Don't get to read too much, but I talked to some seamen out in Seattle once. They'd hit a couple of Russian ports. Way they talked about things there sure sounded like them Russian cops rousted folks as bad or worse than they do here. The way them folks lived didn't sound all that good either.

"I've listened to some of these Commies spoutin' off in the jungles and you can't talk to them damn fools. They jes figger they're right and everyone else is wrong." He grinned briefly. "I'm just ornery enough that when I hear some bastard like that talk I'm agin him. And I happen to think Roosevelt's gonna bring this country out of it. May be a bit too late fer me, but I do believe it's gonna happen." There was no suggestion of bitterness in his voice. It was just the way things were.

I went to sleep that night thinking about Jeff and the thousands of men like him whose lives had been uprooted and shattered by the Depression. I resolved again, as I had on the hillside in Connecticut, that I would not work with my hands and my back for the rest of my life. I would get an education somehow.

The next morning Jeff cooked us bacon and eggs for breakfast.

I felt as if I knew this man well and I trusted him, but as usual I was traveling with my money inside my shoes and I didn't volunteer information along those lines to anyone.

I did have fifteen cents change in my pocket and, after I had helped him square away the camp, I pulled the coins out and extended my hand.

"Jeff, this is about all I can spare, but I want you to have it."

He looked at me. "Didn't invite ya down here to get paid, son."

"I know you didn't, but this has really been a great camp and two good meals. That's the least I can do."

He still hesitated.

"Look, Jeff, I want you to have it. I'm not broke, okay?"

"All right, Russ, if you insist." He smiled. "If I had the dough to spare I'd a paid you jes for the company!"

I smiled back, we shook hands, and I was on my way.

# 35

The rides were so infrequent now that I took anything that came my way if it was going in my general direction. This had the effect of depositing me at times in what seemed to be the end of the known world. London, Texas, was one such place.

The main street was two blocks long. Not a person was in sight. Tumbleweeds were blowing aimlessly along the empty streets. Dust settled on the fronts of a few nondescript stores. There was a one-pump gas station at the far end of the town where the road headed off across the barren landscape.

That night I wrote: "I landed in London about noon today. If I ever kill a man, London is the place I'll head for. No one would ever find me there. No buses, no railroads, no traffic. Just a dusty, windswept little cattle town."

The rancher who had given me the lift into London meant well, but he had no reason to think in terms of my travel requirements.

For a moment, looking down the main street of this godforsaken little town, I felt a rush of panic. How in the hell was I going to get out of here?

Then I saw a small United States Post Office about a block away. The flag above it was snapping briskly in the breeze. I decided that was as good a source of information as anything here in London, Texas.

An older man was sitting at a battered wooden desk in the corner working on some papers. He wore a green eyeshade and black sleeve guards that ended at the elbows of his white shirt.

"Excuse me, sir, is there a railroad anywhere near here?"

"Nope."

He had swung around in his swivel chair when he heard my voice and stared at me intently.

"You a stranger here?"

I thought I had heard obvious questions in my life, but this one had to be the most.

"That's right. Any buses through here?"

"Nope."

"Mister, I'm trying to get to San Angelo and I haven't seen any cars on the road since that rancher dropped me here."

I could see a glint of amusement in his eyes now.

"Wal, son, you done picked a poor place to travel from. But there's a mail truck leaves here every day at four."

"Where does it go?"

"Menard. Cost you four bits."

There was a map of this part of Texas on the wall. I studied it hurriedly. Menard was only about twenty-eight miles away, but it was located on what looked to be a bigger highway than the one I had traveled on to London. Fifty cents seemed downright outrageous for a twenty-eight-mile ride but, at that moment, I would have paid practically anything to get out of there.

"I got the money. Are you sure I can get a ride on it?"

"I'm sure. Last time Bill had a passenger to Menard was three months ago."

The mail truck was a battered, old Model A, but it got me to Menard and, by a series of short lifts, finally to Eden, Texas—without a doubt the most whimsically named community I had ever seen. It was larger than London, but an Eden it was not.

I finally made it to San Angelo and caught a way freight to Big

Spring, Texas. This was West Texas country now and as empty and lonesome as any I had ever seen. I managed to find an empty boxcar, and had it to myself as the freight rattled along.

The Texas Pacific did not have the hostile reputation of the New York Central and the Santa Fe, but it was not the Great Northern either. I had heard that there would be railroad bulls in the main divisions, like Big Spring, and to beware.

I dropped off on the eastern side of the yard as the freight was slowing. There was a hobo jungle, not too far from the right-of-away, situated by a small stream that meandered by the railroad division. I followed the light of a flickering fire and I found one hobo sitting there, staring into the flames.

He looked up as he heard my steps. His voice was wary.

"Evenin', Mac."

"Evening. Mind if I get a little heat?"

It was close to midnight then and cold.

"Help yerself."

"I'm looking for a freight to El Paso. Anything heading that way?"

"Yep. That's where I'm headed myself. Supposed to be a hot-shot. Makin' up in about four hours about half a mile down the line. That's why I ain't sleepin'. Goin' to see if I can spot an empty box on that freight and I'll sack out in it then."

"I'm really new in these parts. Mind if I join you?"

He chuckled briefly. "Well I do know this goddamned yard. Sure, yer welcome."

He was not a particularly talkative type so I didn't push the subject. I sat down on the ground by the small fire, trying to keep warm. Neither of us talked.

I must have dozed off despite the cold because I was awakened by the sound of his standing up and slinging his blanket roll. I scrambled to my feet, slinging my valise over my left shoulder with the carrying line.

He simply jerked his head, moved off, and I stumbled along behind him.

It took us a long time in those early morning hours, and it seemed to get colder and colder.

We located the train, unmistakably made up with a caboose at the end, about fifty cars long—and not an empty boxcar in the whole line.

We finally climbed into a gondola loaded with gravel, and I huddled down by myself at the rear end of the car in the space between the sloping load and the back end of the gondola.

It was just daybreak when the train started moving. The so-called hotshot turned out to be a way freight stopping at what seemed to be every siding in West Texas. As cold as it had been the night before the sun was beating down unmercifully by noon, and I was unbelievably thirsty.

I dropped off the car and approached a section shack at one point when we were stopped at a siding.

A tough-looking section hand was standing in the doorway.

"Excuse me, sir, could I get a drink of water here?"

He looked at me contemptuously.

"All the water gets hauled in here, 'bo. We got none to waste on bums."

That was the first time I had ever known of anyone refusing a person a drink of water, but there was no point in arguing under the circumstances and I returned to my gondola. The sun continued to beat down. I began to worry. I had been eating regularly enough so that hunger wasn't bothering me, but I had a very real concern about how slow this freight was moving west, and just when I would ever get some water to quench the thirst that was consuming me now.

I was by myself at the rear end of the gondola, and I wrote in my diary to pass the time: "I have never seen such barren, godforsaken country as we passed through today." Then darkness came, and it was as uncomfortably cold as the day had been hot under that sun. I wrapped myself in my blankets and that helped. About midnight I could feel the train slowing but it didn't stop. I clambered to the side of the gondola and saw a sign on the right-of-way as we rumbled past—Van Horn, Texas.

My mouth was so dry that I could hardly swallow. The thirst did not seem as bad as it had been during the daylight hours, but the rebuff at the section shack really had me worried. At the moment, it seemed to me that thirst was a far more devastating experience than hunger, and I was seriously concerned about when and where I would ever get a drink of water in this country.

About 2 A.M. I was awakened by the clanking jolts of the train slowly coming to a stop. My gondola had stopped near a division sign, Allamoore, but there was not the slightest sign of habitation—nothing but a windswept, arid landscape stretching in all directions under the starry sky. We were stopped on a siding, and I could see the main line to the left of the siding stretching into the distance. I wondered sleepily how long we were going to be stuck here and how long this bloody train would take to get to El Paso. I also did not know how long I could last without water. In the distance I saw an engine light rolling down the main line heading east. I stared at it idly, thinking we should not be parked here too long, just long enough to permit the main line to clear. Then I stiffened and a chill ran down my back. I suddenly realized that it was a single engine and, as it chugged by my gondola, I realized it was the same locomotive that had pulled this freight onto the siding at Allamoore. We were stuck in the middle of nowhere.

As I sat there despairing, I heard the sound of voices about fifty yards from the siding. I looked in that direction, and a moment later I saw a flicker of light and then the flames of a small fire.

I kept watching, and gradually saw one figure after another walking from the train toward the fire. There were a lot more hoboes on this train than I had realized.

I got my valise repacked with my blankets and then climbed over the side, dropped to the ground, and started walking toward the fire.

There were about thirty hoboes scattered around what was now a roaring blaze. I saw the two large railroad ties crossed over a fiercely burning center, which I knew had to be the oil-soaked waste from one or more of the lubricating boxes on the freight cars. I felt another chill run down my back. I had heard about the hotboxes caused when hoboes used the waste from the boxes to start fires, thereby depriving the car wheels of the lubrication required to keep them from locking. I also knew that the Texas Pacific didn't stack those railroad ties by its right-of-way to make a fire for hoboes. It struck me that this whole group could be in serious trouble before long.

As I drew near the fire I heard a large man talking. He had his hands extended to the fire. "Those bastards wouldn't even give me a lousy drink of water. Hope they get a hotbox on ever' one of these goddamned cars when they pull her out."

There were mumbled murmurs of assent, and I realized that I wasn't the only one who had been refused a drink of water.

A voice came out of the darkness. "When ya think they gonna move this freight?"

The large man standing closest to the fire replied. "Damned if I know, but this is a loaded train, all of the boxes are sealed. They can't let her sit here too long."

About then I began to wonder just what "too long" could mean. I honestly didn't believe I could make it through another day without water.

This group was remarkably good-natured and relaxed, considering their predicament, but how long would that last?

In the flickering light of the fire, I saw what I had heard about on the road but had never seen. A very large man, he must have been at least six feet five, was standing on the far side of the fire. On one side two pretty young black girls were huddled up to him. On the other side was a pretty young blonde. A hobo pimp—and, although I knew better, I felt a certain admiration for him. Even with his size and looking plenty tough, I wondered how he kept control of his enterprise in this hobo world that existed outside the bounds of ordinary society.

Off by myself, to one side of the fire, I got my map out. It was difficult to study in the flickering light of the fire, but it looked to be about ten miles back to Van Horn. There was a major highway paralleling the right-of-way, and somehow, some way, I had to get a drink of water. I did not relish the prospect of a ten-mile hike over that highway but, the more I thought about it, I liked even less the prospect of being here with this group of hoboes who had challenged the property rights of the Texas Pacific railroad. Given the circumstances, I didn't think any of this bunch would be particularly interested in sex, but three girls, with their impressive-looking pimp, added one more potentially explosive element to the situation.

Without saying a word to anyone, I put my map back into the valise and quietly moved out of the circle of light cast by the roaring fire.

It was a long miserable hike but, just at daybreak, I saw the lights of Van Horn in the distance. At the west end of the town there was a diner and, all by itself, a large truck parked next to it. I was really hungry by now, but it was my need for water that drove me.

I stopped long enough to get two dollar bills out of my shoe and then I walked in.

I sat at the counter as the pretty young waitress placed eating utensils before me and a glass of water! She looked at me in amazement as I gulped it down without stopping.

"Boy, y'all really thirsty!"

I started to reply but my voice came out a croak. I simply nodded, and pointed to the glass. She got the message and returned with another glass of water, which I downed just as fast as I had the first. Finally, I felt almost human again.

I leaned back in the fixed counter stool and studied the menu.

"I'll have the stack of hotcakes and the pork sausage, please, and another glass of water."

She gave me an amused look. "Comin' right up!" She had the glass of water in front of me in a moment, and I drank it more slowly, savoring every drop.

There was only one other customer in the diner, sitting two stools down from me. He was a husky, good-looking young man and had to be the driver of the truck parked outside.

"Ain't seen anybody that thirsty in a quite a spell. Where ya been?"

I turned to him, thinking quickly of how I had made my way across New York State by looking for truckers in diners just like this, and trying to look as pleasant as possible.

"Well, I just hiked here from Allamoore. Haven't had any water since..." I paused, trying to remember. "I guess the day before yesterday. I was really thirsty."

"Sure as hell could see that. Y'all headin' east?" It was a logical question, given where I had hiked from, and I felt a surge of disappointment. It seemed that he was about to offer me a ride in his direction.

"No, as a matter of fact, I'm heading for El Paso. Got stuck at Allamoore when the Texas Pacific left my freight on a siding."

"Would y'all like a lift to El Paso?"

I could hardly believe my ears. "Would I! That would be great." The stack of cakes and the sausage were in front of me now. "Are you in a hurry to get started?"

"Hell, no. Take yer time. I'll have another cup of coffee, then we'll get goin'.'" He pointed to his empty cup and the waitress filled it for him. He leaned toward me and shoved out his hand. "Name's Tom Becker. That's my rig parked outside."

"Glad to know you, Tom. My name's Russ Hofvendahl."

With that raging thirst quenched, I realized that I hadn't eaten for a couple of days either, and I wolfed down my breakfast.

A few minutes later we were on the highway heading west.

Tom had done his share of hoboing and, like practically every trucker I ever talked to, was interested in my travels. I guessed it was their vagabond instincts that made them truckers in the first place. He nodded as I told him why I had decided to hike back to Van Horn.

"Good move, Russ. There's no water at that damn siding. I drive this stretch about once a week haulin' from Dallas, and I've seen more than one bunch of hoboes stuck there." He shook his head. "Poor bastards."

We were just then passing the freight on the siding, and I could see the hoboes sprawled around the fire, which was still blazing.

It had taken us about fifteen minutes from Van Horn to reach the siding from which it had taken me three long hard hours by foot. As we rolled by I had an unbelievable feeling of satisfaction. I had not expected to get this lucky but, with my stomach full, that terrible thirst quenched, and El Paso just about two hours away now, I was on top of the world. I really had made the right decision this time.

Tom spoke as we neared the outskirts of El Paso. "Ever been in Juárez, Russ?"

"No. Like I told you, this is the first time in this part of the country for me."

"It's only ten o'clock. If y'all ain't never seen it, worth a visit I think."

"Why do you say that?"

Tom glanced at me and grinned.

"Wal, you can find señoritas all over that town for a quarter for one thing. I dunno exactly. I been over the bridge a lot of times. Damn near ever' time I get to Paso. I like the food and the music, it's jes different, believe me."

I *was* feeling a bit horny, come to think about it, and Tom's description of the Mexican town just across the Rio Grande River was intriguing.

"You know, Tom, I think maybe I'll do that. Man, I never realized how big Texas is. I've been just about a week getting across it. But I got the time to spend a few hours in Juárez."

He nodded his head, keeping his eyes on the road. He was a native Texan and, like all of them, any reference to the size of his home state pleased him.

"Think y'all will enjoy it, Russ. Be careful now when you hit the Santa Fe north. Like I told you, they killed a couple of hoboes in the Dallas yard last week, and the Texas Pacific ain't as tough as the Santa Fe."

"Believe me, Tom, I'll watch it. You really think I've got to stick to the rails now?"

"Wal, that depends. Traffic gets purty scarce out this way, and y'all do want to get home to California from what y'all tell me."

"That's right."

His tone was reassuring. "Didn't mean to scare you, Russ. I do believe the freights will get y'all to the West Coast faster. Jes be careful!"

"I promise, Tom. This has been a real break for me. God knows when I would have gotten to El Paso if it hadn't been for you."

"My pleasure, Russ. Like I tol' y'all, I've been there myself."

We were at his loading dock by then, on the dusty outskirts of El Paso.

"The bridge is about a mile down that street. Don't carry that bag of yours into Juárez. Be careful, buddy, and good luck!"

I found a bus station about halfway to the border and stowed my bag in a locker for a nickel. I was off for old Mexico. It was November 19, 1938.

# 36

As I walked off the bridge onto the main street in Ciduad Juárez, I could feel an excitement that was almost palpable.

I could hear the mariachi music, lively, catchy and melodious, sounding from the doors of the numerous bars. Colorful neon signs advertised the various bars and restaurants and many people were on the street.

I hadn't walked half a block when the first youngster, he must have been all of ten years old, was clutching my sleeve.

"Chu like my seester?" He made the unmistakable and universal gesture—his right forefinger quickly moving back and forth through the circle made by the index finger and thumb of his left hand.

I had no Spanish, but Tom had cautioned me against being led astray by these street urchins. I declined with a firm "No, gracias," as Tom had suggested, and strode along.

Then there were three more, all clutching at my arms.

One made a gesture of smoking a cigarette. "Chu like marijuana, sí?"

That was the last thing I was interested in. Our fifth grade teacher, Mrs. Ryan, had inculcated in me, and I am sure all of my classmates as well, a total fear of any narcotic. "Drug fiends" was the term she used for those who had started down the long slide to degradation with the first puff of marijuana. I suspect that Mrs. Ryan enjoyed a drink herself—there were some mornings in that class when I was sure I could smell liquor on her breath as she bent over my desk to scrutinize my classwork. Still, she opposed narcotics with a fervor that had left me incapable of experimenting with anything along those lines.

I continued to walk as briskly as I could, with my entourage offering me their sisters and marijuana, jumping around me, hustling diligently. Finally, by the end of the second block, they were convinced and, one by one, they dropped off.

From the open windows and doors of the restaurants I could

227

smell the appetizing aroma of corn tortillas. I had developed a fondness for Mexican food in the Mission District of San Francisco, and that delicious smell brought on a wave of hunger and homesickness that was, for a moment, quite overwhelming.

Then I addressed one of the main reasons I was visiting this border town. I had found it hard to believe Tom's description of the availability of Mexican girls in the adobe houses not far off the main street, but he had been very explicit.

"I'm tellin' ya, Russ. Y'all jes walk down one of them side streets until ya see an open door with a pretty señorita sittin' there in the doorway. Don't go knockin' on any closed doors now because average workin' folks live there too. Don't worry, them gals are there!"

When the crowd of young boys had finally deserted me, I walked another block or two down the main street and then turned off on a narrow, unpaved alleyway. The houses were all one-story adobes crowded together, and I was alone. A block and a half from the main street of Juárez, I found what I was seeking.

There was an open door to my right and a very pretty Mexican girl sat there in a chair tilted back against the door-jamb. I stopped as I reached her and she gave me a most inviting smile. I was still a bit uncertain—this looked like a private residence after all, not like the established bordellos of San Francisco.

She removed all doubt. Standing up she made the same unmistakable gesture with forefinger through the circle, smiled sweetly and said "Two beets, okay?"

I had the quarter in my pocket. Tom had warned me not to pull out a dollar bill and expect any change, and I nodded enthusiastically.

She moved very quickly then, putting the chair inside the room, closing the door behind me, and walking over to the narrow bed that was the only other piece of furniture in the rather small room just off the street. From the rear of this adobe I could hear other female voices speaking in Spanish, but in obviously an everyday, commonplace context. I did not hear any male voices.

I handed the señorita my quarter, she stepped out of her shoes, stretched out on the bed, and pulled her skirt up and spread her legs. This was about as fast and direct as anything I had ever experienced and I responded in kind.

It didn't take long and, feeling as lustful as I did, it was remarkably enjoyable. What added to my pleasure was the fact that she seemed to enjoy it too.

We lay there together for a moment when it was over, and she stroked my cheek murmuring, "Muy bueno, bueno."

I am sure not more than ten minutes had elapsed from the time I first saw her until I was out the door, heading back to the main street.

With one hunger satisfied, I concentrated on the other. On the opposite side of the street I had walked into Juárez I saw a restaurant. There were garish neon signs up and down this thoroughfare, and I walked into Restaurante El Pollo.

American money was interchangeable with the Mexican here in Juárez and the menu had English translations, with the prices also stated in cents as well as pesos. The day was cool and comfortable, and I ate at a table just inside a large open window where I could watch the passing scene as I ate. I devoured a wonderful chicken enchilada smothered in guacamole sauce, a chile relleno that was just as delicious as the enchilada, and cooled the fiery food with sips from a bottle of Tecate beer. The entire repast, including the beer, cost me another quarter. I sat there feeling about as good as I had felt on this whole trip.

I was relaxed and feeling the afterglow of that lovely encounter with the señorita, my stomach was full, and I was enjoying the beer almost as much as the food.

Added to my physical sense of well-being was a feeling of accomplishment at having crossed the gigantic state of Texas in just about one week.

I noticed a post card stand on the counter by the cash register and walked over to select a post card to send to Aunt Doris. I selected one captioned "Bird's Eye View of Ciudad Juárez, Mexico," and returned to my table to write. It was rather idealized, of course, looking more like a painting than a photograph. I did not remember seeing all that greenery of trees shown on both the El Paso and Juárez sides of the depicted full-flowing Rio Grande River, which was only a small stream this time of year, at least where it ran under the bridge I had crossed. Still, as evidence of my foray into a truly foreign country, it occurred to me that it probably would please my aunt more to receive the picture post card than a completely realistic depiction of this colorful city.

It was the last time I wrote to her on the trip. As usual, my message was brief and as reassuring as I could make it:

*Dear Aunt Doris,*

*Everything swell. Had a little trouble getting across Texas. Heading for Arizona in about two hours. Say hello to everyone for me.*

*Love, Russ*

As soon as I mailed the card, I headed for the International Bridge to resume my journey westward.

# 37

The weather was becoming colder all the time, but the sun beat down and it wasn't too bad during the daylight hours. It was tough hitchhiking with very little traffic and it took me five hours, involving four relatively short rides, to make it from El Paso to Las Cruces, New Mexico—a distance of about fifty miles.

I made up my mind then, the Santa Fe and its railroad bulls notwithstanding, I was going to have to hit the rails again.

It was about six-thirty in the evening, and dark, when I literally bumped into a man as I turned around the corner of a boxcar in the Santa Fe yard in Las Cruces.

He let out a startled gasp. "Hey, Mac, watch it!"

"Sorry, I didn't see you."

I got a strong whiff of wine from his breath and backed away. His speech was slurred but understandable.

"There's a freight headin' north 'bout midnight. I aim to be on it."

"I'm heading that direction myself. Do you know where they're making up?"

He gestured vaguely down the track. "Tell ya what, why don' ya come to my place and get some chow 'fore we catch that rattler."

He didn't seem to be the most reliable source of information, and it made absolutely no sense to me for him to be talking about catching a freight north, and then talking about his place. I assumed he probably had a jungle camp somewhere off the right-of-way, and I was hungry by then. I followed him out of the yard. Somewhat to my surprise he headed for a collection of small houses not too far from the railroad tracks. As he weaved along it became obvious that he was bombed. At one point he stopped and shoved out his hand. "My name's Gene. What's yours?"

"Russ. Nice to meet you. You live near here?"

He nodded and continued on. Then he was pounding on the

door of a small, flimsy-looking one-story house. I could hear a woman's voice. "That you, Gene?"

"Yeah. Open up!" His tone was peremptory.

The door swung open and I saw a tired-looking woman of about thirty-five standing there.

Gene lurched into the room. "Gert, brought a friend with me. We need some chow."

I hesitated in the open doorway. I was totally unprepared for this. "It's okay, ma'am, I didn't realize..." My voice trailed off.

She stared hard at me for a moment, then stepped away from the door, and nodded. I walked into the room in time to see Gene swaying into the small bedroom just off the living room. He collapsed on the bed with a huge sigh.

She shut the front door, stared at the bedroom, and then swung on me. "You been drinking with Gene?" Her tone was accusing.

"No, ma'am, I just met him a little while ago in the railroad yard. When he invited me to eat I thought he was talking about a jungle camp. I had no idea..."

She was pretty, but I could see the tired look on her face and hear the weariness in her voice. "What's your name?"

"Russ. I really don't have to stay."

"It's okay, Russ. Seems like about once a month Gene gets likkered up and decides to hit the road again." She smiled a tired smile. "He most often passes out, like now, and never does it, but it's a worry. I can tell you ain't been drinking. I'd rather have you sit a spell than some of those drunken bums he brings home. Are you hungry?"

I hesitated for a moment. "I don't want to impose, but I am, as a matter of fact."

"I got some stew cooking. I was waiting for Gene to come home, but I doubt he'll be eating anything for a while. Let's go into the kitchen."

For the next two hours we talked and I learned about their lives. Gert was a waitress, Gene was a good carpenter when he could get a job, which wasn't too often, I gathered.

They just barely made it on Gert's wages, supplemented occasionally by Gene's odd jobs. Then, periodically, he would get drunk on cheap wine and decide to hit the road again. I had the feeling that it was an expression of desperation—a feeling that he had to break away from this drab existence, and not due to any real problems with his wife.

We had just finished the stew, which was quite delicious, when I heard a loud knocking on the door.

Gert stiffened. "Russ, I'm sure that's one of those winos he gets drinking with. Will you answer the door, please?"

I swung the front door open and saw a man standing there, swaying slightly. He blinked in the sudden light. If anything, he was further gone than Gene. His speech was slurred.

"Where's Gene?"

I answered firmly. "He's sleeping it off. You better be on your way."

His tone was belligerent. "Who the hell ya think y'are? Gene and me are buddies." He started to come through the door.

I planted myself in his path. He was a good-sized man but, given his condition, I wasn't too worried. I saw him draw back his right fist. I simply pushed hard with both hands on his chest and he went sprawling on his back.

I tried to sound as tough as I could.

"I told you, Mac. Gene's sleeping it off. Now get out of here!"

The fall had obviously stunned him. He got on to his hands and knees, then finally upright, gave me one baleful stare and lurched off.

When I shut the door and turned around, Gert was standing there, her right hand pressed to her mouth. "Oh, Russ, I'm so glad you got rid of him. Gene's a good man when he's sober, but I don't know how much more of this I can stand. You're welcome to stay the night. You can sleep on the couch here in the front room."

"I really appreciate that, Gert, but I do have to get moving. Gene said there was a freight heading north about midnight. Is that right?"

"Every night they make it up. It's about a mile down the line from here." The cafe where she worked served a good number of railroad workers and her information was reliable.

"What about the railroad bulls? Will they be watching that freight?"

"From what I hear it's not too bad here in Las Cruces. It's tougher farther north in Rincon and Belen. Albuquerque is where the main line west connects up. I hear the closer you get to Albuquerque, the harder it is."

By then it was getting close to midnight. She gave me a firm handshake and a sweet smile. "If he brought home more friends like you, Russ, I wouldn't mind."

"Thank you, Gert, and I really did enjoy that stew."

I headed for the midnight freight. I found it just where Gert said it would be. I reconnoitered carefully and saw no railroad bulls.

It was a fairly long train, and I found an empty boxcar toward the head end. That is, I thought it was empty when I climbed in.

There were two hoboes in the car who kept absolutely quiet until I had walked to the far end of the boxcar and started to stretch out in my blankets.

"Where ya bound for, Mac?" The low voice coming out of the blackness inside that cavernous space startled me.

"North. I want to catch the main line west to California out of Albuquerque."

"Same place we're headin'. Hope I didn't scare ya. Wanted to make sure it wasn't a bull shakin' down this car before I said anything."

"You did scare me. I thought I was by myself until I heard you."

It was another hour before the freight got under way with the usual jerks and clanks, working down the line until we were rolling. By then I had dozed off, but the movement of the train awakened me and I opened my eyes.

I saw two figures at the open door of the boxcar, and as we rolled through a lighted crossing I could see that one was a man about forty, the other was younger, close to my age.

I got up from my blankets and walked to the open door where they were standing, swaying with the movement of the train. They were both about my height. The older man had a strong jaw and regular features. He looked directly at me once, and I was reassured by his calm, intelligent gaze. It seemed to me that this was a man who could be relied on. The younger man was about the same height, but more slightly built. He looked very much like the other, and I assumed they were father and son.

"You guys know anything about Rincon? I've heard that it starts getting tough with the railroad bulls the farther north we get."

The older man nodded. "Me and my son heard the same thing. We haven't been over this line before."

I remembered what he had said about heading for California. This was the first time that I could recall meeting any hoboes who had the same long-range destination as myself. It was a small breach of hobo etiquette, but at least I wasn't asking them where they had been.

"My name's Russ. San Francisco is home for me. How come you're heading for California?

"My name's Bill, this is my son John. We got folks in L.A. Hope to Christ we can get jobs there."

He may not have had as much experience on the road as I had, but he sounded intelligent and careful. Somehow or other I wanted someone else to be making the decisions just then.

"You got any ideas on what to do when we hit Rincon, Bill?"

"I hate like hell to jump off a moving boxcar, it's a high jump from the door level. But I don't think we got any real choice. I'm damn sure the bulls there'll be checking all the empties. I figure we jump off just as soon as this rattler slows enough, then pick her up on the way out. They usually park 'em long enough at a division for us to get to the other end and wait it out."

I shivered slightly and it wasn't from the cold. I didn't much like the idea of leaving a moving train either. Jumping off a moving car from the ladder at the front end was never easy, but at least the lower rung was closer to the ground and, by hanging on with one hand, you could face forward with the direction of travel and have better control of what you were doing.

Thinking about what was coming made it difficult for me to sleep. Finally, after about an hour, I stowed my blankets in my valise, tied the carrying line so it would cross my back with the valise in front to help break a fall, and rejoined the other two.

John was standing at the open boxcar door. "I just saw a milepost with 'Rincon' on it, Dad. Think we're getting close."

The words were hardly out of his mouth when we felt the train start to slow with a series of jarring clanks.

"Okay, boys, let's get ready." Bill was taking command firmly. "Russ, you better go out that left door by yourself. We don't want three of us dropping off the same side. You can go when you want, but I've done this jump a few times so I'll go first when I think it's safe. I'll holler so you'll know if it'll be any help to you."

"Thanks, Bill, it may be."

I shoved the left door all the way open, and peered ahead. It was still quite dark, but our boxcar was near the head end of the train, and the engine light would inform me if the right-of-way was clear of switch handles or anything else that could kill me if I leaped off at the wrong place. There was nothing to do but wait now as the train continued to slow.

I sat in the open door, my valise swung across my chest. Suddenly I heard a shout from the other side of the car. "Now!"

I looked down at the roadbed that seemed to be rushing under my feet. My God, I thought, this is too fast. Over the noise of the train, I could hear the sound of someone hitting the gravel, then about two seconds later I heard the same sound.

For a moment I tried to decide which was worse—being nabbed by a Santa Fe railroad bull or breaking a leg leaping off that moving boxcar.

Well, I thought, the hell with it, I've got to go. I edged off the floor until the right side of my buttocks was just barely hanging there. I faced as much forward as I could and jumped. I turned forward as my left leg hit first, then my right with a gigantic stride, another mammoth leap with my left, and then I was flying through the air. I landed hard on my valise, the wind knocked out of me, my hands cut by the gravel in the roadbed, but alive.

I just lay there as the train rolled on by until finally the red and green lights of the caboose went blinking down the tracks.

I got to my feet a bit unsteadily, crossed the tracks, and looked back. Bill and John were approaching me. Bill spoke first.

"You make it okay, Russ?"

"Yeah. How about you guys?"

"We're okay, but I'm jumping off a ladder next time if I got anything to say about it."

It worked out pretty much the way Bill had planned it. We got off the tracks and made our way around the siding where our train was now halted. As Bill had anticipated, two sets of railroad bulls were methodically shaking down the whole train. They had powerful flashlights that they shone into the empty boxcars, between the cars, anywhere a hobo might be hiding.

It was bitterly cold, and my teeth were chattering so, I could hardly talk.

"Y...you th...think we can pick up that em...empty again, B...Bill?"

He shook his head. "Not a chance. We're goin' to have to catch this one on the fly out."

"Jesus, Bill, we can't ride the ladder or the top in this weather, we'll freeze to death." The urgency of our situation seemed to give me more control of my speech.

I could just barely make out his features in the light from the engine.

"You're right, but they got some empty cattle cars on this train. The top hatches won't be sealed on the empties. We get into one of them, we'll be okay."

About then we heard the highball from the engine. She was

ready to roll. This time I had my valise slung across my back to leave my arms free to grab the ladder.

In his quiet way, Bill had taken command of our small group. "Okay, Russ, John, let's spread out now. You each spot a box you can catch on the front end. Remember, there's no gondolas on this train so you got to make it to the top. Then we can find an empty cattle car and get down in it." He broke off suddenly. "Come on, boys, spread out now. I'll head for the caboose end, Russ you get up front, John grab something in the middle."

The train was beginning to move. I ran toward the head end. I spotted a boxcar but, as I started to run for it, I realized the train was already beginning to move almost faster than I could run. The front end of a car approached. In the darkness I could see the ladder on the front end and that is all that I concentrated on. I was running as fast as I could, and I made it onto the bottom rung of the ladder without mishap. I paused for a moment to catch my breath, then started to climb the ladder. As I did so, I realized I had grabbed the ladder on a loaded cattle car. I made it to the top and prayed that Bill would find that empty he was looking for. The wind was so cold, it was almost unbearable. I clung to the catwalk and turned my head to look over my shoulder. I saw the first figure leap from the top of the car just back of mine and then come swaying down the catwalk to drop into a prone position just behind me. It had to be John. "Where's Bill?" I shouted at him.

He jerked his head toward the caboose and then I saw Bill make the same leap and come unsteadily down the catwalk. Just as he reached us, the brightest lights I had ever seen in my life switched on and illuminated us like insects on a miscroscope slide. It seemed as if I could literally feel them burning into my back. Bill didn't hesitate. He flopped down half on top of me. He had to shout to make himself heard. "Lay still, boys, if they don't see movement..."

All I could think of was the hoboes killed the past week in Texas. I froze and tried to pray. After an eternity, we were out from under the lights and no rifle shots had rung out.

Bill wormed his way past me and began to work with the hatch. I had to shout to make myself heard over the noise of the train. "Bill, this car's got cattle in it!"

He was breathing hard from running and working the hatch open. "Can't help it. No seal on this hatch. Couple more minutes up here we'll freeze to death!"

Then I saw him disappear into the blackness below. I knew he was right and I had no choice. I swung my legs through the hatch and felt my left foot catch on the open slatted end of the cattle car. I had hardly swung my way down when John was scrambling down the hatch behind me. Over the noise of the train and the bawling of the cattle I heard Bill's shout. "John, pull that hatch shut!" A second later he had done so, and the three of us were trying to stand upright in a churning mass of cattle.

# 38

The next few hours were about the worst I had ever spent on a freight train.

My right foot was stepped on almost as soon as I had planted it on the floor of the cattle car. The pain was excruciating! I punched the steer as hard as I could in his gut, and he finally stepped off.

The floor of the car was slick with droppings, and the movement of the train made it difficult to maintain my balance. The smell of cattle urine was strong, but the wind whistling through the slatted ends blew most of the stench away.

The pain in my foot turned me cold with fear as I thought of what would happen to me if I lost my balance and went down in that moving, stomping load of cattle.

The inside of the car was not as dark as a boxcar because of the slatted ends and sides, but it was difficult to see. Then I heard Bill's voice shouting at me, coming from somewhere to my right.

"Russ, you okay?"

I hollered back. "I guess so, but my foot's really hurting where I got stepped on!"

"Try to move back here with us!"

I pushed and shoved my way through the cattle until I could touch Bill's shoulder.

The animals were disturbed by our presence, and their bawling and the noise of the train made it difficult to hear him.

He shouted into my ear. "John's standin' right next to me. For God's sake, stay on your feet!"

Suddenly, I felt the train starting to take a curve to the right. It threw the whole load of animals to the left of the car. I could feel that tremendous weight pressing on me from the front of my body, inexorably forcing me backwards. The same thing was happening to Bill and John, and I heard them gasping for breath as that live weight crushed against us. We had one steer between us and the left side of the car, and he let out an indignant bellow as we were pressed into him. His body had enough give that, just as I thought we were going to be flattened in a standing position, the cushioning of that steer absorbed some of the force, and then the train straightened out again.

I was breathing hard, and I really didn't know how long I could survive.

"Bill, how long to Belen?"

"About three hours I figure."

My heart sank. Bill spoke as reassuringly as he could under the circumstances.

"Look, we got this cow between us and the side. If we take a curve the other way, it's just him that's going to be pressing on us. Think if we can work our way to the middle of this bunch, we won't have that much weight either way she curves. Let's try it. Hang on to me, now. John, you try to get in the middle of this car."

I grabbed onto his jacket and began to follow him down the length of one steer and across the bellowing heads of others. Just as we reached the center of the car I felt a hard kick on my left shin. The pain was so great that my leg collapsed and I started to slip down, but Bill had felt my grip slacken and reached back for me and held me up.

"Whatever you do, stay on your feet!"

"I'll try," I gasped, "but Jesus that hurt."

Finally, the three of us were standing shoulder to shoulder, facing the right side of the car, pressed up against one steer, another pushing us from behind.

Bill was a man of courage and intelligence. No hobo in his right mind ever rode in a load of live cattle, and he had never done it before. But he had figured out just about the only way we could survive in that car. Centered in the cattle, we had only half as much weight of beef pressing on us as the first time, and we had the cushioning effect of about the same amount of live steers between us and the side of the car when a curve threw us in that direction. It never got easy, but after awhile it seemed as if we would make it somehow.

As the hours dragged on, I could feel my legs trembling with fatigue. It seemed as if I had spent my entire life standing up, sandwiched in a constantly moving, bellowing herd of cattle. One saving factor was the warmth of their bodies—at least we weren't freezing to death.

Then, when I had reached the limit of my endurance, the sun came up in a crimson-and-gray-streaked glory over the New Mexico desert. Somehow, just being able to see Bill and John, as the dawning light came through the slats of that cattle car, helped.

I saw Bill study his son to his right and then turn to stare at me. The cattle were quieter now, and he didn't have to shout to make himself heard.

"We got to figure this careful now. Sure as hell don't want to be caught climbing out of a loaded car. Just as soon as we see the milepost for Belen, we got to start moving out."

I knew he was right but, at this moment, I didn't see how I could muster the strength to climb up the end of that car and out the hatch. I did know we had to get out of there. If we were seen climbing out of that load of cattle, there was no way we could ever convince anyone we had not committed the cardinal sin—breaking a seal.

Just then I heard John shout. "We're coming into Belen, Dad, saw the milepost!"

"Okay, boys, let's go!"

I am sure he realized how exhausted I was and how I was feeling. He must have felt much the same himself. It would have been easy enough for him to leave me in that car, but he did not.

Roughly, he started pushing me to the front of the car. I moved as fast as I could, but it was tough going forcing my way through the herd. When I finally stood just under the hatch, I looked up despairingly.

Bill saw the look on my face.

"Come on, son, we're all bushed, but we got to get out of here. Start climbing!"

I don't quite know how I made it, but little by little I climbed up the slatted end of the car. Then, with the hatch just above me, my left hand slipped, and I think I would have crashed to the floor of the car, but I felt Bill's right shoulder shoved hard against the upper part of my legs. He was breathing hard too, and I knew I had to get out somehow.

"Get out, Russ, you can do it!" he yelled.

With one last effort I pushed the hatch open, crawled out on the catwalk, and lay there exhausted. Then Bill and John were out, and Bill was leading the way down the catwalk toward the caboose end of the train. He turned and shouted at me. "Come on, Russ, there's a box just behind this one! You climb down that ladder and get ready to jump. We've got to get away from this car!"

Again I knew he was right, but the thought of making that jump from the cattle car to the boxcar had me petrified. I watched them go and finally got unsteadily to my feet. I took one look at the head end, the Belen division was coming up.

I forced myself down the length of the car, steeled myself when I got to the end, gritted my teeth, and jumped. I landed with both feet on the catwalk of the boxcar as the train started to slow, and the first jolt threw me down. For an awful moment I thought I was going all the way off, but I caught the catwalk with both hands and hung on grimly.

Bill and John had already started down the ladder. It would have been better if we were each on separate cars, but there was no time for that now. My valise was still slung across my back, as it had been this whole miserable night. Very carefully and slowly I inched my way across the top of the car, grabbed the iron rung on the top, and felt for the ladder with my feet. I looked below and saw that Bill was getting ready to drop off. John was on the ladder halfway between us.

I saw Bill drop off, running with gigantic strides on the roadbed. Somehow he stayed on his feet.

A few seconds later John dropped off, and he made it standing, too.

The train was really slowing now and I got to the bottom of the ladder quickly. I leaped off and found it easier than I thought it would be to keep my balance. I did not go sprawling and, for an instant, I felt a surge of relief. This was about the only good thing that had happened all night.

I took a deep breath and looked toward the end of the train. I could see Bill and John standing there quite a distance from me. I waved to let them know I was all right. As I stood there, expecting an answering wave, I saw them suddenly run across the maze of tracks, going as hard as they could to get off the right-of-way. I was dumbfounded.

Then I heard the voice behind me, cold and hard.

"Well, Mac, don't have time to run down them other bums, but I sure as hell got you!"

I turned and found myself facing about the toughest-looking railroad bull I had ever seen.

# 39

He was about six feet tall, muscular, with a strong face and cold gray eyes. He wore whipcord trousers, a creased Stetson hat, and a corduroy jacket lined with sheepswool. His gun belt was buckled around his waist, the revolver hung on his right hip, the holster cinched to his leg with a strip of rawhide.

As I stood there facing him, my heart in my mouth, I saw him sniff.

"You been sleepin' in a barnyard or somethin? Jesus, you stink!"

I felt a real chill of fear down my spine. There was no way I could admit that I had ridden a loaded cattle car into Belen, New Mexico.

"Haven't had a chance to wash up in quite awhile."

Luckily, he decided not to pursue that subject. "You look a little better dressed than most of the bums I catch. Bet you got money on you." He stared hard into my eyes.

"I got a little, but I need it to eat on. I'm heading home to California."

"Well now, I got somethin' to say 'bout that. Let's just go over to the depot and buy you a ticket. Headin' for California, are ya?" He continued to stare at me. "I'll bet you could buy a ticket all the way to Gallup and that'll get ya a good long ways west."

"I don't want to buy a ticket. I told you I need the money to eat on."

I could see he was beginning to work up a head of steam. "Goddammit, I told ya you're gonna buy a ticket. Get movin'!" He pointed toward the yellow-painted depot about a quarter mile away.

I started hiking toward it, my nemesis walking about two feet behind me. I really had no idea how this was going to end, but the closer we got to the depot, the more determined I was that I was not going to spend any part of the seven dollars I had left on a damn railroad ticket.

He marched me right up to the ticket window. This time I didn't say anything. I just shook my head. I could see the veins in his neck stand out. Finally, he took a deep breath.

"Buddy, you're a stubborn son of a bitch, but so am I. Thirty days for trespassing on Santa Fe property is just the beginning. I'm goin' to get some coffee now. When I get back, you don't want to buy that ticket, we're headin' for the Justice of the Peace."

The minutes ticked by. He could watch me through the window of the depot restaurant, and I did not dare try to run for it.

I saw him light a cigar as he finished his coffee. Then he was standing in front of me. "Well?"

Once again I shook my head.

"Okay, let's go."

As we walked out the depot front entrance I had the worst idea I had had in a long time. It suddenly occurred to me that I was in the custody of a Santa Fe railroad bull. Once we got off the Santa Fe property his authority had to end.

I waited until we were across the street and obviously clear of the depot and the surrounding area. I stopped and faced him.

"I'm not going any farther. We're off the railroad property now. You can't make me do anything."

"Well, I'll be goddamned! You serious?" He took the cigar out of his mouth and looked at me as if he could not believe what he was hearing.

"I sure am."

"Well now, mister, I want to show you something." He reached into the pocket of his jacket and pulled out a badge.

My heart sank as I read the inscription: "Deputy Sheriff" across the top, "Bernalillo County" across the bottom. I could see the county jail looming.

His next words absolutely amazed me. As I looked at him, I saw something like reluctant admiration in the cold eyes.

"You didn't know it, but we got a full house in the jail right now. That's the only goddamned reason I'm not takin' you in. Mister, if I ever see you near Santa Fe property again..." He stopped talking for a moment but his meaning was clear. "Now get out of here!"

I didn't say a word. I started walking up the street, wondering if he was just trying to set me up for an attempted escape charge. I didn't even dare look around. My heart was pounding as I walked rapidly, resisting the impulse to run. Finally, I turned a corner two blocks down the street, stopped, and peered carefully around the building. He was nowhere in sight and I was free.

I didn't want to spend any longer in Belen than necessary. I wasn't about to try to catch a freight out of that yard, and I didn't want to try hitchhiking either. I saw the bus depot a block away and I made up my mind. Albuquerque was only about thirty-five miles north, and I could buy a bus ticket for about fifty cents.

Half an hour later I had cleaned off my shoes and the lower part of my trousers in the bus-station washroom. As nearly as I could tell, I no longer carried the smell of the cattle car, and I was waiting for the next bus north.

Finally I was on my way out of Belen. My legs began to tremble as I realized just how close I had come. If it hadn't been for the jail being full, I could have been locked up right now.

After a while the trembling subsided and I relaxed as the bus rolled along. I looked at the high desert scenery where it seemed as if the sky was closer than anywhere I had been yet. An hour later I was in Albuquerque.

# 40

Albuquerque was centered in an expanse of open country that stretched to the far horizon in all directions. Toward the north, the outline of mountain ranges was barely visible as the sun set in a breathtaking explosion of scarlets and golds. Then it was dark and the thin air at this altitude seemed to intensify the cold I could feel penetrating my clothing.

I found a diner and enjoyed a good steak followed by apple pie à la mode. My pleasure in the food was tempered by a concern I felt over where I would spend the night. All the clothes I wore, and my two blankets, would not provide much protection from the biting cold.

I walked for about twenty minutes through a modest residential neighborhood when I saw a Catholic church about a block away. As it was a weekday evening, there was no reason for the church to be open, but I felt that making my bed for the night somewhere on the modest grounds of that small church would be safer than anywhere else in this city.

I scouted the church carefully. It was locked tight, but I found a place in some sparse bushes on the side of the main building. Across from where I was preparing to bed down for the night there was a lighted window in what I assumed was the priest's residence.

I had just rolled myself tightly in my blankets when I heard footsteps approaching. Then I felt my shoulder being gently shaken.

"Would you care to sleep indoors, out of the cold?" I could hear the trace of Irish brogue. "I could see ye gettin' ready to sleep out here and it's too cold for that."

I sat upright in my blankets. "Yes, sir, I really would!"

"Well now, I can let ye sleep in the parochial school. I'm Father O'Brien and this is me parish. Sure and I'm sorry we don't have a bed to offer ye, but at least it's warmer in there than it is outside in this cold."

"That'll be great, Father." By then I was standing and I could see a smallish man dressed in black coat and trousers, with a black garment inside his coat that covered his chest, and the white clerical collar above it. He had a fringe of white hair outlining his bald pate and wore wire-rimmed spectacles.

"Are ye Catholic now?"

For a second I was tempted to lie about it and then I felt ashamed of myself. This kindly priest had offered me shelter out of the goodness of his heart and did not deserve to be lied to. There were Catholics in my family. I had occasionally attended Mass as a youngster, and the "Father" came naturally to my lips when addressing a Catholic priest.

"No, Father, I'm not."

He led the way across the dusty yard, past his small frame house, to a somewhat larger one-story building.

He unlocked the front door to the school, stepped inside, and switched on the light. We studied each other for a moment without saying anything.

"'Tis a hard life for ye, my son, isn't it?"

"It's not all that easy, Father, but I'm doing okay. I'm on my way home to California now."

"I see so many young men like ye. At least ye have a home to go to. Me school's not all that big, but 'tis a bit warmer in here than out in that yard. Ye can sleep anywhere that suits ye, son."

"Thanks, Father. Is it okay if I use the lavatory to wash up in the morning?"

"Of course, of course. Just come by to let me know when ye're leaving so I can lock up in the mornin'."

The hard wooden floor wasn't really as comfortable as the ground outside, but the difference in temperature more than made up for it. I drifted off to sleep wondering about why some men became railroad bulls and others became priests.

When I knocked on Father O'Brien's door in the morning to let him know I was leaving, he insisted on my sharing breakfast with him—a modest meal of oatmeal mush and coffee.

There was no housekeeper and he cooked for himself. As we sat there in his small kitchen I had to satisfy my curiosity.

"Father, I've heard a lot of Irish cops in my hometown that talk like you. Are you from the old country?"

"Yes, lad. County Kerry. Me folks had a small farm near Lake Killarney." The *r*'s rolled off his tongue and I was surprised to see his eyes misty behind his glasses. "Ah, 'tis lovely there."

I thought of this kindly man, living now in a place that must have been as different from his birthplace as any place on earth could be. I remembered the green fields, the blue lakes, and the gently rolling hills of Ireland from my grammar school geography book. I thought of the sere New Mexico landscape I had traveled yesterday and wondered what it was like for him in this dramatic but harsh environment with its Spanish-Indian culture.

"How did you happen to end up here?"

"We go where we're ordered, son. I serve God wherever I'm sent."

My next question was blunter than it should have been. "How do you like it here, Father?"

He paused for a moment. "Ye know, I've not had anyone ask me that in the twenty years I've served this parish. I do miss the old sod."

It struck me that, in his own way, Father O'Brien must be as lonely as my friend Jeff living under the bridge by the Llano River back in Junction, Texas.

"I'd sure like to see Ireland some day. What was it like where you lived near that lake?"

That opened the floodgates. He insisted on pouring me another cup of coffee, poured one for himself, and leaned back in the kitchen chair. In a way, he seemed to be talking more to himself than to me as he described the beauties of his native Ireland, the food he enjoyed, the lively village market days, and all else that was a far world away now.

Given the spartan furnishings of his home, I was sure that there was little money to spare in this parish, and the likelihood of his ever returning to Ireland was small indeed. I decided not to ask him *that* question.

Finally, after about half an hour, I pushed my chair back from the table and stood up.

"You know, Father, I've really enjoyed hearing about Ireland, but I've got to be pushing on now."

"Sure and I've enjoyed the tellin', me boy. It's been a long time..."

As we said good bye he cautioned me. "There's good folk in this town, son, but they're a bit hard on them that don't live here. Watch out for the police now."

"I will, Father, and thanks again for everything."

I wasn't sure just what I would do. I knew how difficult the hitchhiking would be, but after that last ride on the Santa Fe I wasn't much in the mood for catching a freight again.

The decision was taken out of my hands. I thought I was keeping my eyes open for the police and my valise didn't mark me as an obvious hobo.

I was walking down the main street in a westerly direction when a car stopped just ahead of me. My heart sank when I saw the "Albuquerque Police Department" marking on its side.

"Okay, mister, climb in." The voice was authoritative as the driver called out through the open window on the passenger side.

I hesitated momentarily.

"Don't try running, get in!"

The tone was sharper now, more peremptory.

I decided to get into the police car.

"I wasn't doing anything, officer."

"Know you weren't. But you sure as hell don't live here in Albuquerque, do you?"

There was no point in trying to lie about that. I simply shook my head.

He put the car in gear and started down the street. He glanced at me briefly, but I could see he was studying me closely.

"Just relax now. I could arrest you for vagrancy, but I'm not. Just going to give you a small lift out of town." He paused for a moment to give emphasis to his next words. "But I tell you something, mister, once I drive you out of town, if I ever see you in Albuquerque again, it's gonna go hard with ya. Understand?"

I nodded dumbly and we drove in silence about two miles out of town. As he was slowing down he spoke for the last time. "You know, mister, I don't really like doing this, but I got my orders to keep drifters out of this town."

He didn't have to say that, and even though I was feeling totally helpless about what was happening to me, I felt a certain sympathy for this cop. He really did dislike what his orders compelled him to do.

There were five other men strung out along the highway and I was deposited at the far end of the line.

Hour after hour I waited, watching the men back down the highway vainly trying to catch a ride. There wasn't much traffic and no one even slowed down. I began to feel as desperate as I had ever felt on this trip west.

By three in the afternoon I had been stuck out on that lonely highway for six hours. The wind was whistling, carrying the cold off the snow-topped mountains to the north. In another couple of hours it would be dark, and the temperature would really drop.

I thought about what that police officer had said about being found in Albuquerque again and I knew he meant it. I weighed the possibilities in my mind. The chances were that he was off duty by now. Still, this seemed to be a standard routine for the Albuquerque police. They must accomplish their sweep every morning and, even if I didn't encounter the same officer, one of his cohorts had to know I had been ridden out of town earlier that day. The result would be the same in any event.

I looked around at the stark, cold landscape; I could literally freeze to death out here, and there was no way I was going to hitch a ride on this highway with five men ahead of me.

I made up my mind. Somehow or other I had to get back into Albuquerque and, much as I disliked the idea, try to catch a freight. I was the last one ridden out of town this morning and there had been no police cars out here since then. I would hike this highway back toward the city, and then detour off the main road when I got within a half mile or so of the outskirts. Much as I disliked the prospects, just making up my mind helped.

I picked up my valise and started hiking. Almost all of the men I passed were so cold and disheartened they merely looked at me without saying anything as I walked by.

The last one, first in the line of men and nearest the city limits, did hail me.

"Where you bound fer, Mac?"

"Albuquerque."

"Them cops will lock you up and throw the key away!"

"That's if they catch me. I sure as hell don't plan to stay out here and freeze to death."

He just shook his head as I walked on.

Even though this was a major highway, no more than five cars passed me in the half hour it took to get where I intended to detour off the highway and back into Albuquerque. They went racing by and I didn't even bother to stick out my thumb.

I stopped and surveyed the landscape. There were no side roads connecting with this main highway. I would have to strike off across the desert. I didn't mind the prospect of hiking off the highway, but I realized that in this clear, thin air, I would be visible for quite some distance in that empty landscape, and I might be better off to wait for darkness before leaving the highway.

No sooner had I made this decision when I saw a truck approaching. It was the first truck I had seen all day. With no hope at all, I stuck out my right thumb, tried to look as pleasant as possible, and waited. It wasn't rolling very fast—probably about thirty-five miles an hour. Unbelievably, as I held my breath, it slowed and stopped. I was into the cab almost before it stopped moving.

The driver was a pleasant-looking man with curly dark hair and brown eyes, about thirty-five years of age.

He spoke first as I hopped in.

"Just goin' as far as Gallup. Will that help you?"

"God, yes, mister, anything to get me out of Albuquerque."

The truck was a flatbed with slatted sides and back, open on top. I caught a whiff of the manure on the bed of the truck. It was a cattle truck, the vehicular equivalent of the cattle car I had ridden into Belen.

The driver grinned. "Them Albuquerque cops run you out of town?"

"They sure did. Me and five other guys strung out down the road aways."

"That's what I thought. I make this run about once a week and every time I see the same thing. Think those other guys want a lift?"

"They sure do, mister. This is really nice of you."

"Been on the road myself. I know what it's like. Goin' to be cold back there, but I'll pick 'em up. Don't like to have more than one guy in the cab with me, though."

And so he did. After the first traveler was gestured into the back of the truck, the others came running, and then we were on our way, with my five fellow travelers in back, hunched up as close as they could get to the cab to break the icy wind.

When the last one was aboard and we were rolling again, the driver glanced at me.

"My name's José Garcia. What's yours?"

He had used his last name and I returned the gesture. "Russ Hofvendahl. José, I can't tell you how much I appreciate this. Do you do this every trip?"

"Yep. I know how these Albuquerque cops run the guys out of town. I been stuck myself a few times. Like to do what I can to help."

"How far is it to Gallup?"

"'Bout a hundred and forty miles. We'll be there about eight tonight."

"Is Gallup as tough as Albuquerque?"

"No, it isn't. Matter of fact, there's an empty kiln in a brickyard this side of town. Guess they figure hoboes can't do any damage to it and they even have a stove in it. That's where I always drop the guys I pick up on this stretch."

The contrast between the bleak prospects that had confronted me just a few minutes before, and now to be assured of a warm place to sleep a hundred and forty miles farther west, was unbelievable.

The truck was old and beat up, but it was warm in the cab from the engine heat. Once in a while I felt a twinge of conscience about the five men huddled together in back. Then I thought about what they would have confronted it if had not been for José Garcia, the Good Samaritan. It wasn't any colder back there, but for the wind, than it would have been for them stuck in that lonely country west of Albuquerque.

It was just after eight when José pulled off the road and turned off his engine. I could hear the voices from the rear of the truck. "Where the hell are we?" "Is this as far as we're goin'?"

José called out to the men from the open window. "Guys, this is 'bout as far as I go anyway. This here is the Gallup brickyard. There's an empty kiln right there with a stove in it where you can bed down for the night."

I was out of the truck by then, and watched as the men, half-frozen, laboriously climbed over the slatted sides and dropped to the ground.

Talking louder than was necessary, I called out to the driver. "José, you really saved our lives. Thanks a million!"

It had the desired effect. All of them then crowded up calling out thanks and appreciation. I didn't believe José Garcia did this for our thanks, but I wanted him to know he was appreciated. There would be other groups of stranded men on that highway west of Albuquerque, and I wanted him to go on helping them.

He beamed at us, waved once, started his truck, and rolled off down the road.

I looked around and saw six beehive-shaped structures spaced in a large open area. To one side was a high stack of finished bricks. A short distance from where we stood a flickering light illuminated the entrance to one of the brick kilns. That had to be the one José had described with the stove in it.

The entrance was low and narrow, but I eased myself through and was surprised by the space inside. As nearly as I could tell, it was about fifty feet in diameter. A small stove stood in the center with a chimney running up to the top of the kiln. A fire was crackling cheerily in the stove, and it threw off enough light for me to see that there were another six men in the kiln. Some were lying down, some were sitting.

The five who had traveled in the back of José's truck huddled around the stove trying to get warm, and again I felt a twinge of guilt at having ridden so comfortably in the cab.

I made my way to the back of the kiln where a man sat with his legs stretched out, his head touching the inward curve of the kiln.

"Mind if I spread my blankets here?"

"Y'all go right ahead. Plenty of room."

I could hear the Southern drawl that I had enjoyed listening to as I traveled through the South. In the dim light he looked about my age, rather slightly built.

"My name's Russ. Where you from?"

"Virginia." He shoved out his hand and gave me a firm handshake. "Craig's my handle. Nice to meet ya, Russ."

He sounded as if he truly meant it.

"You know anything about this place, Craig? It's practically a hobo hotel."

"Not really. Ah came in on a Santa Fe freight this afternoon and one of the 'bos told me about it. He's been here before. Guess the owner's jes a nice guy. He's not usin' this kiln anyway, so he rigged it with the stove and chimney."

"This weather it's a good thing he is a nice guy. Must have saved a lot of hoboes from freezing to death in the winter out here."

"Where y'all headin', Russ?"

"California. That's home for me. Where you bound for?"

"I'm headin' for California too. Hope Ah can get a job out there. Got an uncle who's livin' some place called Pomona."

"Do you know anything about the freights west out of Gallup?"

"Should be one made up about nine tomorrow morning. This weather Ah'd rather stay off them rattlers, but Ah don't reckon there's any other way Ah'm goin' to make it to California."

"Mind if I follow along with you, Craig? I don't know anything about the yard here."

His voice was courteous and friendly. "Not at all, Russ. Glad to have the company."

Little by little the murmuring voices of the men faded away. I stretched out in my blankets and drifted off to sleep, with the flickering light from the stove the last thing I saw before my eyes dropped shut.

# 41

The next morning Craig shook me awake.

"Come on, Russ, we gotta check out that freight west."

The kiln was comfortably warm and I awoke refreshed by a good night's sleep.

When we made our way out of the small opening of the kiln and emerged into daylight, I got a good look at Craig for the first time. He had curly brown hair, blue eyes, and an engaging grin. He seemed to be in good spirits just about all the time and I enjoyed being with him. Like me, he was carrying a good-sized bag, not a bed roll. I noticed that a carrying line could be tied to the handle of a soft canvas valise that was large enough to contain his blankets. He looked about nineteen or twenty years of age.

Craig led the way to the railroad yard where he had dropped off a freight yesterday. There was no sign of railroad bulls, and we could see a switch engine shunting various types of boxcars, gondolas, and others onto a long line of cars standing on a siding.

"It's going to be at least a couple of hours before she's ready to roll, Craig. I know damn well it won't do much good, but why don't we try the highway for a while."

"Suits me."

We walked through Gallup, and I was fascinated by the number of Navajo Indians I saw. Some wore colorful blankets thrown over their shoulders against the cold. I could see the silver and turquoise of belt ornaments and circlets holding the thick braided hair of the men. There was an occasional cowboy, bowlegged and a bit awkward afoot with high-heeled boots. Somehow this looked more like the real West than any place I had seen yet.

Just as we reached the outskirts of town I saw a car with Arizona license plates in a small gas station.

It might not do much good, but it was sure worth a try. I walked over to the driver sitting behind the wheel.

"You heading west, sir?"

"Sure am. I'll take you all the way to Flagstaff for a dollar."

Although I had not run into this situation before, I had heard that it was not uncommon for drivers to require payment for a lift. Some of them were just about as broke as the men on the road.

Craig was standing right behind me and heard what was said.

"Will you take both of us for a dollar?"

"Nope. I'm having it tough myself. I gotta collect enough for gas. There's plenty of guys on the road be happy to pay. That's about two hundred miles to Flagstaff."

Craig spoke slowly. "Guess that lets me out. Ah don't even have two bits."

I was down to six and a half dollars now. Even a dollar would make a large dent in my remaining money. Still, a ride two hundred miles in a car through that high desert and mountain country in winter, not freezing on a freight train, was worth it.

I looked at Craig. I didn't owe him anything, but the forlorn look on his face jolted me. Suddenly, I remembered Finn Bering giving the last food we had to that starving young fellow in the old passenger car up in Saskatchewan. The circumstances were different, but I had the money and I made up my mind.

"Okay, mister, you're on. I'll pay for both of us."

He was a smallish man, about forty, with sharp features.

"Let's see your dough. I'm not doin' this on credit, believe me."

"Just give me a minute." Quickly I ducked behind the service station, pulled off my left shoe, and took out three dollar bills, leaving three of them in my shoe. I put one of them in my pocket and clutched the other two as I returned to the car where the driver was still sitting, waiting for me. Craig was standing by the passenger side with an unbelieving look on his face.

"Okay, mister, here's your two bucks, let's go. Get in, Craig."

He shook his head as if he couldn't believe it. "Russ, y'all don't have to do this."

"I know, but I want to. Come on."

The car was a 1930 four-door Oldsmobile that had seen better days. Craig climbed into the back seat and I took the seat in front.

Perhaps it was the fact that I had paid for our passage, or maybe it was just the certainty of one long lift west—whatever the reason, I enjoyed that traveling about as much as I had any ride since I had left New York. I thought of what Finn had told me about making someone feel good by providing an opportunity to give. For me, right then, just one of those dollars wasn't all that easy to give up, and paying over two of them reduced my remaining bankroll by one-third. Perhaps it was the magnitude of my generosity that made me feel so good now. I guessed that is what Finn Bering would have decided anyway.

The driver was not a talkative type at all. He never told us his name or asked ours. He did volunteer that he lived in Flagstaff and made the round trip from there to Albuquerque about every two weeks, on some type of business that he didn't describe.

However, as taciturn as he was, he had a typical Westerner's pride in the natural wonders of his home state.

About seventy miles out of Gallup he raised his voice to make himself heard.

"You guys ever hear of the Petrified Forest?"

We both shouted a no back at him.

He kept talking, his voice raised. "Well, we're goin' right through it. Old trees turned to stone. If you want, I'll stop for a minute and you can pick up a sample." He smiled briefly. "What the hell, you're payin' for the ride, might as well give you the tour."

"That'll be great, mister," I shouted back at him. I vaguely remembered reading about this phenomenon and, in my mind's eye, I pictured groves of trees like the towering redwoods in the John Muir woods across San Francisco Bay in Marin County. I got rather excited thinking about what we were about to see.

I raised my voice again. "Are the leaves stone too?"

He gave me a peculiar look and simply shook his head. About ten minutes later he pulled off to the side of the road. "Okay, here we are."

We climbed out of the car, looking for the stone forest. Instead, I saw acres and acres of lengthy pillars of stone. Since he had been thoughtful enough to give us this look I did not voice my disappointment, but it sure wasn't anything like what I had imagined it to be. Still, it was interesting to see the clearly defined bark and trunks of what had once been gigantic trees—now turned to stone.

Craig and I were off by ourselves. Our tour guide had remained in the car. Craig spoke to me in a low voice.

"Geez, this don't look like any forest Ah evuh seen. Jest a bunch of rock."

"Yeah, I was expecting something different too. Let's get a sample anyway, long as we're stopped."

We both picked up pieces of the stone that had defined markings of the bark of trees they had once been—eons ago.

When we returned to the car the driver looked at us inquiringly. "Well, what did ya think of it?"

I didn't want to offend him. "Uh, real interesting. We each got a sample."

We rode in silence for ten minutes or so. Then he spoke again. "I s'pose you guys never heard of the Painted Desert either."

We both agreed that we never had.

"Well, we're comin' into it pretty soon now. Real purty."

I turned toward him and raised my voice. "Will we be stopping?"

"Nope. No need to. We'll be drivin' through it for quite a spell. Just wanted you to know what you're seein'."

After my disappointment with the stone forest I wasn't expecting much, but this time the panorama was spectacular.

It was desert country with buttes and mesas thrusting up at intervals across the stark landscape. In the distance the desert floor was a blend of pastel pink and yellow. In serrated rows of limestone in the mesas and buttes, there were startlingly bright strips of red, blue, and brown. It truly did look as if some heavenly painter had splashed the colors on this empty, open terrain—painting the land-scape with lavish abandon.

I could hear Craig speak from the back seat. "Man, Ah nevuh seen anything like this!"

The driver nodded with satisfaction. "Drive this stretch every couple of weeks, and I never get tired of it."

We were crossing the southern end of this magnificent panorama and, all too quickly, we had left the Painted Desert behind. Another half hour and we started to climb through the foothills leading to the mountains where Flagstaff was located. We drove through pine forests, and I could smell the clean, distinctive scent of the trees. The window on the passenger side would not fully close and the fresh mountain air filled the car. The dusting of snow on the floor of the forest made it a lovely scene, but it also made me think of what the temperature was out there. I reflected on what it would be like exposed to the elements in this country this time of year. Once again I pushed the thought out of my mind. I was becoming quite adept at controlling my thought processes—mainly disciplining myself to enjoy the present, and not worry unnecessarily about the future.

It was about five in the afternoon when we rolled into Flagstaff.

"Where you guys want me to drop ya?"

I spoke up. "If you pass near the train depot that would suit us fine."

A few minutes later he stopped about a block away from the passenger depot, a yellow building with brown trim. He left the engine running, waited until we were out, and then drove off with a wave of his hand and not another word.

We watched him disappear down the road.

Craig spoke first. "Not the friendliest guy Ah evuh seen by a long shake." Then he shivered. "Ah can feel the cold in mah bones. Sho do 'preciate y'all payin' for that ride, Russ."

"That's okay, Craig. Like I told you, I wanted to do it."

I was warmed by his sincere gratitude but, at the same time, I felt a small chill of apprehension. I enjoyed his company or we wouldn't be traveling together. By tacit understanding, we were temporarily partners on our journey west. There was no way I was going to buy food and not share it with him. But that four dollars and change I had left had to last me for what I estimated to be a tough eight hundred miles home to San Francisco. I had not said anything one way or the other to Craig, but I guessed that he thought I had used my last two dollars to buy our ride to Flagstaff. I was in no financial position to feed both of us, but I would be damned if I would beg for food while I still had money.

"What's eatin' ya, Russ. Y'all been real quiet." We were walking toward the depot and I hadn't realized how absorbed I had become in my own thoughts.

"Uh, nothing. Let's see if we can get a line on a freight out of here."

"Okay, but first I'm goin' to buy us dinner!" With that he walked into a small store near the depot and returned a moment later holding two Hershey chocolate bars aloft in his right hand.

I was touched, and a bit ashamed. That ten cents he had spent on the candy had taken a bigger bite out of the small amount of cash he had than the two dollars I had spent for our ride.

Still, Craig was a cheerful type. "We find us a drinkin' fountain somewhere, Russ. Lot of water with that there candy bar and we done feel like we ate a ten-course dinner!"

It wasn't that good, of course, but it was true to a certain extent. The chocolate bar provided quick energy, and drinking a lot of water with it did fill the stomach, and eased the pangs of hunger—although the feeling didn't last all that long.

We learned that there was a westbound freight scheduled through Flagstaff the next morning about ten. We hung around the depot until it was dark. Then we cautiously eased our way in. The interior was dimly lit and practically deserted. We could see rows of benches and only one ticket agent reading a newspaper behind his grilled window at the far end.

I whispered to Craig. "It's pretty warm in here. I don't think we're going to find any better place to spend the night than to stretch out on one of those benches. You're carrying a bag too. We don't look too much like hoboes."

Craig had walked over to the nearest bench while I was talking. Then he looked at me with a small grin. He spoke quietly.

"Y'all right about this being a good place to spend the night, Russ, but we sho' ain't goin' to stretch out on these benches. Take a look!"

I could see what he meant. Every bench in that depot was divided by armrests spaced about two feet apart. There was one position, and one position only, in which those benches could be occupied—sitting bolt upright.

I sat down on one of them and tried to slide to the edge, with the back of my head against the top of the bench. The top wasn't high enough for that.

I really thought, briefly, that someone had specifically designed those damned benches to prevent a tired wanderer from getting a good night's sleep. Then, more reasonably, I realized that this was meant to be a passenger-train waiting room, not a haven for Knights of the Road.

I spoke again, in a low voice. "You know, Craig, I wouldn't mind spreading my blankets on the floor here, but I don't think we better chance that."

"You're right. Long as we'uns jest settin' here on one of these danged benches, Ah don't think anyone'll bothuh us. It's too damn cold to go lookin' fer some other spot to bed down. Let's try it."

In some ways it was about as tough as any night I had spent on the road. Just as I dozed off, my head would drop down and I would snap awake again. My buttocks were numb from the smooth, hard wooden surface. I tried in vain to slide far enough to the edge of the bench to rest my head on the back, but that wouldn't work either.

I must have slept some because, after many hours of fitful dozing, I was surprised to see the faint light of day slowly lighting the depot. The long night was over at last.

# 42

It was just getting light when we walked out of the depot, and the cold morning air pierced like a knife.

Craig's teeth were chattering just like my own. "W...w...want to try the h...highway, Russ?"

I nodded and we headed west on the main street out of Flagstaff. More and more I was bedeviled by the thought that Craig believed I had spent my last money to pay for the ride to Flagstaff. If I had just said something yesterday when he bought the candy bars. It was pure self-interest that had stopped me—the realization that I couldn't feed two of us all the way to California with my remaining money. The irony of the situation suddenly hit me. Thinking of Finn's generosity, a moment that seemed a lifetime ago now, had prompted my impulsive gesture. Now it seemed as if that very generosity was going to doom me to beg for food, which I detested, or force me to sever my hookup with a good-hearted companion, if I was ever going to be able to buy food for myself again. And just how in the hell do I do that, I wondered to myself. To make matters worse, Craig had, from time to time, commented almost reverently about my generosity. He had made it clear that no one he had ever met on the road had spent his last dollar to make it easy for him—his partner Russ was one in a million.

Finally, I gave up thinking about it. I remembered all of the days without food I had endured on the road, and decided another day or so wouldn't kill me. Something had to work itself out.

When we reached the western edge of Flagstaff, my heart sank. There were at least six hitchhikers spaced out on the highway, and not one car heading west had passed us as we walked out of town. Shades of Albuquerque!

I stopped abruptly. "This is no good, Craig. Let's see if we can catch that freight they were making up this morning."

"Whatevuh y'all say, ol' buddy."

We walked quickly back toward the depot. Just as we got near it we could hear the highball from the engine.

"Come on, we gotta move!" All I could think of was getting out of Flagstaff. I started running toward the track. I had my carrying line for my valise already tied, and I slung it across my back as I ran. When we reached the main line the freight was beginning to roll. I knew that Craig had plenty of experience catching freights on the fly. We would automatically stay out of each other's way. I took a quick look up and down the track. No railroad bulls were in sight.

I started to jog along the right-of-way, timing my movement to the speed of the train. Craig had dropped back two car lengths and was doing the same. The train was picking up speed all the time.

Then I saw a boxcar moving up on me, and I knew that if I didn't catch it right now, it would be too late. Running as hard as I could, I grabbed the iron on the front end with both hands and jumped for the bottom rung. I made it neatly, and hung there for a moment breathing hard. I looked back down the line of cars and saw Craig at the bottom of a ladder on a boxcar two cars back. We were really moving by then and that cold mountain air was freezing me. My hands were so numb I didn't feel as if I could hang on much longer. Once more it seemed as if I had placed myself in a position where I would either freeze to death on the train or get killed rolling off it. Despairingly, I looked back down the line of cars and suddenly saw Craig waving at something behind him. He had one arm thrust through the ladder and was gesturing and pointing, with the other, toward the caboose end of the train. For a second I was absolutely baffled, and then we started to curve to the left. We were on the left side of the train, on the inside of the curve, and now I could see it. Just behind Craig's boxcar was a gondola which was only about half full of gravel. I realized what Craig was trying to tell me. If we could make it to that gondola, we had a chance to survive. On the side of the boxcar, or the top, we would never last.

The sight of that gondola gave me new hope and I started climbing the ladder. The iron rungs were so cold it felt as if they burned my bare hands. Finally, I was on the top and I sprawled out to catch my breath. I had seen the brakemen leap from top to top on a moving train—like agile mountain goats. I had done it myself not too long ago, but it was not an experience I wanted to repeat. I realized that I had no choice now; it was either make it back to that gondola or freeze to death in the rushing, freezing mountain air of Arizona.

I could have walked the catwalk on top of that boxcar, but I preferred to crawl. I had never traveled over a rougher roadbed. I would have to stand up to make that leap from the top of one boxcar to the next, but I wasn't going to tempt fate by walking when I could crawl.

When I reached the end I got to my hands and knees, then stood fully upright, swaying unsteadily with the motion of the train. I looked behind me toward the front of the train, to make sure we were on a straight stretch of track and not heading into a tunnel which, if it caught me in a vertical position, would kill me for sure. It was clear. I held my breath and jumped. The distance wasn't all that great, probably not more than three feet. But jumping from a standing position on a bouncing, moving catwalk, to land on the other side on an equally unsteady boxcar top, took some doing. I barely made the end of the catwalk and fell to my knees, grabbing the sides of the catwalk with all my strength. I crawled the length of that boxcar, stood up at the end, and once more leaped across. Finally, I made it to the end of the boxcar Craig had caught.

I peered over the edge and saw his upturned face, eyes anxiously searching for me. When he saw me, he let out a yell. "Come on, buddy, we all got it made in this heah ol' gondola!"

The gravel rose to a mound in the center of the car and then sloped down to each end, leaving space behind the front end where we would be out of the freezing wind. Craig was standing there as he stared up at me.

This was going to be more dangerous than jumping from the top of one boxcar to another. I checked my carrying line to make sure my valise was securely slung. Then I hollered to Craig. "Okay, I'm coming down!"

Gingerly, I eased my body to the edge of the boxcar, hanging onto the hand grips on top until I could feel my feet touch the rungs of the ladder. Then I started down. When I reached the bottom I swung around to the short ladder on the end. Craig was watching me intently. The last thing I needed just then was his worried shout. "Russ, watch that couplin' when y'all step across, lotta slack in it!"

I stepped from the short ladder onto the moving coupling, teetered there for a second, and then made it across in two quick steps—fearing any instant that moving steel monster was going to snap its jaws shut on one of my shoes. I grabbed the top of the front end of the gondola and hung on grimly. Craig wasn't hollering now, we were face to face. "Y'all almos' there, Russ."

There was a three-inch ledge on the leading edge of the car. Carefully I eased across, sliding my hands along the top of the front end of the gondola, placing my feet on the narrow ledge. I reached out and grabbed the short ladder on the front end. After that it was easy. I climbed the ladder, rolled over the end of the car, and dropped to the bottom.

"Jesus, Craig, that was downright stupid—us catching this freight on the fly. Thank God you saw this gondola."

He looked at me indignantly. "Speak fer yo'self, ol' buddy, I saw this gondola when Ah grabbed the iron on the box. Damn train was goin' so fast Ah couldn't wait any mo'. Had to grab that box then. That's what Ah was wavin' to y'all about."

I stretched out on the gentle slope of the gravel and took a deep breath. The sun was bright in a cloudless, deep-blue sky. Once out of the wind it was almost warm, but not quite.

Craig said, "When we took that curve back aways, Ah looked toward the caboose end. Ah really think we caught us a through freight. Must be a hunnerd cars on her."

That was good news in terms of making distance west, but the empty feeling in my stomach reminded me that all I had had to eat for almost two days now was one chocolate bar. Somehow we had to get some food.

"Let's take a look at my map, Craig. See if we can figure out where we're bound for."

I pulled my battered map out of my valise and we both studied it, sitting on the gravel, out of the icy wind.

"This is a highway map, but I think the Santa Fe main line more or less follows the same way. Looks like Williams is the next division, probably about twenty-five miles, then Ashfork."

I concentrated on the map. God willing, this freight was a hotshot that could take us all the way into California. It wasn't rolling all that fast through these mountains, about twenty miles an hour, I judged. There was only the one main line. We were bound to be shunted to a siding from time to time. I guessed that if we were lucky, and if this *was* a through freight, we should reach the Arizona-California border about dark—making allowance for the time spent on sidings. I made up my mind. After all, I had not told my companion that was my last two dollars.

"Craig, we're bound to be shunted to a siding somewhere along here. If we're lucky, and if there's a store anywhere near, I'll buy us some grub."

He looked at me in astonishment. "Y'all still got some dough? Ah thought that ride to Flagstaff done cleaned y'all out."

"Not quite. When we hit a siding, keep your eyes peeled for a store."

I pulled my blankets out and burrowed a space in the fine gravel more toward the center of the load. It was still out of the wind, and lying on my back wrapped in my blankets, my buttocks fitting the space I had squirmed into, I was warm and comfortable. I was just high enough on the load of gravel to see out over the side if I raised my head. Most of the time I looked up at the sky through the green forest which bordered the right-of-way. I could smell the clean scent of the mountain pines, and see the snow lightly covering the forest floor, when we traveled through a cut, with the mountains rising above us first on one side and then the other.

Thinking about home, feeling totally contented as the miles west went rolling along under us, I fell sound asleep. Last night the bench in the Flagstaff depot had effectively deprived me of sleep, and the effort of catching this freight, and finally getting back to this blessed gondola, had just about exhausted me.

I was awakened by Craig shaking my shoulder. "Man, y'all sho sawin' wood. Ah wish Ah could sleep like that. This heah freight's slowin' down. Ah think we's gettin' near a sidin'." He looked at me a bit anxiously. "Y'all *did* say to look out fer a store?"

I shook my head to clear the cobwebs. "That's right, partner, where do you think we are?"

"Dunno, but y'all been sleepin' more than an hour. Reckon we may be close to Williams."

I could feel the train slowing. The sound of the wheels crossing the rail joints was longer spaced now. Then we felt the jolts of the cars shoving into the couplings as the train slowed more and more.

We both saw it at the same time, a milepost with "Williams" painted on it. Staring toward the front end, we could see a maze of tracks ahead of us and then the engine veering off to the right. Far down the track was a switchman levering the switching section open for us.

Standing there, looking out over the side of the gondola, the cold air was like a dash of ice water in my face and I was immediately wide-awake.

Now we were just barely moving, and I felt the thump as our car passed over the switch and rolled onto the siding.

Craig was pointing excitedly. "Glory be, Russ, there's a lil' ol' store right up the tracks aways."

I looked at where he was staring. The highway was now paralleling the tracks. Sure enough, about a quarter mile away, just about where I figured we'd be stopped, there was a one-pump gas station and next to it a small grocery store, on the other side of the highway.

When our train finally came to a complete stop, we looked cautiously over the side, sighting down the length of the train in both directions. There wasn't a railroad bull in sight. Then we checked the other side. No one was on the ground. In this weather I was sure the brakemen and the conductor were warming themselves at the potbellied stove in the caboose. There was no work for them to be done on this siding, and a local switchman would switch us back onto the main line when our time came.

We listened carefully in the sudden stillness. Up ahead, about twenty-five cars, we could barely hear our engine huffing steam. We neither heard nor saw the through train, for which we had been shunted off.

I made up my mind. I hated to leave my bag and blankets in the gondola. You never knew just how long a freight would be parked on a siding. Still, it would be downright insulting to Craig to stow my blankets and take the bag with me—as if I was afraid he would steal it.

"Okay, Craig, I think we're going to be here at least fifteen minutes. You watch our stuff. I'm going to buy us some grub."

The look on his face said it clearly—wondering why he deserved the good fortune to be traveling with such a generous, moneyed partner.

Quickly I pulled myself to the top of the front end, scrambled down the ladder to the roadbed, and headed for the small country store Craig had spotted.

As I walked in I could smell the cheese and cold meats. I began to salivate and I could hear my stomach growl. I guessed I must be even hungrier than I had thought I was.

There was a kindly looking man standing behind the counter at the rear of the store, looking at me.

I pulled my dollar bill out of my pocket and laid it on the counter.

"Mister, I want a couple of orange Nehis and all of the food I can buy for ninety cents—like bread, cheese, and stuff like that."

"You off that freight, son?"

I hesitated a moment, but I felt sure I could trust this man.

"Yes, sir, you got any idea how long it's going to be stopped on that siding?"

"Least half an hour, maybe longer. You're waitin' for the passenger train out of L.A. to come through. All right, let's see what we got for you. How 'bout some Swiss cheese and ham, will that suit you?"

"Sure would, but that's kind of expensive isn't it?" I was looking for quantity now and had been thinking more in terms of baloney.

"Don't you worry about it." Then he took a large chunk of Swiss cheese and placed it on a slicing machine. Slice after slice I watched it mount on the sheet of wax paper as he expertly pushed the cheese to the blade, and pulled the holder back for the next slice.

"Gee, mister, how much is that?" I did like Swiss cheese, but I wanted some of that ham too, and I thought worriedly that he probably had already exhausted the ninety cents I had left after the two bottles of orange pop.

He looked at me again and switched off the slicing machine.

"Son, I told you not to worry about it, didn't I? I've been purty lucky here with this store. Got a nice trade, what with the loggers and the trainmen; once in a while a tourist stops. See a lot of you young fellas down on yer luck." He smiled. "That freight gets parked on that sidin' 'bout three times a week. I don't often have one of you boys come in here wantin' to buy food." He paused again and looked at me. "If they're not bums, and willin' to do a little work, none of them leave here hungry either. So I'm goin' to fix you up with enough ham and cheese to keep you goin' for a while."

I must have been looking at this good-hearted grocer much the way Craig had looked at me a little while ago. This world was full of generous people, I decided.

He returned to his slicing machine and I watched the mound of ham grow on the wax paper. All I could do was shake my head.

As he wrapped the cheese and ham, placing them in a brown paper bag with the bread and the two bottles, I suddenly thought of something.

"Isn't there a deposit on those bottles?"

"Yep, but don't worry about it. Don't expect you're likely to be back this way again for a while, are you?"

"Guess not. I just want you to know how much I appreciate this."

His tone was gentle. "That's all right, son, I can tell you're grateful. But I don't do it fer that. I feel purty lucky these days, and I like to help when I can. Where ya headin'?"

"I'm on my way home to San Francisco. You got any idea where that freight train's heading?"

"Sure do. One like it comes through three times a week. You'll be going through Ashfork, then Kingman, drop down to Needles in California, and across to Barstow."

"Barstow! There's nothing there."

"That's right, but what the railroad men tell me is that they break up this particular freight there. Part of it'll go on to L.A., part of it'll head north for Frisco and Oakland."

"Are there any railroad police here in Williams?" I was careful not to say "bulls," and I tried to make my question as casual as possible.

"You're not the first one who's asked me that. Not as far as I know. I gather from what the boys like you tell me it's tough east of here, that right?"

"How come they're not out here too?"

"I don't really know. I guess they figure they've pretty well cleaned off the freights back around Albuquerque. Then too, this time of year there's not too many fellas like you on those trains. Maybe they think the winter'll get what they miss. Anyway, I don't think you'll have much of a problem from here west. Still, I'd keep outta sight much as I can if I were you."

I picked up the bag and looked at him. "I can't tell you how much this means to me. All of this food—and what you just told me. Looks like I'll be back in California by tomorrow sometime."

"Good luck, son, and do be careful."

I stopped at a water faucet just off the right-of-way and had a long drink of water.

As I got near the gondola where Craig was waiting for me, I heard the drawn-out *whohoohoo* whistle of the eastbound passenger train. I quickened my pace and then called up to Craig.

"We got groceries here, partner. Give me a hand with this bag." I stood on the ladder and handed the bag up to him.

He took the bag from me and I dropped down into the car beside him.

"Man, what y'all got here?"

"Wait'll you see. A real nice guy owns that store. He gave me a lot more for my money than he had to. You like Swiss cheese and ham sandwiches?"

"Oh, Lordy, do I? The way Ah feel right how Ah could start chewin' on some of this gravel."

We tore open the loaf of bread and the wrappings of the cheese and ham. Craig's eyes widened when he saw the quantity. "Mah Lawd, Russ, y'all must 'a spent a fortune theah."

"Nope, that's just a buck's worth from a very nice guy."

I hadn't thought about a bottle opener, but Craig quickly snapped both tops off using his belt buckle.

Just as we bit into our first sandwiches, the passenger train came rushing by on our left, sounding the highball as it cleared our siding. A few moments later I heard the coupling clanks starting from the front end, and felt the jolt as our gondola started to move. The long drawn-out whistle from our engine hung in the clear air, and we were on our way again—heading west for California, not too far now.

# 43

We rolled ourselves in our blankets and stretched out on the gentle slope of gravel to watch the mountain scenery roll by. The rhythmic clickety-clack of the wheels on the tracks was a sound that soothed my spirit, a continuous clipping off of the miles westward toward home.

I looked up at the blue sky through the trees and saw an eagle soaring effortlessly, high above us, keeping pace with the train. His graceful shape was a dark silhouette etched against the azure heaven.

Craig broke into my reverie.

"Y'all evuh see any orange trees in California?"

"They don't have them much up north where I live, but my Aunt Doris has one in her backyard. Don't get any oranges from it you can eat, though. I was in Southern California once and I did see the orange groves. Why do you ask?"

"My Uncle Tim wrote and said that's all ya can see for miles 'round Pomona. Ah've nevuh seen one in my life. Jest sounds kinda innerestin'."

It was almost the first time we had had a chance to talk since we joined forces in Gallup. I learned that he came from a small farming community in southwestern Virginia. Times were tough there and Craig had decided to follow his Uncle Tim west to California. He was twenty years old, but this was the first time he had ever been away from home. He had never seen an ocean, and was fascinated by my tales of the sea as well as by my travels since last July.

We fell silent after awhile. I never would have guessed I could enjoy a ride on a freight this much, and a Santa Fe train at that!

It seemed as if we were pulling up a grade most of the time, but the slow speed of the train didn't bother me at all. I was relaxed, contented, and at peace with the world.

Craig looked at me and smiled. "Y'all evuh heah 'The Big Rock Candy Mountains', Russ?"

"Sure have, why?"

"Ah dunno. This here ride makes me think of it some way. It's so pleasant and easy here in the sun, this ol' freight sorta moseyin' along."

"You're right. Do you know the words? All I can think of is the 'lemonade springs and the bluebird sings'."

"Lemme try." He had a clear tenor voice and almost perfect pitch. And indeed he did know all the words. Somehow, winding through that beautiful mountain scenery, the old hobo ballad never sounded more right to me, the sound of the wheels on the tracks a perfect background. Snug and warm stretched out in my blankets, I took a deep breath as he reached the chorus and sang along with him.

> Oh the buzzing of the bees
>   in the cigarette trees round
>   the soda water fountains
> Where the lemonade springs
>   and the bluebird sings
> In the Big Rock Candy Mountains

Then Craig finished the rest of it himself, singing of a land so fair and bright, where the boxcars all are empty, and the sun shines every day.

I had never really reflected on the meaning of the words before. As I thought about them, I realized the song was not a celebration of the life of a hobo in any way. It was a wistful paean to the promised land—cast in the terms most meaningful to a Knight of the Road—blind railroad bulls, empty boxcars, and jails made of tin where you can bust right out again.

It was about one in the afternoon when we were shunted to a siding just east of Ashfork. We were almost out of the mountains now. In the far distance the pale brown of an arid landscape reflected the light.

We saw a water faucet just off the right-of-way and, after a good long drink, filled the now-empty pop bottles. Then we climbed back aboard our gondola, and I studied my map.

"Looks like the Santa Fe's been following the same way as Route 66, Craig. I don't think it's likely to change now."

He was peering over my shoulder, studying the map with me.

"That guy back at the store done tell y'all we oughta roll right into Barstow on this freight, didn't he?"

"That's right. Let me try to figure the distance." I did some mental arithmetic, adding the miles between towns as shown on my highway map. "Looks like it's a hundred miles to Kingman from here, 'bout sixty miles south to Needles, and then a pretty straight shot to Barstow for another hundred and fifty miles or so."

"That's some more than three hunnerd miles, Russ. How long y'all figger it'll take us to make Barstow?"

"Well, it looks like we're just about out of the mountains now. The engineer can really crank it up if he wants to. If we just rolled steady, I'd guess we could make it in about seven hours. Probably three times that long the way we get shoved off on these sidings. Probably some time tomorrow morning."

The same thought was in both our minds, and I spoke it aloud.

"I figure we got enough grub for four more sandwiches, Craig. We have one each tonight sometime, and then one each tomorrow morning. There seems to be a water faucet somewhere on every one of these sidings, and we got these pop bottles to fill. We'll make it in good shape."

Craig looked at me again, gratitude shining on his face. To my relief, he didn't make any reference to my generosity this time. Just shook his head and murmured, "Gonna miss y'all, ol' buddy, when we split up."

"I'm going to miss you too, Craig, but we'll connect up again some day."

We both knew how improbable *that* was, and both of us somewhat embarrassed by the sentimentality, fell silent.

A moment later, we heard the highball from our engine and the jolting clanks of the couplings starting from the head end, and moving toward the caboose end, as we rolled onto the main line west.

Almost immediately, it seemed, we were crossing arid desert. We had left the Arizona mountains behind us and the somber landscape had a quieting effect on both of us.

Craig had not followed the same route I had across Texas, but he had crossed much of the same type of wasteland I had, only farther north.

We rattled along in silence for about half an hour and then, as usual, Craig spoke up.

"Man, Ah *nevuh* seen country like this. Even makes ol' Texas look purty!"

I should have kept my mouth shut, but getting so close to my home state affected my judgment.

"You're right, but we're getting pretty close to California now. It's bound to get better then."

"Y'all really think so?"

"Well, I've never been in Needles or Barstow, but it's got to look better than this." It was the next morning before I realized how wrong *that* belief was.

The hours passed more slowly but, whenever the barren landscape started to depress me too much, I reminded myself that I was on the last leg home now. Three times we were switched off onto sidings and, finally, we were in Kingman about six that night. The freight was shunted to a siding for hours and I began to worry about whether this was in fact a through freight to Barstow.

When darkness fell, the bitter cold came with it and I really started to worry.

"What do you think, Craig? Do you suppose the man could have been wrong—about this freight not breaking up until we get to Barstow, I mean?"

"Ah jest dunno. They not been doin' any switchin'. This heah ol' freight's still made up the way we caught her in Flagstaff. Haven't seen anything else headin' west. Ah think we bettuh stick with this gondola."

"You're probably right. But I don't want to try sleeping until we know one way or the other."

Craig spoke up again. I could just barely see his face in the darkness, but I caught a flash of his white teeth as he grinned at me.

"Ah don' want y'all to take this wrong, Russ, but Ah think we buttuh double up our blankets and bed down together, or we not gonna make it in this heah weathuh."

"You're right." I grinned back at him. "Even if you *were* a jocker, no one could get it up in this weather!"

I could hear him chuckle. "Let's get the gravel leveled out heah at the front end, roll up and try to get warm."

Using our feet and hands, we got a level area in the gravel spread out as near to the front end as we could. Then we put our four blankets together and lay down under them, side by side, to wait it out. It wasn't the warmest I had ever been in my life, but the difference was remarkable. The warmth of Craig's body and the doubling of the blankets really helped, and I was sure we would survive the night.

After an eternity we heard the long whistle of our engine and felt the train begin to move. Laboriously, I dug my watch out of my pocket and, as we moved under some yard lights, I saw that it was just 10 P.M.

"Is it okay if we sleep now, ol' buddy? Ah been layin' heah tryin' to figger whethuh them damn benches in Flagstaff or this heah' gravel's the most comfortable bed Ah've evuh had."

"Well, I tell you, Craig, that was a hell of an idea you had about doubling up on our blankets. Now that we're moving again I'd pick this gravel over those damn benches any time. Least we can stretch out here. Let's try to get some sleep."

I was awakened three times during the long night as our freight rolled off onto a siding and clanked to a halt.

The last time it seemed as if we stopped almost as long as we had in Kingman, but I was past worrying about it then.

Dawn was just breaking as we finally started to move. Craig was sleeping soundly, and I eased my way out from under our blankets as carefully as possible so as not to awaken him.

Away from the warmth of our burrow, I was trembling almost uncontrollably, but I clambered to the far end of the gondola and relieved myself on the gravel.

The sun came up in an explosion of scarlet and yellow across the eastern sky, with some long narrow clouds on the distant horizon reflecting the spectacular colors. Balancing with the motion of the train, I suddenly heard a different sound beneath me. We were crossing a railroad bridge and my heart leaped. I peered over the side and, sure enough, it was the Colorado River beneath us, now reflecting the light of the rising sun. California was just on the other side.

# 44

As I stood there gazing at that beautiful sunrise, shivering in the cold morning air but with elation in my heart, I heard Craig clambering over the gravel toward me.

He was coming to the caboose end of the gondola for the same reason I had earlier, and I grinned as I heard him mutter. "Man, it's so damn cold my pecker done shriveled up. Can't hardly find it!" Then I heard a long sigh of relief as his water splattered on the gravel, small sounds against the background noise of the train.

"Where are we, Russ?"

"Crossing the Colorado River, going to be in California pretty soon."

I saw him stare at the moonscape we were heading into, as the freight rumbled across the bridge, and shake his head once.

"Y'all *did* say it was gonna be purtier heah?"

"Look, I thought it was, but I was wrong okay?" I was annoyed at the implied criticism of my home state, and more than a little chagrined at the arid vista of California stretching to the western horizon. I thought of the Okies who had migrated to the Golden State in great numbers, fleeing the Dust Bowl, not too many years before. Many of them were still coming west in their beat-up jalopies, and the great majority came over this Route 66. I wondered what *they* thought of their first glimpse of the promised land. At least I knew that somewhere, northwest of this godforsaken terrain, the green mountains of the Coast Range ended at the San Francisco Peninsula, with the beautiful, sparkling bay at the foot of the precipitous hills of my white city. I felt a need to justify myself, and explain all this to my obviously disappointed traveling companion.

"Come on, Craig, let's get back in the lee of the front end and get some chow."

We made our way over the load to where we had made our bed the night before. I sank down to a seat on the gravel, pulled one of the pop bottles filled with water out of the gravel where we had placed it, and tilted it up for a drink. Nothing happened. Puzzled, I brought it down and studied it. Right at the top it was frozen solid. Craig was watching me.

"What y'all doin', Russ?"

"Trying to get a drink of water, but it's all ice at the top."

"Man, Ah knew it was cold las' night, but Ah nevuh thought it was *that* cold!"

The sun was up now and shining directly onto our open-topped gondola. I moved up the gravel and worked the pop bottle into it so it stood upright in the sunshine.

"I tell you, Craig, I didn't know it was that cold either. This sun feels good now, though. I wasn't all that thirsty anyway. Don't think it'll take very long to thaw out in the sun."

I sat down again and pulled the brown paper bag of food out of my valise. There were just four slices of bread left, but fortunately the remaining Swiss cheese and ham was more than enough for two great sandwiches.

I spread the pieces of bread out on the paper bag and, even though I had paid for this repast, I was careful to let Craig observe just what I was doing. The Swiss cheese was divided into two equal stacks, and then I did the same with the ham. All the time he was watching me hungrily. Finally, I placed a mound of cheese and one of ham on one slice of bread, placed the other on top of it, and mashed the sandwich together so it could be eaten. At that, it compressed just barely to a size that could be bitten into.

"No point in trying to save any more, Craig. We should be in Barstow in four or five hours now, and this'll last us till then."

He didn't quite snatch the sandwich out of my hand, but it was a third gone before I had mine assembled and took my first satisfying bite.

By the time I finished my sandwich, the ham and cheese had made me really thirsty. I glanced at the bottle and I could see the water in it jiggling with the movement of the train. I pulled it out and had a long satisfying drink. Then I passed the bottle to Craig and he did the same.

We had left the railroad bridge behind now, and were heading north toward Needles, paralleling the Colorado River. I stood up and looked ahead over the side of the gondola. In the far distance I could see a green oasis. That had to be Needles.

Then I wrapped myself in my blankets and stretched out in the sun.

"You know, Craig, that was pretty dumb—me thinking it was going to be better just as soon as we reached California. I knew there was a desert down this way, I just didn't know there was this much of it."

"That's okay, ol' buddy. Can't blame y'all fer this country." Then a bit anxiously he said, "Y'all think mah uncle was givin' it to me straight—'bout them orange trees, I mean?"

"Like I told you, I've only been down there once, but he's not lying. There are miles and miles of oranges groves, all laid out in rows. Real green and pretty. Up north, where I live, we don't have the orange groves, but we've got other orchards. In the spring the blossoms are beautiful, and San Francisco Bay is something else! Sure wish you'd seen that part of the state first instead of this."

It suddenly occurred to me that Craig still had aways to go from Barstow to Pomona. Not nearly as far as I had to travel, but he was just about flat broke.

"You got some way to reach your uncle if you get hung up?"

"Sho' have. He's got a telephone *and* a car. He done wrote and said if I get within a hunnerd miles of Pomona, jest call him collect and he'll come fetch me. Ah still got two nickels left and Ah only need one. All Ah hafta do is find me a pay telephone."

"Let's take a look at my map."

We both studied it and I could hear the excitement in his voice. "Man, it looks like it's jest 'bout eighty miles from Barstow to Pomona. If this ol' gondola gets hooked up fer that part of the country, Ah want to ride it as fer as Ah can, so's not to put Uncle Tim to any mo' trouble than Ah need to. But it sho' looks like Ah got it made now!"

I think I was just about as relieved as he was. I had been worrying about him, knowing how broke he was. For some reason, neither one of us had laid out the last leg for him when we were studying my map yesterday in Ashfork.

My moral responsibility for Craig was finally coming to an end.

About half an hour later we rolled on to the inevitable siding just east of Needles. With the freight stopped there in the desert sun, we were finally warm and comfortable, rolled up in our blankets. I guessed that the temperature still wasn't that much above freezing.

The town of Needles looked literally like an oasis—a swatch of greenery resting on the desert floor about a mile ahead from our siding.

We were only on the siding about twenty minutes when a west-bound passenger train came roaring by on the main line. A few minutes later, we began to move.

Both of us started at the sight of a hobo rolling over the end of the gondola just as we were picking up speed. When he dropped into the car and stood up, he looked as surprised to see us as we were to see him.

"Well, howdy, didn't think there were any other 'bos on this freight."

I spoke up. "Far as we can tell, we're the only ones on this train. Been on it since Ashfork yesterday morning."

"This time of year, I'm not surprised. This here gondola's damn near the only car on this freight you can ride without freezin' to death." He shoved out his hand. "My name's Jack, where ya bound?"

"Glad to know you, Jack. My name's Russ. This is my partner, Craig. I'm heading for San Francisco. Craig's on his way to Pomona."

He settled down comfortably on the gravel. He had a large blanket roll, sturdily tied with cord. He was about thirty years old, with a weathered complexion, and friendly brown eyes. His hand-clasp was strong and firm. His Levi's and denim jacket were worn, but clean and not threadbare at all. He was strongly built, and projected an air of quiet competence.

"Well, Craig's on the right train. Won't quite make it, but San Berdoo's just a hop and a jump away from Pomona."

"You traveled this line before, Jack?"

"Every year 'bout this time. I'll be pickin' oranges in Southern Cal not too long from now."

I could see Craig's eyes light up when he heard "oranges".

"Did y'all say pickin' oranges?"

"That's right. I been workin' for the same grower the last three years. Usually come through a bit earlier, 'fore it gets so damn cold on this desert."

I spoke up again. "A guy back in Arizona told me they'd break up this freight in Barstow. Is that right?"

"Sometimes they do. Sometimes they don't."

He grinned briefly. "Word I have is that this one'll stay made up right into San Berdoo. That's why I been waitin' for this one rattler."

I reached in my bag for my map and pulled it out. "Looks like San Bernardino is only about twenty miles from Pomona. Is that right?"

Jack nodded. Studying my map I asked him, "Is there much in the way of freights heading north out of Barstow?"

"Yeah, should be at least one every mornin'. I've made that run quite a few times when I head north for the spring fruit pickin'. But I tell you, Russ, you think you been cold here. Just wait'll you go through Tehachapi this time of year from what I've been told." He shook his head. Then he brightened. "Come to think of it, I've always found a lot of empty boxes on them freights headin' north out of Barstow. Should be okay. I wouldn't try it, even in a gondola this time of year, if I was you. You ought to be able to catch an empty boxcar though."

Somewhat relieved I replaced my map in my valise. "How are the railroad bulls in Barstow?"

"No problem right now. I think they figure the weather'll take care of any 'bo damn fool enough to ride a freight through this country in the winter."

We were rolling through Needles now, and then the freight really began to pick up speed on the long straight tracks heading west.

We all stretched out comfortably on the gravel in the sun. It was warm enough now, out of the wind at the end of the gondola. The sun was shining down on us, and Jack didn't have to break his roll to get his blankets out.

I was a bit dismayed by his grim reference to the weather going through the range of mountains, between Barstow and the San Joaquin Valley, on the other side of Tehachapi.

Jack was quite willing to give us the benefit of any information he could but, other than that, he simply wasn't much of a talker. The miles jolted along beneath us and we rolled steadily westward.

We were shunted to a siding only once, for about thirty minutes, and then, when the main line cleared, we chugged west again.

Jack broke the silence once.

"We should be hittin' Barstow in about an hour now."

"They won't be rolling this freight right through a main division like that will they, Jack?" I was in no mood to jump off another freight on the fly.

"Hell, no. This freight's goin' to be parked there for awhile. I'll let you know when we get in where to look for a rattler north."

My mind relieved, I lay back on the gravel and my thoughts drifted back over the trip from New York. I pulled out my diary to leaf through it and was startled to learn that today was November 24, 1938—Thanksgiving Day. I had simply lost track of time the last few days, but I was able to place the date from my diary.

It was then about one o'clock in the afternoon and, like metal to a magnet, my thoughts were pulled to my aunt's home at 85 Justin Drive in San Francisco, where my aunts, uncles, cousins, and assorted relatives—all twenty-five or more of them—would be gathering just about now. I could see her husband, Mike Phillips, "Pop" to everyone in the family, holding forth on a political issue. He would be sharply challenged, most probably by my Uncle Herb Hofvendahl, not to mention my Uncle Jerry Sleight. As much as I loved them all, I recognized their contentiousness, but remembered as well their warmth and generosity. Suddenly, I was really missing them.

I could smell the aroma of the mounds of white meat and dark meat, expertly carved by Pop and served on a huge platter. I could taste the delicious dressing, a specialty of my aunt's. My reverie had me all but drooling, and then I returned to reality—riding a load of gravel in a gondola on a freight train, jolting over the desert approaching Barstow, California.

For a moment I was feeling a bit sorry for myself, and then I thought about Jack, and the thousands of men like him on the road. I wondered how long it had been since he had enjoyed a family feast on Thanksgiving and whether he ever would again.

It wouldn't be long to Barstow now and, I realized, another parting. So many good-byes I had said to so many good people— Fritz Hoffman and his family on his lonely farm in Saskatchewan, and Finn Bering at that jail in Portal, North Dakota. The memory of that farewell, and how close I had come to seeing Finn at Ellis Island, still caused a wrench that was almost physical. I thought about Sally, and how genuinely concerned she had been about my bruised torso. I felt a warmth, and a stirring, thinking about her soft hands applying the liniment to my aching back and what *that* led to. I remembered Howard Schroeder with his generous, open, good nature, and how he had shared his provisions with me; how overwhelmed he was setting foot on a Great Lakes steamer when I introduced him to a ship. Edie, and what she had taught me, was a part of me. I still ached remembering that good-bye. Izzy Cohen, and how he had appreciated my hard work. I recalled now with gratitude what that brief interlude on his Connecticut farm had meant to me, not the least of which was Rebecca Cohen's wonderful food. I thought of working with George Adams at the dry-cleaning plant in Harlem, what a truly decent person he was, and how we had enjoyed that fried chicken together. Sheila Lessin was totally different from Sally and Edie but, in her own way, she too was unique. My mind ran on thinking about these people who had touched my life—too briefly it seemed, but I would never forget one of them.

Soon I would be saying good-bye to Craig. As I thought about that, I glanced over to where he was stretched out on the gravel slope. I was surprised to see him looking at me intently.

"We'all goin' to be splittin' up purty soon, ol' buddy. Ah won't nevuh forget what y'all done fer me, Russ."

I was embarrassed by his obvious emotion and the fact that he truly meant it. I remembered something I had read once about the American Indian. If a brave saved a fellow warrior's life in battle, then *he* had the responsibility for that life he had preserved from then on.

There certainly wasn't that kind of bond between us, but the help I gave him when he needed it was critical and he realized it.

As the train started to slow Jack stood up and looked over the side of the gondola.

"This is Barstow, boys. Just thank God you don't have to live here!"

Looking forward to the maze of tracks fanning out ahead of us across the arid landscape, I could see one set of tracks heading off in what I judged was a northwesterly direction. Jack saw where I was looking.

"That's where your freight'll be headin' out on, Russ. Think we're goin' to roll by it apiece, but they'll be making up that freight somewhere 'bout this afternoon and tonight. I'd get off hereabouts if I was you."

We were only doing about two or three miles an hour. It would be simple to drop off now.

My valise was already packed and I had the carrying line on. I slung it across my back and turned to Craig.

Jack was watching us. He was an understanding man, and he

looked at us sympathetically. "Don't worry, Russ, I'll make sure your buddy here gets to Pomona."

Craig grasped my extended right hand in both of his and clasped it hard. He tried to say something and then he turned away quickly. I wasn't doing any better myself at talking.

A moment later I was on top of the end of the gondola, then halfway down the outside ladder on the front end. I stood there for a moment, then called out, "Good luck, Craig!" He turned and looked at me, and tried to grin. I could just barely hear him. "You too, ol' buddy."

I hung on the ladder on the side and dropped easily off the gondola that had carried us so far.

I stood there watching the train rolling away from me. Craig was on top of the load of gravel now—waving at me. I waved back, and then the freight curved slowly to the left and he disappeared from my sight.

# 45

That last sandwich this morning had been most satisfying, but I wanted to provision myself for what lay ahead.

I sat down on the ground and took my last three dollar bills from my shoe. In one way I felt downright affluent being this close to home now, and with that kind of bankroll left. Then again, those three singles seemed rather flimsy to me, and I sure couldn't risk losing any one of them. I thrust the bills deep into the right-hand pocket of my jeans and trudged into town.

Barstow, in the best of times, could not be described as a booming metropolis. Today it looked absolutely deserted, and then I remembered it was Thanksgiving Day. There was only one grocery store I could see, and it was locked up tight. I saw a coffee shop down the street, also closed and dark. I hadn't felt too hungry until I confronted the locked doors of the store, and the closed coffee shop, and realized that it would be some time tomorrow, probably some-where north of Barstow, before I could buy food again. That realization made me ravenous immediately, but there was no help for it.

I retraced my way back to the yard and across the maze of tracks to the far side of the rails bearing north, which Jack had pointed out to me. About two hundred yards away, I saw a figure sitting on the ground, his back to me resting against a bedroll.

As I got near him I realized, somewhat to my surprise, that he was a young black man. It dawned on me that he was the first black I had seen on the road since I left New York.

He got to his feet as I reached him, and I could see him eyeing me rather warily.

I spoke first. "Hi, you heading north by any chance?"

He nodded without saying a word.,

"You got any idea when there'll be a freight out of here for Mojave?"

"Sho do."

He was taller than me by a couple of inches, with a strong, muscular build. His complexion was a rich brown. He had regular features, and kind-looking brown eyes, but he sure wasn't talking much.

I shoved out my hand.

"My name's Russ. I'm heading for San Francisco. Where you bound for?"

He hesitated a moment before grasping my hand and then, when we shook, I could feel the strength of his grip and the calluses on his hand.

Finally he smiled and it lit up his face.

"Mah name's Henry, Russ. Real glad to meet y'all. Ah'm headin' fo' Fresno. Got a brothuh up theah."

"So when's the next freight out of this place?"

"Dey tell me theahs a way freight gonna be makin' up in 'bout half hour. Thas what Ah'm waitin' fo'."

It turned out that Henry was right. A short Santa Fe freight, not more than twenty-five cars and a caboose, was gradually switched together and coupled up not too far from where we waited.

There were at least five empty boxcars, and not a railroad bull in sight.

"Looks like we're going to have this rattler to ourselves, Henry. Let's climb in one of those empties."

About half an hour after we were aboard, we heard the highball from our engine and were on our way.

It was about sixty miles to Mojave across the flat desert land-scape, and we made it in less than two hours with no stops. Jack had told me that the Southern Pacific railroad ran numerous freights out of Mojave over to Bakersfield, and from there many of the trains rolled north up the San Joaquin Valley. As easy as the Santa Fe had been since we caught that freight out of Flagstaff, probably due to the freezing weather, the Southern Pacific had a reputation, much like the Great Northern, of not making life miserable for hoboes. I guessed that it had something to do with the same type of agricultural-economic factors that operated in the prairie states. The farmers needed the transients to work the wheat and other harvests, the railroad hauled the crops, and those freight trains were the only practical means for the needed workers to get from one location to another. Here in California, the vast stands of orchards required fruit pickers and the Southern Pacific, by tacit understanding, transported a large number of them.

I hoped to make it from Bakersfield to somewhere near Stockton and then catch a Western Pacific freight into Oakland.

Henry and I sat back from the open door of the boxcar, as much away from the freezing wind as possible, with our backs against the side of the car. He sat on his bedroll, and I sat on my valise to absorb some of the jolts as we rattled along over the roadbed.

He didn't volunteer anything but he did answer any question I asked.

"Where you from, Henry?"

"Yazoo City, Mississippi."

"Where?"

This time he really drawled it out. "Yaaazooo, man, ain't y'all nevuh heah of dat place?"

"Sure haven't. Whereabouts is it?"

"Mississippi delta. Lots of cotton grown dere."

I learned that he had followed almost exactly the same route I had. He and his older brother in Fresno were the last two children in a large family. His father had sharecropped cotton until his death several years ago. Then, after his death, Henry's mother had gotten a job cooking for a prosperous white family in Yazoo City. Henry had continued to labor at farm work in the rich delta fields but, urged on by his mother who sounded like a very determined lady, he had saved every dollar he could until he figured he had enough to stake him for the trip west. Much like George Adams, as strong as the attachment was to his birthplace in Mississippi, he was determined to escape the South.

He didn't complain, and I assumed a great deal from the little he did tell me, but I gathered that there simply was no point in a black man trying to hitchhike. He had made it all the way from New Orleans by freight. He confirmed what I knew from my own observation. There *were* very few blacks on the road. Ironically enough, it seemed that the lower the economic level, the more bigots there were. This must have been a lonely trip for him, always keeping to himself, alert, in the South at least, not to use the wrong water fountain, avoiding police of any description.

We had a lot to talk about, having traveled the same route, although it had taken him about three times longer than it had me.

"When you were in El Paso, did you cross the bridge and go into Juárez?"

He looked at me with a big grin. "Ah sho did. Dey don' seem to mind cullid folks down dere. Ah..." He broke off abruptly.

Little by little I was figuring out things. It just made good sense for Henry to be very cautious meeting any strangers, and particularly white ones. I guessed that my speech and my proffered handshake had convinced him that I was not a white supremacist. The way he grinned, when I mentioned Juárez, was a distinctly male communication. I was sure he had entertained himself, in one of the back streets of Juárez, exactly the same way I had with one of those pretty señoritas. Still, he didn't know me *that* well, and he was not going to take a chance on my reaction to his telling me about a sexual experience with a white woman.

I tried to prod him. "You what?"

"Uh, Ah smoked one of dem marywanna cigarettes."

This really shocked me. I had never talked to anyone who had taken this first irreversible step on the slippery descent to degradation. Mrs. Ryan's dire admonitions raced through my mind.

"Marijuana!"

Henry nodded, his eyes half-closed, a dreamy smile on his face. "Yassuh! Sho did. Mattuh fact, Ah done bought five of dem tokes. Gottem in mah roll."

"Jesus, Henry, what was it like?"

I think my horrified fascination surprised him. He was twenty-three years old and, growing up in a black, deep-South environment, I am sure he was, in some ways, much more experienced than I was in terms of women and hard liquor.

He looked at me with mild surprise. "Made me feel kinda dreamy lak. Sorta floatin' happy. Better'n dat white lightnin' Ah drunk back home. Sho no hangovuh from dat lil' ol' smoke."

"Yeah, but..." My convictions were being shaken. I had started to ask him if he didn't feel the grip of this addiction; if he didn't realize he would soon be a dope fiend. Then, the realization that this wouldn't be very polite, combined with Henry's obviously relaxed acceptance of his dangerous foray into drugs, stopped me.

Then *he* prodded me. "Y'all was sayin'?"

"Well, I just wondered how it made you feel," I finished rather lamely, since he had already told me that.

"Lak Ah said, sorta floatin'." Then he remembered something else. "One thing, it sho made me hongry fer sweets. Ah bought fo' candy bars aftuh Ah had dat smoke. Jes chomped em all down!"

It was about four in the afternoon when we rolled into Mojave. I could see the mountains with the snow on them, northwest, beyond Tehachapi, in the clear air.

As the freight slowed we saw what passed for a hobo jungle in these parts. There was a campfire site with a rough tripod above it and a sizeable stack of firewood nearby. Henry saw it the same time I did.

"We jes find some watuh now and Ah'll cook us up dinnah..." He broke off and pointed to a water faucet just off the right-of-way.

"Come on, Henry, let's get off here. This'll make a good camp for tonight. She's just barely rolling."

We eased off the boxcar and walked over to the campsite.

"Ah'm sho glad whoevuh was heah rustled up dis much wood. Ah can feel dis cold in mah bones."

I watched, fascinated, as he broke open his roll and sorted out cooking utensils and food. He was fully equipped, and again I thought of how self-reliant he had to be to travel, separated by the color of his skin from the normal camaraderie and sharing of the road.

"All Ah got is taters and mush, but it'll fill us up. If y'all don' mind, fetch us some watuh." He handed me a gallon container with a wire carrying handle that had been fashioned from a lard can.

I walked over to the water faucet, filled the can, and returned. By the time I got back, Henry had a good fire started and soon it was a roaring blaze. It felt good facing it, but my back seemed to be turning to ice.

Henry took care of everything. He peeled the potatoes and

asked me to hand him the water so he could boil them a bit before frying them.

The water had been sitting away from the fire, not more than five minutes, and when I picked up the can I saw a thin film of ice on the top. Henry saw it when I handed the can to him.

"Lawdy, knew it's cold, but man…" He looked a bit anxious, and I knew he was thinking the same thing I was—if it was below freezing in daylight, what was it going to be like after dark.

As had become my way of addressing problems, I put it out of my mind for now.

Henry's provisions were remarkably complete. He had a can of olive oil to fry the potatoes in, and he had brown sugar for the mush.

Sitting by the fire that food tasted exceptionally good and it sure was filling. After we had eaten I got another can of water for heating over the fire and cleaning our eating gear.

Then I pulled the diary out of my valise. Henry looked at me curiously.

"What y'all got theah?"

"It's just a diary I began keeping since I left New York. I figure it'll be easier to show my aunt this than to tell her about the trip."

He shook his head, but was too polite to comment on the strange traveling companion he found himself with.

My fingers were almost too numb to hold my pencil, but it seemed to me that this holiday required some acknowledgment. For Thursday, November 24, 1938, I wrote:

*Had fried spuds and oatmeal mush for dinner. So cold, any liquid set away from the fire freezes almost immediately. This is the first Thanksgiving I can ever remember that I haven't had dinner with the folks. Oh well, I'm thankful that at least I'm in California and not too far from home, but I can think of better places to celebrate Thanksgiving than over a campfire in the Mojave Desert.*

# 46

We sat as close to the fire as we could as night fell. The stars in that clear cold sky looked like diamonds set against a dark-blue velvet backdrop. The wind was not strong, but it was steady, and it felt as if the chilled, icy air was being forced through my clothing and deep into my body.

I was genuinely worried now. The temperature, at below freezing in daylight, felt as if it had dropped another ten degrees with darkness. We would not survive the night out here on the desert floor.

I could see some empty boxcars spotted not too far from our fire. Occasionally, a switch engine nudged another car into the growing line. The collection of railroad cars was on a track at the outside edge of the yard, and some distance from the single set of rails bearing north toward Tehachapi. There was no real way to know whether this was the train we were looking for until a caboose was coupled onto one end of the train or the other. I felt sure that if the caboose were hooked on the end to my left as I faced the tracks, placing the head end closest to the tracks heading north, this would be our freight.

As I saw the switch engine far down the yard nudging a caboose along, I realized that our salvation lay inside one of those empty boxcars—if this was in fact our train bound for Tehachapi.

I was standing by then, staring hard at the approaching switch engine. Henry was, if anything, even more miserable than I was. While it got cold in the Mississippi delta country in winter, he had told me, it was never anything like this.

"What y'all lookin' at, Russ, jes dat ol' switch engine?"

"We're not going to last the night out here in this weather. If that's our freight for Tehachapi, I sure as hell know what we're going to do."

I think the cold had numbed our reactions and speech more than I realized. He did not immediately say anything. Laboriously, and slowly, he got to his feet and moved over to where I was standing. He stared at the approaching engine and caboose.

"What we'all goin' to do iff'n dat's de freight we want?"

"We're going to find us an empty box and, if we're lucky, one with some packing cardboard still in it. If we get in, and get the doors closed almost all the way, it should be at least some warmer than out here."

I was thinking about something else too. I remembered what a remarkable difference it had made last night when Craig and I had doubled up on our blankets and shared our bodily warmth. Henry and I could do the same tonight, and it could save our lives, but it wasn't quite that simple. I put the problem out of my mind for the moment.

I kept staring at the caboose being shoved along and finally I knew—this was our freight. About three hundred yards down from where the assembled cars were standing, the caboose rolled over a switch, pushed by the yard engine, and up the tracks to the far end of the train. Almost gently it seemed, from this distance, we watched the caboose coupled into position. That train was a Southern Pacific freight bound, sooner or later, for Tehachapi and Bakersfield.

"Come on, Henry, grab your roll and let's find us a boxcar with some cardboard in it."

Slowly we walked toward the line of cars. There was no feeling in my feet by then, and I was afraid that I would stumble over something and really hurt myself.

The doors to the first boxcar were open. As nearly as I could tell in the darkness, there was no dunnage at all—wood, cardboard, or anything else in it. It was absolutely empty. The second car was the same. Henry was walking ahead of me and reached the third car first. We really weren't worried about railroad bulls at all now, but there was no point in asking for trouble. Henry kept his voice low, but I could sense his excitement.

"Lawdy, Russ, dere's lots of cawdbawd heah. Dat's gotta hep to keep us warm!"

Both of the doors were about half open and I could see what he meant. Large, random pieces of cardboard were strewn about on the floor.

We climbed into the car and, as always, the sheer immensity of the inside of an empty boxcar impressed me. Our quiet voices echoed and the ends of the car disappeared in the darkness.

We decided to close one of the doors completely and leave the other open about three feet. This would avoid the draft of air created by the two open doors opposite each other. Leaving one door partially open would make it certain that the noise would awaken us if any train crew started to slide it shut and trap us inside.

We stacked a pallet of cardboard pieces in the middle of the floor and just back from the partly open door. It was then about nine o'clock, and I decided to bring up the subject of us sharing our blankets.

I knew very well what my friend from Virginia would think of such a sleeping arrangement. Craig was one of the most pleasant, companionable, and easy-going persons I had met on the road. Yet I knew how horrified he would be at the very thought of rolling up in his blankets with a black man, or that his friend Russ would do so.

Whatever Craig thought, or would think, was only a background for the concern I felt now about how Henry would react when I suggested it.

It seemed apparent that he trusted me, and we *had* done a lot of talking. He had fed me this Thanksgiving Day, and I hoped he thought of me as a friend. I certainly considered him to be my friend. Then, there was that other thing—I smiled as I remembered how Craig had suggested that we roll up together in our blankets.

Standing by the open boxcar door, I could just barely make out his features.

"Henry, I don't want you to get the wrong idea." I deliberately used just about the same words Craig had, "I would a hell of a lot rather roll up with one of those señoritas in Juárez than a big lug like you. But if we don't double up in our blankets, even out of the wind in here, we could still freeze to death."

There was a momentary silence. Then, to my relief, he grinned at me.

"Sho nuff, Russ. Dat's a good idea."

So we wrapped up in our four blankets on the pallet of cardboard, and the bulk of Henry's body created even more warmth than Craig's.

I drifted off to sleep thinking about what Craig would say if he could see me now.

It was about five o'clock in the morning, and still dark, when I was awakened by the clanking jolt as the couplings stretched from the head end first, the noise moving to the caboose end, and we were on our way. The long whistle of our engine sounded lonely and mournful out here on the Mojave Desert, but my heart leaped. This was just about the last leg now.

Once we were moving I was wide-awake, and so was Henry. We rolled the door back a bit further on the right side of the car as the sun came up in the east. It was a spectacular dawn of long gray streaks of cloud, separated by pale yellow horizontal banners, topped with flaming crimson that stretched across the eastern sky. We moved the cardboard to the closed door on the left side of the car, and sat there with our backs against it, wrapped in our blankets, watching the landscape go by.

We rolled out of Mojave at about forty miles an hour and then, within minutes, we slowed measurably and our train was laboring up a grade. I stood up once to look out forward, saw the mountains ahead of us, and realized we would be climbing all the way to Tehachapi. Soon, the entire landscape was blanketed with a mantle of white snow. It didn't look too deep, but it softened the contours of this rugged, barren country and, from the interior of the boxcar, the soft, clean vista seemed to actually relax and rest my eyes.

We climbed for about two-and-a-half hours, grinding up a grade that had remarkably few horseshoe curves. It was a steadily rising grade, curving around the mountains occasionally, but mainly our freight was chugging steadily upward.

The landscape was a pristine white now, an untouched blanket of snow, and we were both feeling the cold. Still, out of the wind inside the boxcar, it wasn't too bad, and I kept reminding myself that we would be in Bakersfield in the San Joaquin Valley in just a matter of hours.

It was about 8 A.M. when we rolled by a milepost too quickly to read it from inside the boxcar. I jumped up, leaned out the door and read "Summit" on the sign disappearing from my view down the track.

I knew almost nothing about the topography of this part of my home state. Still, I knew in general terms that Bakersfield was located on the floor of the valley and, if we had just crossed the summit of this mountain pass, it had to be all downhill from now on.

Just a few moments later, we were switched onto a siding to permit a long, eastbound, heavily loaded freight to clear us on the main line. We were only there fifteen minutes and then we were on our way again.

About ten minutes after that, we rolled slowly by a yellow and brown painted depot. "Tehachapi - Elevation 3793 feet" was painted in white letters on the sign on the side of the building.

It seemed as if we started to descend almost immediately. The grade down from Tehachapi was very steep for a railroad, and now we went through one switchback turn after another. Some were tremendous, sweeping horseshoe curves when, even on this relatively short train, we could see our own caboose on the curve behind us through the open door of our car, as it rolled along down the mountain.

About ten o'clock in the morning I could feel the air just a bit warmer than it had been. Maybe it only seemed that way because the snow had just about disappeared from the ground, but obviously we were beginning to get close to the foot of the mountains now.

I thought of the food I had intended to buy in Barstow yesterday afternoon, and how I had dined instead on fried potatoes and mush. I would soon be in Bakersfield, with a straight shot up the valley to Stockton, and then across the rolling green hills of the Coast Range into Oakland. Even with slow connections, I had to be home in San Francisco sometime tomorrow, and I still had three dollars in my pocket.

My stomach was growling again, and the full feeling produced by yesterday's repast had long since disappeared.

We had not been talking much, just sitting there with our backs against the boxcar door, watching the scenery roll by. I broke a long silence.

"Henry, you like cheeseburgers?"

"Ah sho do, why?"

"Well, when we get into Bakersfield we're going to find a creamery, and I'm going to treat you to a feed. If you hadn't had that grub in your roll yesterday, I'd really be hungry by now."

"Can y'all 'ford it?"

"Sure can. You're closer to Fresno than I am to the City, but it's not far for either of us now." My appetite and my imagination took over. "What's your favorite milkshake flavor?"

"Ah haven't had too many, but stro'berr Ah guess."

"Really? Mine too! You know it's been so damn cold I never even thought about something like a milkshake, but now I can just taste it washing down a big bite of cheeseburger. I like my milkshakes rich and creamy, but thin enough to drink. We'll top it off with apple pie à la mode." I was sure we would find a creamery somewhere in Bakersfield, where each component of the feast I was planning would cost ten cents. Even if the cheeseburgers and the shakes each cost as much as fifteen cents, it still wouldn't be as much as a dollar to pay for both of us. That would leave me more than two dollars in my pocket.

Henry chuckled. "Man, Russ, y'all make it sound good. Ah wasn't too hungry til jes now when y'all started talkin'."

Then he stopped rather suddenly and looked at me. "We gonna be able to find a place whea dey serve cullid?"

"Hell, yes, Henry, you're in California now, not Mississippi."

"Ah know's dat, but mah brothuh, Ed, wrote once. He said it's better'n back home, but dere's still lotta folks out heah don' care much fo' us cullid."

I thought briefly of the cosmopolitan city I called home and its diverse ethnic neighborhoods—Chinatown; North Beach and its large Italian settlement; Russian Hill. Then I thought of the Fillmore district where the black population of San Francisco was concentrated. I realized with a start how little attention I had paid to what was a day-in, day-out pervading fact of life for my friend.

With a small chill of apprehension, I remembered the elegant coffee shop and restaurant in the Hotel St. Francis. I had seen them from their entrances in the years I had worked at the hotel. I couldn't afford to buy a meal there myself so I had never been inside to dine, but I could not remember ever seeing a black guest seated in either the coffee shop or the restaurant. My next thought was even more chilling. I had never spent any time in the San Joaquin Valley, but I knew, in a general sort of way, that it was heavily populated now by the migrants from Oklahoma and Arkansas, among other places. Thinking about it, I was sure they had not left their prejudices behind when they crossed the border into California. Suddenly, I had the feeling that, once again, my mouth had raced ahead of my mind. But now I was determined, Henry was probably salivating just like me after listening to my detailed description of the food I would provide and, by God, he was going to have it as far as I was concerned. I made my tone as casual as possible.

"Just don't worry about it. I'll handle it."

His look and his tone of voice were still doubtful, but he merely said quietly, "Okay, if y'all say so."

About half an hour later we were on the floor of the valley. The weather was cool, but markedly warmer than it had been in the mountains. I stowed my blankets in my valise and secured the carrying line. Henry had stowed his gear in his blankets, and his roll was securely tied and ready to sling.

I stood in the open door of the boxcar and saw the milepost, "Bakersfield," just as I felt the train start to slow.

"We might as well ride her till she stops, Henry. Should get us closer to town. From what I hear, we don't have to worry about railroad bulls in the SP divisions."

When the train stopped, we dropped off the boxcar, and stood there for a moment getting our bearings. We were in a main railroad division at the eastern edge of the maze of tracks. Not too far away I could see the modest skyline of downtown Bakersfield.

Just off the right-of-way a clump of willow trees was growing next to the embankment. It was directly in line with where we wanted to go to find the creamery I was seeking, and I led the way.

I slid down the embankment and through the trees, which were not too dense a growth, with Henry directly behind me.

I walked right into a small group of six hoboes seated around a fire. Normally I would stop to visit, and get the latest word on freights heading north. This time, with Henry hard on my heels, I was somewhat surprised to see these men anyway, and then I saw the wine jug being passed around. At just about the same instant, I noticed an empty gallon jug lying on the ground, and I heard the Southern drawl.

It was the same sounding voice I had so enjoyed listening to while traveling through the deep South, but this time the words and the tone were ominous. I felt a chill run down my back.

"Ah'll be goddamned! Lookit that nigguh, and he's gottuh nigguh-lovin' white boy with him."

I stopped so suddenly, Henry walked right into me. I could literally feel the tension in his muscular body.

As outraged as I felt, I wasn't about to take on six of them, no matter how much cheap wine they had put away.

The ground leveled off in all directions and I knew we could run for it if we had to, but the problem at the moment was that we were right in the middle of the group we had accidentally stumbled into.

I had my valise slung across my back, and Henry had his bedroll slung across his, so our hands were free.

Then the hobo who had spoken was on his feet, directly in my path. He was swaying slightly, and I could smell the cheap wine, and see his bloodshot eyes in a mean-looking face. He was a good-sized man, quite a bit bigger than I. I tried to be diplomatic, even though the rage was burning in me, keeping my voice as friendly as I could.

"Look, Mac, we don't want any trouble. We're just heading into town."

I started to walk around him, but he moved to plant himself in front of me again.

I had been concentrating so hard on him that I didn't realize for a second that three of the others were also on their feet, more or less surrounding me. At the same time, Henry had quietly and quickly slipped away and was outside the circle now, watching warily, his body tensed, his hands hanging loosely.

There was nothing else to do then. As I tried to walk around the hobo, I felt my left shoulder grabbed roughly by one of them behind me. As he spun me around, the pent-up rage exploded, and I threw a right fist into his face with all the weight of my body behind it. I could feel the jolt all the way to my shoulder. I felt a fierce surge of joy when I saw the blood from his shattered nose spurt and run down his chin, as he stumbled backwards.

The next minute or so was a whirling melee of shouted curses, wild swings, and moving bodies. Suddenly, I became aware of the fact that Henry was planted to my right, standing shoulder to shoulder with me. It was all happening so fast that I didn't have time to focus on anything, but I saw Henry, out of the corner of my eye, throw a left hook, followed by a right cross, which put the big bastard who had started this flat on his back. The two who had been sitting on the ground started to get to their feet at one point but, when they saw the big hobo go down, thought better of it and stayed where they were.

Suddenly, one hobo just in front of me ducked his head and drove it into my body. The force of the blow to my stomach knocked the wind out of me, and I found myself on the ground, flat on my back, gasping for breath. My valise broke the fall but, for a second, I was stunned and helpless. I saw him draw his right foot back. As if in slow motion, I could see that heavy work shoe crunching into my head, smashing my facial bones, maybe killing me.

Then, magically it seemed, his foot stopped in mid-air at the same instant that I heard the crack of a clean uppercut, as Henry's right fist caught him on the point of his chin. He went down, flat on his back, like a pole-axed steer.

There was only one left capable of fighting, and he backed off now, joining the one I had punched out first—away from us with the two who were still sitting on the ground. There was pure hatred in their eyes, but this fight was over.

No one was going to stop us now. We edged out of this misbegotten camp, always facing them, until we were clear. We walked toward town, as rapidly as we could, neither of us saying anything for quite a while.

# 47

It was a long walk to downtown Bakersfield. My right hand throbbed, and I gingerly explored it with my left hand. As nearly as I could tell, no bones were broken. My stomach ached too, from that butt in my solar plexus.

For a little while, after we had left the jungle camp behind us, I was really high. We had beaten the bastards—we had shown them! Then my spirits started to sink. It was more than my physical woes. I had been feeling so good rolling into Bakersfield on that freight—thinking about treating Henry to the feast I had planned. Why had that no-good son-of-a-bitch started it? We weren't hurting him. We weren't looking for trouble. Just because Henry's skin was a darker color than his—and mine—that was no reason to start something.

I could not sort it out in my mind. All I knew was that I had been looking forward to treating Henry and, I must admit, myself, to some special food. I almost cried aloud in my anguish. Why did people have to spoil something that simple, something that would hurt no one?

We were almost in downtown Bakersfield when it suddenly hit me that I had been totally lost in my own emotions. I had not even considered how Henry was feeling—and he had, quite literally, probably saved my life.

We were out of the fields adjoining the SP railroad division by then, and walking on a sidewalk. I stopped abruptly and grabbed him by the arm.

"You know, buddy, you saved my life back there. That bastard was about to give me the boot. He could have killed me."

His expression was somber.

"Dey's de fust white men Ah evuh lay hands on."

What he said surprised me. I just wasn't expecting that. I didn't know quite what to say, but I probably said the best thing I could have said.

"I can't think of a better bunch of bastards for you to lay hands on, Henry. How did it feel?"

292

He looked at me for a moment, then that smile, which lit up his face, turned on. "Real good, Russ, real good!"

All of a sudden I was feeling better. It was as if we had left that scum completely behind us; somehow or other we were cleansed.

"Henry, you remember that feed I told you I was going to buy us? Well, we're going to have it now!"

Again, he looked at me, some doubt and apprehension in his eyes. He didn't say anything.

For once I thought about him instead of myself. "Henry, we may be in California, but I'll check it out first. I promise. Okay?"

"Dat's good, Russ. Y'all handle it."

We continued to walk through Bakersfield and then, about half a block away, I saw a sign—"Nick's Creamery."

It was exactly the sort of place I had in mind. From what I could see from the outside it looked large, prosperous, and clean.

When we reached the front entrance I hesitated for a moment, and Henry simply dropped his bedroll on the sidewalk, sat down on it with his back against the wall, and looked at me. "Y'all find out, heah?"

I nodded and walked in. There weren't many customers this time of the morning, but a large muscular man was working busily at a wide grill. He was dressed in white trousers, short-sleeved white tee shirt, and had a white chef's cap cocked rakishly on his head. At the moment he was flipping pancakes on one part of the large grill, gently easing some eggs over on another, and babying some sausage links carefully next to the pancakes.

A middle-aged waitress at the far end of the creamery was serving a customer.

I walked up to where he was working so busily. I stood there until he had the current orders neatly placed on plates, waiting to be picked up by the waitress. When he was done he turned around, and I could see his flashing black eyes, his blue jowels, probably shaved two hours ago, but sprouting again. He stared at me intently.

"What can I do fer ya, mistuh?"

"Can I speak to the owner?"

"Yer lookin' at him. Nick Bouzakis, that's me. What-d'ya need?"

"Well, I want to get something to eat, for me and a friend of mine."

"So what's the problem? This is the place to get fed." He paused for a moment, eyeing me a bit suspiciously. "Ya got the dough to pay fer it?"

"Yes, sir, but my friend's colored." I all but choked on the words, but I was not about to subject Henry to any more indignities. "Is it okay if he comes in here and eats with me?"

Nick Bouzakis looked at me unbelievingly. "Fer Chrissake, what color is he, purple? Ya got the dough, ya get fed in Nick's place!"

It occurred then to him that this was a real problem for me. In a more gentle tone he said, "Kid, you and yer friend sit where ya want. Nick'll see ya get fed. Okay?"

I hurried outside to get Henry.

"It's all right, come on in."

He still looked a bit doubtful, but picked up his roll and followed me into the creamery.

Nick took over now. He personally sat us in a booth by a large plate glass window that overlooked the sidewalk. He smiled at us in a friendly way. "You guys need a menu?"

I shook my head. "I don't really think so. We'd like cheeseburgers and strawberry shakes to start."

"Marsha!" he bellowed to the far end, "these guys want strawberry shakes." Turning back to us. "How d'ya like 'em?"

"Well, I like mine so I can drink it, you know, not too thick."

Nick Bouzakis gave quick directions to Marsha, who obviously handled the milkshake part of this operation. She was a motherly looking lady who gave us a pleasant smile as she poured the milk into the metal containers, followed by the scoops of strawberry ice cream.

"Wait'll ya taste my cheeseburgers. They're the best!" He returned to his grill, and soon I could hear the juicy hamburgers sizzling, watch the golden cheese melting on them. An absolutely heavenly aroma of frying onions drifted from the grill.

In practically no time, Marsha was pouring a thick, creamy strawberry milkshake into a tall glass in front of me, and another into a glass in front of Henry. The condensed moisture glistened on the outside of the metal containers from which she poured. We each took a cold, delicious swallow, and then the chef arrived at our booth with the cheeseburgers. They were superb! The cheese was melted on top and became one delectable whole with the hamburger, the onions, and the bun that had been perfectly toasted on the grill.

Nick Bouzakis stood there, hands on his hips, watching us eat. This was a man who obviously took pride in his work. When we were about halfway through the cheeseburgers and the milkshakes, I looked at him.

"This is really great, sir. We're thinking about apple pie à la mode for dessert."

He broke into a huge grin and nodded vigorously, his chef's cap bobbing. "I really enjoy watchin' good eaters in my place. You guys are two of the best! Would you like that apple pie kinda warm—so the ice cream sorta melts on it?"

We were both fairly well-fed by then, but the chef's description of warm apple pie, with the vanilla ice cream melting on it, spurred us on. It seemed as if Nick Bouzakis enjoyed watching us eat almost as much as we enjoyed putting it away.

I used a spoon to scoop up the last bit of that wonderful apple pie juice, mixed with melted vanilla ice cream now, and leaned back in the booth blissfully.

Henry was giving his apple pie and melted ice cream the same devoted attention.

We hadn't said a word about the fight since we had edged out of the camp. Now there was a question I *had* to ask him.

"You know, I didn't have time to watch much of anything, but I did see three of those punches you threw. Where did you learn to fight like that?"

"Evuh since Joe Louis be champ, lotsa us cullid boys feel maybe we kin do it too. Back home Ah fought in smokuhs at de Elks Club 'bout ever week or so. Dey pay us dolluh each fer sho, two dolluhs if'n Ah win." He smiled proudly. "Ah always won!"

"I can believe it. Sure glad I had you on my side, Henry!"

The food was on the expensive side, but it was sure worth it. The total was ninety cents for both of us. After I paid at the cash register, I went back to our booth, left a dime for Marsha, and then we were on our way.

By unspoken agreement, we headed for the north end of the yard, as far as we could get from where we had gotten off the freight earlier this morning.

There was a freight made up, almost all empty boxcars, with the engine on the head end pointing north. Just as we reached the tracks we heard the bell ringing and saw the brakeman on the ground at the caboose signal with his lantern. I knew there was just one direction it would be going—up the San Joaquin Valley to Fresno, and eventually to Stockton.

"Come on, Henry. This is our freight. Let's get aboard." Even as I spoke, the train started to move and the brakeman swung aboard the caboose. We sprinted for the nearest empty boxcar and scrambled aboard. A moment later, we heard again the long *whohoohoo* of the highball, and we were rolling north.

The valley floor was as flat as a pool table and, at this time of year, there were no remaining signs of the crops that had been harvested earlier. The freight never made more than about thirty miles an hour, but we were never shunted to a siding either. The mileposts defined our progress north—McFarland, Delano, Tipton. When we left Goshen behind, I got out my map again.

It was about two in the afternoon then. It looked like Fresno was about fifty miles due north.

"Well, Henry, you got it made now. Should be in Fresno in about an hour and a half."

That wonderful smile lit up his face again.

"Sho nuff, Russ. Nevuh though Ah'd be pullin' in lak dis, with mah belly so full. Man, Ah kin still taste dat food!"

I smiled. "It was good, wasn't it."

He was seated on his bedroll, I was seated on my valise, just opposite the open door, watching the valley roll by. In the distance we could see an occasional farmhouse, always the tall stand of eucalyptus trees nearby, the windbreaks for the lonesome-looking farms.

As we neared Fresno, the landscape became more inviting. There were miles and miles of vineyards, occasionally growing in orderly rows almost up to the railroad right-of-way. We hadn't stopped once, all the way from Bakersfield, and I was certain this freight had to stop in Fresno. I had a momentary concern for Henry—it would be a real disappointment for him if this train rolled right on through—going too fast to safely get off, and he had to beat his way back.

Then, almost as I had the thought, I could feel and hear the couplings jolting together, as we began to slow, and the milepost for Fresno moved across my line of vision through the open boxcar door.

We both got up and stood in the open door as we rolled into the Fresno division.

Once again, I thought, another good-bye. My feeling of sadness at the thought of saying good-bye to Henry was lightened this time. There would be no more good-byes this trip, this was the last one. Tomorrow, at the latest, I would be home.

Still, as always, there was the sense of loss at the prospect of bidding farewell to a person who had, however briefly, been an important part of my life. Important—for a moment I thought of his powerful fists and how he singlehandedly had saved us—that was a bit of an understatement. If it had not been for his fighting prowess and his loyalty—I thought again, as I had before, of how easily he could have run for it. Instead he had stayed there, fought it out shoulder to shoulder with me.

The train had stopped now, and Henry picked up his roll and slung it across his back. It seemed almost as if he was avoiding looking at me.

Then he faced me. "Ah think if y'all stay raht on dis freight, she goin' lak a through train, y'all be in Stockton in no time."

"I think you're right, Henry. Well, you made it. Won't be long you'll be seeing your brother."

We were both having a problem trying to say what we were feeling.

Then he extended his hand. I gripped it hard.

"Y'all a good man, Russ, Ah won't fergit."

"I won't forget you either, Henry. Good luck!"

He dropped off the car and strode away. When he cleared the edge of the tracks he stopped and turned. He waved once, I waved back, and then he too disappeared from my life.

# 48

The freight stopped in the Fresno yard for about half an hour, and then we were rolling north again.

I studied my map. It was about a hundred miles to Stockton. I knew the Western Pacific ran from there into Oakland. It was going to be after dark when we got into Stockton. This close to home I was not going to take any chances on catching the wrong train in the darkness. I would find an empty boxcar, if possible, to sleep in tonight and I should be home in San Francisco tomorrow.

A friendly switchman in Stockton directed me to the Western Pacific yard, a smaller complex of tracks than the Southern Pacific's. I thought about how I had actually walked up to the passenger ticket window in the Great Northern depot in North Dakota and was given directions for the next freight out. It was almost like that now, with the train crews being friendly and helpful.

I had a steak dinner in an all-night diner near the yard. It cost me fifty cents, but I wasn't worried about money now. I returned to the yard and went to sleep on a pile of cardboard in an empty boxcar, thinking about how I would be sleeping in a bed tomorrow night.

A short Western Pacific freight was made up and heading due west out of Stockton by nine the next morning.

I was the only hobo on the train, as nearly as I could tell, and I never enjoyed a ride by sidedoor Pullman more. We crossed the floor of the valley, and then began to wind through the hills. It looked as if there had been an early rain because the hills were green, and the air was fresh and clear.

It was a beautiful, late Indian summer day, warm and balmy. I looked at my map for the last time and reckoned I should be in Oakland some time around noon. With the weather so pleasant, I sat in the open door of the boxcar, my legs dangling, and breathed deeply of the clean, country-scented air. Almost before I knew it, we were chugging through Niles Canyon, not too far from Oakland now.

The right-of-way through this gently rolling country was not constructed on a grade that was anything like the Tehachapi grade we had climbed, and descended, yesterday. Still, the tracks did run along a right-of-way carved mainly out of the side of a hill. There were a lot of curves, and the engineer nursed us through carefully.

The sun sparkled off a creek at the bottom of the canyon. The terrain was heavily wooded now, unlike the first hills we had entered coming out of Stockton. Suddenly, I had an overwhelming sensation of having done this before, of now repeating an experience I had had at some other time and place. The feeling was so strong and intense and so pleasurable, I could not account for it. Then, I had the answer.

In the middle of Golden Gate Park, there is a children's ride on small scooter-like vehicles. As a little kid it had been one of my all-time favorites. Getting on at the top of a fairly high and steep hill, I descended by gravity, never too fast, down and down, through the sun-dappled trees, on a curving concrete runway. It had been at least ten years since I had enjoyed that ride, but I had never forgotten it.

Now I realized that, as we dropped down through Niles Canyon, this is what made me feel as if I had lived this experience before. Despite the difference in scale between this boxcar and the kiddie scooter of my childhood, I was just as happy and carefree now as I had been then, so many years before.

Then we were out of the canyon and rolling into the outskirts of Oakland. There were several ways I could reach San Francisco, including taking the Key System train over the newly completed Bay Bridge, or a ferry from the Key System terminal jutting into the bay. But these were not my choices.

The nickel ferry was the longest and best ferry boat ride on San Francisco Bay. It started far up the Estuary, at the Oakland terminal, proceeded down the waterway, past the ships of Oakland and Alameda, out into the bay, past Yerba Buena Island, under the bridge, and finally to the terminal at the Ferry Building. *That* was how I was going home.

It was a half-hour walk from the railroad yard to the ferry terminal, and I just made the one o'clock ferry. It took about forty-five minutes to go down the Estuary, cross the bay, and dock at the ferry building. I enjoyed every minute of it.

I stood out on the bow with the clean salty breeze blowing over me, the white skyline of San Francisco etched against a blue sky, visible in the distance across the sparkling bay. This *had* to be the most beautiful place in the world.

I was really hungry now. I hadn't had anything to eat since my dinner in Stockton last night, and I thought briefly of getting something in the ferry boat's dining room on the top deck. Then I thought of my Aunt Doris's turkey dressing and all that went with it. I remembered from past Thanksgivings how much of her huge repast was left over after the holiday dinner. For no good reason, I was sure she would be saving a generous part for me, and I wanted to do it justice.

Standing out there in the wind, feeling the surge of the ferry boat driving across the bay, I thought about the home at 85 Justin Drive and how important it was to so many of us.

It was a uniquely San Francisco type of residence, located in the outer Mission. The entire ground floor was a garage, and all of the living accommodations were on the second floor. Aunt Doris and Pop had worked hard, scrimped and saved and, finally, even in the depths of the Depression, had been able to make the down payment on the home of their dreams in St. Mary's Park. Unlike many of the homes in the Richmond and Sunset Districts, which were built right up against each other, 85 Justin Drive had a five-foot space on each side. Situated on a hill, there was a modest view of the far reaches of the Mission District from the front windows. From the windows of the breakfast room, just off the kitchen at the rear of the house, the view stretched to the bay. That breakfast room, with its pull-down wall bed, was the heart of the home—all of our meals were taken there except for the large family holiday dinners, when we ate in the formal dining room.

There were only two bedrooms and one large bathroom, with a shower over the tub. When they moved in with her bachelor brother, Herb Hofvendahl, who had always lived with them, and my infant cousin Marie, it was downright spacious compared with the flat on Octavia Street, downtown in Hayes Valley, where I had first lived with them.

The years went by and the family grew. First, Pop's son by an earlier marriage, Roy, finally came to live with them after a bitter custody battle. He took up residence in a twin bed in the other bedroom with Uncle Herb. Pop's elderly Greek mother, after another family upheaval, came to make her home with them. Pop constructed a good-sized room for her in the far reaches of the basement-garage, and installed an extra bathroom down there. Marie grew into a young lady, and moved out of her parents' bedroom, to take up residence with Grandma Filios in the large bedroom downstairs.

Some time after my return from the Bering Sea, and my Uncle Jerry Sleight's transfer to another railroad division of the SP, I moved in once again. I really hadn't thought much about it before but now, it began to dawn on me how generous my aunt was. As far as she was concerned, there was always room for one more. Room for me was made in the downstairs laundry room with a second-hand day bed. There was a separate entrance to these quarters from the backyard and, given the night swing shift I worked at the St. Francis Hotel, I was able to come and go without disturbing the rest of the family. I insisted on paying for my room and board, and my beloved aunt accepted my monthly payment with the same instinctive understanding she always demonstrated. We both knew that I would be just as welcome without the payment, but we also knew that we both felt better with it.

Thinking about this heterogeneous household now, I smiled when I thought about Grandma Filios. She was a fierce old lady who had emigrated from Greece late in life, and spoke only her native tongue. Pop had emigrated as a young boy of fourteen, had always been self-conscious about his immigrant background, and refused to speak Greek unless it was an absolute necessity. As a part of this rejection of his early background, he had changed his name from Filios to Phillips. My Aunt Doris, running the household in the company of her aged mother-in-law and her own small daughter, did acquire a minimal Greek vocabulary. Characteristically enough, she did not insist that Grandma Filios learn English; she tried to learn to speak Greek.

Then, almost before anyone was aware of it, my five-year-old cousin was fluent in Greek, and she became the conduit of communication between her elderly grandmother and the rest of the family.

Due to my high school and work schedule, I wasn't around the house much but, on the infrequent occasions when we all ate together, the evening meal was invariably enlivened by a spirited, but always good-natured, argument between Pop and Uncle Herb. They argued about every conceivable subject, from the latest murder trial in San Francisco to politics, and every topic in-between. They had been doing it when I first joined the family almost eight years ago, and they were still at it when I shoved off last summer. I am sure they both would have felt a tremendous void in their lives if they were deprived of their verbal jousts.

I did not see much of Grandma Filios but, whenever I saw her and my cousin Roy in close proximity, the tension was palpable. He had a way of getting under her skin that would generate a torrent of speech in her native tongue, accompanied by the expressive gestures of her southern European homeland. Roy was a remarkably handsome young man, six months older than I, and with a wicked sense of humor.

Knowing full well that his grandmother did not speak or understand one word of English, he would face her, in the middle of one of her tirades, assume the sweetest smile, and most angelic expression he was capable of, and address her in absolutely insulting terms. "You goddamned old bitch, I'm getting tired of your yammering. Why don't you just shove it!" All delivered in the softest, most courteous voice he could manage.

Grandma Filios was no fool, and I am sure she must have figured out what was going on long before I unexpectedly stumbled on them in the kitchen one day.

Her excited shrieking, juxtaposed with Roy's pleasant smile and gentle voice delivering the most insulting remarks he could think of at the moment, were just too much for me. I absolutely broke up and, as I stood there laughing, Grandma made one more violent gesture in Roy's face—I am sure it was a Gypsy death curse at the least—and indignantly flounced down the stairs to her room.

Fortunately, Grandma Filios liked me, I learned from Marie, and she apparently bore me no ill will for this particular incident.

In an odd sort of way, since I was less than an hour from home now, I was more homesick than I had been at any time since I had left on the S.S. *Dagmar Salen* months before. I was really missing my family.

We docked at the Ferry Building at one forty-five. I walked off the front end as soon as the mooring lines were secured, and soon I was on a Mission streetcar heading for home.

At two-thirty I ran up the front steps and leaned on the doorbell. I knew the back door would be open but, somehow or other, it seemed as if this was the way I should do it.

I could hear my aunt's brisk footsteps approaching the front door, then hurrying, and suddenly she flung the door open.

"Oh, Russ, I knew it was you!"

I grabbed her and hugged her hard. Then she held me at arm's length and studied me appraisingly. "You look better than I thought you would."

She was not a sentimental type at all, but I thought I could see tears in her eyes. My vision at the moment was a bit misty too.

She grabbed my hand and pulled me into the house. It was a Saturday afternoon, so both Pop and Uncle Herb were working. She was alone in the house.

She stopped and faced me in the middle of the kitchen. She was fairly tall, with the regular Nordic features, blond hair, and blue eyes of her Swedish father. She always braided her hair in a long braid, and wrapped it around her head. I had never thought of it before really, but standing there looking at her, I thought she looked downright regal—the way a queen should look.

No matter how she may have looked to me, she was the same briskly efficient, no-nonsense lady who kept the wheels of this household turning.

She smiled at me mischievously. "I'll bet you can't guess what I've got saved for you in the Frigidaire?"

"Stuffing, and all the rest—plenty of dark meat?"

"That's right, Russ, but I really think it would be a good idea if you took a shower while I'm getting it warmed up for you. Do you have a clean change of clothes?"

"I got clean socks and shorts in my bag. The rest is okay, isn't it?"

As far as my aunt was concerned, cleanliness was not just next to godliness—it was right up there with it.

"Well, those aren't the cleanest jeans I've ever seen." She reached up and pulled the collar of my shirt away from my neck. "Russ! I don't know if I'll ever be able to get the dirt out of that shirt." Then her tone softened. "You are hungry, aren't you? Take that shower now, put on the clean socks and shorts, and we'll worry about the rest of it later."

That long hot shower felt as good to me as anything I had experienced in a long time. When I had finished, and opened the door to the bathroom, I could smell the aroma of turkey, dressing, hot rich gravy, and mashed potatoes. It was all waiting for me piled high on a plate on the table in the breakfast room. She had put it on the table at the place where Pop usually sat, with the view looking out the window toward the bay.

She was seated there at the table, waiting for me, and I impulsively leaned down, hugged her again, and kissed her.

"Man that looks great! I can hardly wait." I was seated now, preparing to dig in, when she gently placed her hand on my arm.

Momentarily surprised, I looked at her, and this time I could clearly see the tears in her eyes.

She bowed her head and spoke to her Maker. "Lord, thank you for bringing Russ home safely." I could hear a small quaver in her voice. "I've been so worried."

I just looked at her. "It's good to be home, Aunt Doris."

# AUTHOR'S NOTE

My voyage on the schooner *William H. Smith*, described in my book *Hard on the Wind*, awoke in me a love for the sea which led directly to my shipping out on the S.S. *Dagmar Salen*. When I walked up the gangplank of that trim freighter, my seabag slung over my shoulder, the ship's white paint and bright-work sparkling in the sun of the San Francisco Embarcadero, I had no idea where this voyage would eventually take me.

Catching that first freight train out of New Westminster, British Columbia, was not a matter of choice. It was the only way out of town and, as an illegal alien in Canada and a ship-jumping seaman, I had to get away from that seaport fast.

Riding freights is an extraordinarily dangerous form of travel, but it was the only means of transport available to me then. It is a miracle that I survived the adventures unharmed. Today, some of my friends in the National Hobo Association ride freight trains for the sheer excitement and adventure of it. While I admire their courage, I will take the cushions any time.

Over the years, I have been fortunate to ride trains throughout the world—across Europe, the length of Africa to Capetown, the fabled Indian Pacific across Australia—and my love for railroad travel remains undiminished.

In 1966 my wife, Beverly, and I took our two youngest children, Steve and Dave, on a train trip out of Vancouver, British Columbia, via the Canadian National, over exactly the same route Finn Bering and I had traversed so many years before. I know there was no one on that train who watched the mileposts go by more excitedly than I did as we chugged through Red Pass and Yellowhead. The scenery was every bit as spectacular as I had remembered it, and that fourty-four mile stretch of tracks that Finn and I had hiked so laboriously was just as desolate as it was then. Sitting there in the comfort of the lounge car, watching that beautiful scenery roll by, it seemed as if I could feel the pangs of hunger and the broken blisters on my feet as strongly as I had in 1938.

In January 1939, just weeks after my return home to San Francisco, I enrolled at San Jose State University. Despite the delayed start, by reason of the journey described in this book, I carried extra units and graduated with my class in June 1942. My Aunt Doris was there, proudly watching, as I accepted my degree.

Three and a half years in the United States Marine Corps during World War II followed. I served with the Second Marine Division at Tarawa, Saipan, Tinian, and Okinawa, surviving those operations, which claimed so many Marines, without a scratch. I concluded my overseas tour of duty as a part of the first occupation forces in Japan.

After Stanford Law School, following World War II, and courtesy of the GI Bill, I commenced the practice of law in San Jose, California, in 1948, and have practiced my profession there ever since.

As I began to write this book, the memories came flooding back, and the places, people, and events were there in a figurative sense, almost waiting impatiently to be set down and find their place in the narrative.

The post cards, letters, and the diary provided the exact chronological and geographical references for me. At age sixteen, that part of one's mind which absorbs and records new experiences is, of course, a fresh canvas, a more impressionable receptor. The experiences I had on the road in 1938 are indelibly etched in my mind.

Despite some of the harshly negative encounters I had, it seemed to me then, and it seems to me now, as I have described these events, that the warm and generous people I met far outnumbered the others. After a lifetime of practicing law, it is perhaps a bit ingenuous of me, but I still believe that the great majority of people today are just as honest, helpful, and caring as so many of them were in 1938. For those wonderful people I have described in this book—this is my belated thank you.

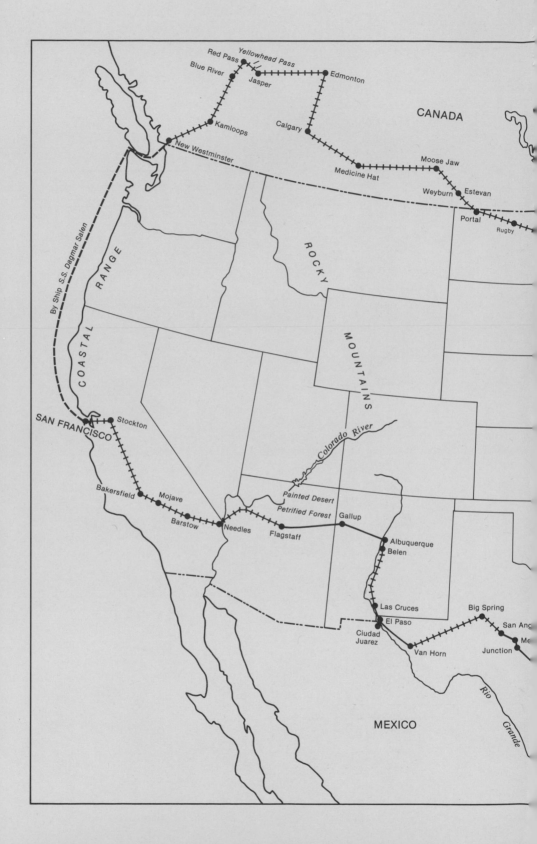